Volume II

ANCIENT MIRRORS of WOMANHOOD

Our Goddess and Heroine Heritage

The original Sibylline Books were the sacred records of the statements of the ancient Sibyl priestesses who foretold the future, and passed judgement by ancient Goddess law. Although the Sibylline Books were supposedly destroyed in the early Christian period, the wisdom and holy decrees that were written in them still live with us today.

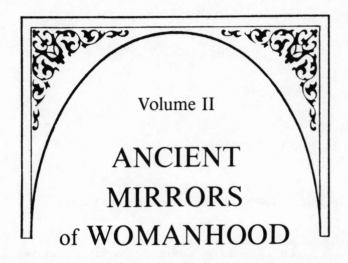

Volume II

ANCIENT
MIRRORS
of WOMANHOOD

Our Goddess and Heroine Heritage

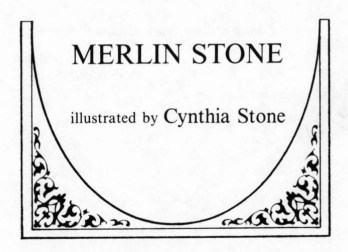

MERLIN STONE

illustrated by Cynthia Stone

NEW SIBYLLINE BOOKS

Library of Congress Catalog Card Number 79-90027

ISBN 0-9603352-1-8

TABLE OF CONTENTS

TABLE OF CONTENTS

TABLE OF CONTENTS

Volume I of Ancient Mirrors of Womanhood includes our Goddess and
Heroine Heritage from: Africa, China, Mexico, Central and South America, Australia, Polynesia, Celtic Europe (including England, Ireland,
Scotland and Wales), Anatolia (land of the Amazons), Semitic Canaan
and Mesopotamia, and the introduction to both volumes.

from the waters of the Indus

-- EAST INDIAN

The thousand named Goddess who sits upon the thousand petalled lotus of the cosmos, source of all energy, She who holds the entire universe in Her womb—manifests Her existence in the many Goddess images of the land of India.

The exploration of Goddess reverence in India is a vast and complex undertaking, the following section able to do little more than skim the surface of the subject. In such a study, it is of paramount importance to realize that Goddess imagery, ritual, and reverence in India are the result of a confrontation and eventual blending of at least two quite different major racial/ethnic groups. The first are the people of the early Harappan culture of the Indus Valley, believed to be the ancestors of today's Dravidians. The second are the much lighter skinned Aryans who began to invade the Indus Valley at about 2000 B.C. To understand Goddess reverence in India, a knowledge of the historical events that encompass the Aryan conquests of the people of the Harappan culture, and the subsequent institution of the caste system in which Aryans appointed themselves as the highest caste, the Brahmins, is vital.

India had been inhabited long before and during the Upper Paleolithic period, producing such cultures as the Soan and the Madras. The neolithic period of agricultural development started in India at about 5000 B.C. By about 3000 B.C., the culture known as Harappan began to flourish. Well built houses of brick, some two stories high, reveal that the Harappan culture spread out over some 950 miles along the banks of the Indus River and its tributaries. A form of writing, including over 250 symbols, was developed, but unfortunately this writing has not yet been deciphered. The religious beliefs of the Harappans are known to us from the enormous number of Goddess statues unearthed at Harappan sites, many quite similar to those found in Mesopotamia.

At about 2000 B.C., bands of nomadic Aryans, probably from the Kirghiz Steppes of Russia, descended upon and conquered many of the cities and villages of the Harappan culture. Accounts of these invasions and the massacre or enslavement of much of the indigenous population were recorded in the *Vedas*, the earliest written material from the Aryans of India. The Vedic writings reveal the extreme patriarchal orientation of the early Aryans, while explaining that their religious beliefs were centred around the male trinity of Indra, Mitra and Varuna. The Vedas also reveal that the native language of the Aryans, Sanskrit, is an Indo-European tongue related to Greek, Latin, Hittite and most European languages, including English. The Vedas also make it clear that the invading Aryans regarded the indigenous population of the Harappan culture as physically and mentally inferior to themselves, despite the obviously advanced cultural achievements of the Harappans as compared to the nomadic life of the Aryans. References to these claims of superiority suggest that the dark skins, smaller stature, and religious and social beliefs of the Harappans lay at the core of these claims—which were used to justify and explain the institution of the caste structure. Most pertinent to the study of Goddess reverence in India are the Vedic passages that refer to the people of the Harappan culture as *Danavas,* people of Danu—and an account in the *Rg Veda* that describes the murder of Mother Danu by the Aryan god Indra.

It is not too surprising that early Vedic writings do not include images of Goddess figures as powerful, or even as especially important. Certain aspects of nature are perceived as female spirits, but these personifications are relatively insignificant in comparison to the descriptions of the male deities. The names of Ushas as the dawn, and Sarasvati as a river, both appear in the Rg Veda, but the important cultural and spiritual aspects later associated with these names are not mentioned in the Rg Veda. The most dynamic female image included in the Vedas is that of Aditi, the Mother of the Aryan gods. This name is especially interesting in that the name Diti, like the name Danu, is associated with the Mother Goddess of the Harappans. The name Aditi literally means 'not Diti'. The use of this name raises the question of whether the importance, or even the image, of Aditi existed among the Aryans prior to their invasion of India. A legend in the much later *Ramayana* describes Indra's destruction of an embryo in Diti's womb. The account explains that all of the other children of Diti had been slain, and that Indra feared that the embryo might be a child who would eventually kill him.

At about the sixth century A.D., two bodies of writings began to emerge, texts that are filled with detailed and dynamic images of the Goddess. These are known as the *Tantras* and the *Puranas* (Ancient Lore). The Brahmanic leaders long resisted recognition of these texts, finally accepting them as writings of a much lesser sanctity and importance than the Vedas. It is in the Puranas, and even more so in the Tantras, that we find the accounts of Goddess as powerful, even as the dynamic force of the universe. This late emergence of Goddess imagery is generally attributed to a survival of ancient beliefs among non-Aryan groups that had been less affected by Brahmanic teachings. We should not underestimate the probability of changes and transformations in much of the material, as it may have been retained over a very long period of time, but the Goddess images and rituals of the Puranas and Tantras may offer some clue to ideas about the Goddess that may be as old as the Harappan period.

One of the areas of India that remained relatively non-Aryan is the Malabar coast of the southwest. Among many of the villages of the Malabar area, worship of the *Ammas,* the Mothers, is still the primary religious concern. Over the last two centuries, the social structure of the Malabar areas has been recorded as matrilineal and matrifocal, while polyandry (one woman having several husbands) was observed among the Nayyars of Malabar in the nineteenth century. It is interesting to note the presence of many woman poets in the collections of Tamil poetry from the Madura area of Malabar, dated to about 100 B.C. Along with women's poems about the feelings of a nursing mother during famine, the feelings of a young girl when a neighborhood boy destroys her sand castle and the joys of palm wine at a village festival—lesbian love appears to have been included as a noncontroversial topic. The poetess Avviyar, author of many poems in the Tamil collections, wrote, "O Bee, fair of wing...among all the flowers you have known, is there any more fragrant than my lady of the lovely hair and perfect mouth? Graceful as the peacock she dwells, rich with love for me." (*Koruntogai 2*)

Other areas that remained relatively unaffected by Aryan Brahmin influences are Bengal and Assam, to the northeast of India. Matrilineal and matrifocal customs still exist in these areas as well, while Goddess names such as Kali, Candi and Chamunda originate in Bengali beliefs. The shrine at Kamrupa in Assam is regarded as one of the most important seats, *pithas,* of Tantric rituals which centre upon the Goddess as the ultimate Shakti. Tantric Yoga groups reveal a quite different attitude towards women in practice, as well as in their theological beliefs. They are one of the few religious orders that include women in the highest positions of clergy. They were the first to speak out against the Aryan custom of *suttee,* a wife being burned upon her husband's death pyre. It is also interesting to realize that caste discrimination is discouraged at Tantric rituals as well as in Tantric beliefs. In contrast to other Hindu tenets, the Tantric texts list 'pride in family' and 'pride in caste' as two major obstacles that must be overcome before enlightenment can be achieved. Tantric sexual rituals, *Maithuna,* are certainly to be compared to the sexual rituals of Sumer and Babylon. In exploring the possible links between the sexual rituals of Sumer and those of India, it may be significant that the sexual rituals of Sumer were enacted by priestesses who lived together in the temple, while contemporary Tantric Maithuna is most often enacted between wife and husband.

In the more narrative Puranas, many Goddess names appear, each associated with specific traits and symbols. They are understood to be aspects or incarnations of the Great Goddess Devi. Devi, in turn, represents the concept of the ultimate Shakti. To fully describe and discuss each of the enormous number of Goddess names and aspects would require several volumes, but some of the better known aspects are included as part of the account of Devi, while a separate account of Kali is included in this section. For those interested in further reading or study, other aspects of the Goddess are: Candi, the fierce; Chamunda, the demon slayer; Annapurna, she of the abundant food; Gauri, the golden one; Jagad Amba, world mother; Ambika, little mother; Kulakatyayani, intuitive wisdom; Bhuvanesvari, earth—to list but a few.

One interesting image that appears in the Puranas is that of the Submarine Mare who holds the fiery ambrosia of passion and anger in her mouth. This image invites comparison with the Celtic imagery of the Goddess as the great mare whose mane can be seen in the foam of the waves of the ocean. Although actual connections between the spiritual beliefs and images of the Celts and the Indians may be remote, and certainly highly speculative, it is interesting to note that the name of the Mother Goddess as Danu occurs in the literature of both India and Ireland.

Wherever a deeper exploration of Goddess imagery and reverence leads, there is no question that the beliefs of India offer us a wealth of information about the nature of life creating deity as female.

SHAKTI

Knowledge of Shakti, literally power, occurs primarily in the Tantric texts. Descriptions of the nature of Shakti might well be used by modern physicists in attempts to describe the nature of pure or primal energy. Shakti reverence is known to this day, especially among the non-Aryan peoples of Bengal, Assam, Nepal and the southern Malabar coastal area. The four most important shrines of Shakti worship are Oddiyana, Jalandhara, Purnagiri and Srihatta, though many other sites of Tantric worship exist throughout India. The concept of Shakti as the serpent of Kundalini Yoga may be linked to the Naga serpent deities of the Dravidian south. The image of the Shakti serpent rising to the Ajna Chakra of the forehead may well be compared to the symbolism of Egypt, in which the Cobra Goddess Ua Zit emerges from the forehead as the Third Eye of Wisdom.

She who holds the Universe in Her womb,
source of all creative energies,
Maha Devi who conceives
and bears and nourishes
all that exists—
She is the ghanibuti,
the massed condensed power of energy;
She is the sphurana,
the power that burgeons forth into action;
She is purest consciousness and bliss,
inherent in the manifestation of all being.

Never can She be known
in Her perfect completeness,
for Her omnipotence is in all
that She continually does.
Do they not say
that even Shiva is unable to stir,
lies as a corpse,
until She grants him Her energies?
In the form of the coiled serpent,
the Bhujangi Kundalini,
She unwinds Herself through the chakras,
through the lotuses of the body,
as She creates Her cosmic serpent spiral
through the lotus chakras of the Universe.

At Her sacred shrine of Kamrupa,
they drink the kula nectar
that is the blood that passes from Her
as the moon passes from the sky,
while those who reach out to know Her
sit in Her circle of worshippers,
the sacred Shakti Cakra Pravartika,
knowing that if they worship Her with full devotion,
She will appear and give what is requested,
as She maintains the many beings of the world.

Some say that there are many worlds,
each ruled by a goddess or a god,
but that there is just the One Great Mother,
the Jagad Amba, the Makara,
Shakti of all existence,
She to whom even the gods bow down
in reverent worship and respect,
anxious for even the dust of Her feet
to touch their waiting heads—
for it is Shakti who is the ultimate source,
the infinite Cosmic Energy of all that occurs,
Maha Devi of the thousand petalled lotus.

DEVI

The word *deva,* or the feminine *devi,* is the Sanskrit word that means
deity, cognate with the English word divine. It literally means 'glowing
with brilliant illumination'. Though the name Devi is from the Aryan
Sanskrit, Her image encompasses many of the names and aspects of the
Goddess as known in non-Aryan beliefs. The names included in this account; Kali, Parvati, Sati, Laksmi, Tara and Durga occur primarily in the
Puranas. The description of Devi that comprises the first paragraph of
this piece is adapted from the *Saundaryalahari,* Flood of Beauty. The account of the defeat of the evil buffalo demon, Mahisa, is drawn from
several of the Puranas, including the *Markandeya* and the *Skanda.*
Though probably coincidental, it is interesting to note that the colours of

the eyes of the Goddess, and the colours of the guna strands of matter, are red, black and white—the three colours used in the cone mosaics of Goddess temples in Sumer.

Whose feet can it be that form the image of the holy crest upon the sacred writings? Who is it that is Supreme Intelligence, second to none? Who is it that is earth, air, fire, water, and yet is the ether of all energy, and yet again is Pure Mind? Who is it that owns the gunas, the very threads of matter of all that mortals see and touch? Who is it that has three eyes, one red, one white, one black, the colours of the eyes the same as those of the guna strands? Who is it that is many sided love, the protection and guidance of a mother who speaks with loving kindness to each and every child that calls out to her in need, yet at the same time is the feelings that bring the body to desire—the sight of the sun and the moon as breasts upon the perfect body arousing the lover to passion? Who is it that daily battles all that is harmful? By whose permission do all other deities have access to their stations? Name Her! Name Her! Luminous with energy, magnificent in Her brilliance, it can be no one but Devi! If She were to close Her eyes for an instant, the entire cosmos would disappear.

Upon the desire for divine wisdom, or safe childbirth, or a healthy infant—She is called upon as Sati. Upon the mountains where She takes Shiva as Her consort, and finds that She must listen to him curse the very one She wants to bless, yet provides Shiva with Her Shakti power so that unless he is united with Her, he cannot move—She who was once known as Sati, She who then lived again as Uma—She who is the daughter of the Mountain Himalaya, She is called upon as Parvati.

Upon the need for special luck, blessings and good fortune, when one turns to She who came forth from the primeval churning of the Ocean, sees Her seated upon the lotus, ever fresh with the cool of the water from the trunks of Her attendant elephants, knowing that She was once the patient Sita, knowing that She returned again as Radha, knowing that She sometimes answers to the name of Sri—She is called upon as Laksmi.

Upon the struggle of each swimmer caught in the tangled waters of the ocean of the world and the contemplation of the

One who will lead each swimmer from the confusion of the wild currents of the sea of life, so that each may rise and blossom as a lotus blossoms on the surface of the waters, upon thoughts of the One who is the Mistress of the Boat of Salvation, the One who guides the shipwrecked to safe shores, the One who is the knowledge, the wisdom, the guiding star, the Prajnaparamita, protecting, rescuing, redeeming Saviour—She is called upon as Tara.

Upon the need for courage, when one considers the righteous conquest of evil by awe inspiring majestic powers that lead the way—She is called upon as Durga. Upon consideration of the passage of time, the span of this life, when asking who is it that takes life only to give it back again, and sees the skin that is like the petals of a blue lotus at night covered with a tigerskin around Her loins, a garland of heads hanging about Her neck, knowing that She sometimes answers to the name of Mahacinatara—She is called upon as Kali.

Long ago in lifetimes past, the name of Durga passed to Devi. But long before that time Durga was the name of the force of evil, the wicked one, the Mahisa Buffalo, who drove the deities from their home in heaven, making them seek refuge in the forests upon earth. Durga destroyed all that was sacred, smashing the holy places where the beings of heaven had once been welcomed. The Buffalo Demon stole the heat from hearth fires, pushed great rivers from their paths, sent rain when rain should not have fallen, held rain back when it was needed most, struck the ocean with his horns, uprooted mountains with his horns, dusted himself with the precious powder of the minerals of the mountains —and dragged off every Goddess of perfection, forcing them to do his housework.

The people cried to Shiva, praying to him, begging him to destroy the evil demon. But the powers of the Buffalo were greater than those of Shiva. Against the evil demon, Shiva was weak. Thus Shiva went to Devi, who sat as golden Gauri, knowing that She was Shakti, knowing that She was the power and energy of the world and that She could succeed where he had failed. But Devi had much to do and thought to rid Herself of yet another task, so She sent the dark Kalatri, guardian of the night, to confront the Demon Durga. It was not long before the truth was clear. Kalatri too was helpless before the powers of the Buffalo. If

the Demon Durga was to be stopped, only one could do the job—
so to halt the evil Durga, mighty Devi then rode forth upon Her
lion.

The demon was prepared for battle. One hundred and twenty
million elephants, one hundred and twenty million war chariots,
one hundred and twenty million horses, and troops beyond
number—all these lay in wait to battle Devi. Mahisa Durga had
made them all. A storm of arrows hailed upon Devi's body, but as
if they were raindrops, they slipped off without harm. The army
of the demon hurled great rocks, as the Buffalo gored Devi's
troops with his horns. The demon's breath stirred up hurricanes,
tearing trees from their roots. The demon hurled these uprooted
trees at Devi, but they fell from Her unscathed body as sand falls
from the crevice of a cliff in a strong breeze.

The Buffalo Durga lashed the ocean with his tail, so that
great waves fell upon the land. Devi's one thousand arms were
each busy with battle, shooting aside one thousand arrows sent by
Durga's troops. Angered at the demon's attack upon the lion that
She rode, Devi threw a lasso about the Buffalo's tail, only to find
that the demon Buffalo itself became a lion. Though She plunged
Her sword through the neck of the lion, it then took the form of a
man, sword and shield in his hands. Seeing this, Devi pierced his
heart with arrows, only to find that the evil demon Durga had
become an elephant.

So it was that the evil being continued to ravage the land. He
created a mountain of wickedness, hurling this at Devi who cut
through its density with Her sword, slicing it into seven smaller
hills. Battle after battle, no one won and no one lost, until the
time that the evil Buffalo took his true form, revealing himself as
the manifestation of all evil. Stripped of all that he had used to
hide, without elephants, without chariots, without horses, without troops, Durga showed himself as Durga—and he too had one
thousand arms.

The battle was fierce. Arms matched arms, as each wicked
hand of Durga challenged each perfect hand of Devi. And then in
the heat of the battle, Devi pulled back in silence. Worrying that
She had admitted defeat, the world watched as Devi stopped to
drink the blood red wine. With surprise, they heard Devi call out
to the evil Buffalo, telling him to roar with laughter, for that
would be his final roar. The world watched as Devi drank the
celestial wine, finishing the last drops. They saw Her place Her

mighty Devi
then came forth

foot upon the demon's neck and heard the roar of Devi's laughter as Her trident pierced the body of the Buffalo—until it lay dead.

Thus the world rejoiced. People shouted 'Victory' and 'Saviour'. And in memory of the time that Devi saved the world from the evil Buffalo, they took his name of Durga and gave it to the Goddess Devi, so that those who speak of Durga know that Durga is but one part of Devi, while remembering the cosmic struggle She fought so long ago.

KALI

Kali, literally meaning Time, is a Goddess name that is traced back to early Bengali beliefs and may be related to Korravai, a Dravidian name of the fierce warrior aspect of the Goddess. Although Kali is worshipped in many shrines and temples of India, literature and general practice make it clear that Kali is yet another aspect of the great Devi. The material concerning Kali is found primarily in the Puranas, both the *Skanda* and the *Harivamsa* used for this account. It is vital to be conscious of the inherent racism in certain accounts of Kali, especially those that state that Her blackness reveals a lesser level of spiritual development, e.g. *Skanda Purana*. Such statements must be seen in the context of Aryan Brahmanic attitudes imposed upon Dravidian peoples, and the caste system in which Aryans assigned the darkest Dravidians to the lowest caste. This aspect of Indian beliefs should not be ignored. It demands that an examination of its presence and intent be made at greater length—if what is truly spiritual, and what is political, are ever to be understood in Indian belief systems.

Black as the petal of a blue lotus at night,
black as the night touched by the light of the moon,
Kali is the essence of Night,
She who is called Sleep,
She who is named Dream,
She who is the joyous dancer of the cremation ground,
She who chooses from among the corpses
which souls shall be released
from the bonds of existence—
to know eternal bliss.

23

She is Maha Kali, Great Mother Time,
She is Nitya Kali, Everlasting Time,
She is Raksa Kali, Goblin yet Protector
during earthquake, famine or flood,
She is Smyama Kali, the Dark One who dispels fear,
She is Smasana Kali, Ever Joyous Dancer
on the corpses of the cremation grounds,
surrounded by wailing female spirits,
a garland of heads about Her neck,
a belt of human hands about Her waist,
blood upon Her lips.

Yet others say that She lives in the triple heaven,
wearing a bodice of gold,
and a string of pearls that glisten like moonbeams,
Her four arms of darkest iron
holding a trident and a sword,
holding a perfect lotus and a pot of honey,
and that Her banner is the peacock's gracious tail,
as peacock feathers adorn Her wrists and ankles.
It is this Kali who dwells forever
on the summit of Mount Vindhya,
born again from the womb of Yasoda,
murdered as an infant girl
by the wicked coward Kamsa,
who seeing Her take Her place in heaven
saw his own violent death—
while She lived on Vindhya, eternal and divine.

Daughter of the Ocean, Mother born of Anger,
wet nurse to invincible warriors,
though they say that death
lingers in the waters of Her womb,
still, full devotions are made to Kali
on the ninth day of each month,
and those who worship with full heart
receive all that they desire.
For who does not know that this is the Kali Yuga,
the Fourth World of bitterness and sorrow,
and that when the Yuga finds its natural end,
Kali shall be there to gather the seeds—
to create the new Creation.

ANASUYA

This most surprising account of the woman Anasuya, literally 'free from envy', is from the *Bhavisya Purana*. As with most Purana dating, estimates on this text vary greatly, ranging from 500 to 1200 A.D.

Woman among women, seldom do they speak of her or her great wisdom and the Goddess powers that dwelled within her, for she spoke of herself as mortal as she sat upon the banks of the Ganges, deep in meditation, calling upon the holy deities.

Yet there are a few who did remember that as she sat there, deep in deepest mind, suddenly three gods appeared before her, those of whom she had long heard, and long been taught to trust. But great was her surprise when Shiva approached upon his Nandi Bull, holding his phallus in his hands. And great was her surprise when Vishnu appeared on his Garuda Bird, thinking only of his physical desire for her. And even greater was her surprise when Brahma appeared, telling of being in the power of Kama's passion and that he thought only of possessing her body.

When she heard their unexpected speeches, of their bodily cravings for her, despite the fact that her husband Atri sat close by her side, she held her silence, for so long had she been taught to hold these gods in great respect. But in response to her respectful silence, the three gods fell upon her with violent attack, determined to take her body forcefully, to use it to satisfy their own desires.

Thus astonished by their actions, her anger raged and rose against them. Though they were the ancient gods that she had learned to worship and revere, she cursed their very existence, hurled insults at their being. Calling them 'The Phallus', 'The Head' and 'The Two Feet', she warned them that all worshippers would laugh at them unless they realized that they were as sons to her, as to any mortal woman. With wisdom, she explained that their uncontrolled desires grew from their ignorance at not recognizing that they were but children to her, and if they desired to be revered as worthy holy beings, they must learn to know her as their mother.

SARASVATI

In the *Rg Veda,* Sarasvati appears as the spirit of the Sarasvati River, a
river that once flowed from the Himalayas into the Indus. Early sites of
the Harrapan culture once flourished along its banks. Today the river bed
lies along the edge of the Thar Desert. In the later *Brhaddharma Purana,*
She takes an anthropomorphic form, presenting the knowledge of writing
to the son of the Goddess Parvati. Her name occurs in many later prayers
and rituals, each providing some of the material included here. At times
described as the wife of Brahma, She is also known as Vac and revered as
the presiding deity of the arts: music, painting, carving and especially
associated with the acquisition of writing.

The echoes of the lovely notes
that She strums upon Her vina lute,
and the clear resounding words
that She plays upon the strings of Her voice,
float across the waters
of the river Sarasvati,
as it flows from the melting snowcaps
of the heaven touching Himalayas.
How fortunate are those who watched
and saw the gracious Sarasvati
seated upon the downy back
of the great white swan,
as the crescent of the moon
glowed from Her perfect brow.

Who was it that remembered
that it was She who brought the gift of language,
the poetry and the words of ancient knowledge,
designing the very letters
of the sacred Devanagari script
whose alphabet forms the garland
from which the holy mantras are picked?
Thus memories were carved in stone—
Sarasvati's holy arms holding the tablets,
Sarasvati's holy hands holding the stylus,
so that none would forget
The Mother of the Written Word.

THE GODDESSES OF ASSAM

Assam, the land of the Khasi peoples, is located at the far northwestern edge of India, on the southern ridges of the Himalayas. This particular account was recorded by Mrs. M. Rafy, who spent many years of her life in Assam, eventually publishing her studies as *Folktales of the Khasis.* The structure of the divine family, as described in this account, appears to reflect evidence of the matrifocal customs that have been observed among many groups of Assam. The image of the moon as brother to the sister sun recalls the Inuit (Eskimo) legend of Sun Sister (see Native American section). Both legends explain the dimmer light of the moon as the result of a brother's sexual attack upon his sister. The details of the funeral rites for the Mother, Earth, is as much a creation story as one of death—one that may be better understood in the context of the topography of the area of Assam.

High in the Khasi Hills, along the banks of the River Brahma-putra, not far from Kulhakangri of the rising Himalayas, ancient stories of the holy family who guide the people are remembered still. For who can forget Mother Earth and Her four children— Goddess Ka Um of the waters; Goddess Ka Ding of the fire; Goddess Ka Sngi of the sun; and their brother U Bnai who shines as the moon.

Thus it is remembered that when Earth's children were very young, the moon shone as brightly as the sun. Young Sun Goddess Ka Sngi appeared faithfully each day, to be the light for Her Mother, resting only when Her day's work was done. But Brother U Bnai was selfish, caring little for the needs of others, seldom doing his family chores. Often, he disappeared for days at a time, staying out late at night accompanied by loose companions, leading a life of indulgence and wasteful pursuits. It was no wonder that Mother Earth was filled with worry, and each time he returned his sisters scolded him, only to find that their words fell upon ears deaf to their concerns.

As adulthood came upon him, U Bnai wandered ever further, often descending to the caverns deep beneath Earth, cavorting there with evil beings who encouraged him in his thoughtless, lazy life. In the darkness of U Bnai's absence, time continued to pass. So long had he been gone from his home in the heavens that a day came upon him that was filled with a longing for the lovely home and family he had nearly forgotten. Deep in memories of home, U Bnai once again flew up into the vast blue heavens.

Though he soon reached the home that he had longed for, his mind was still filled with the wrong thinking and selfishness he had known in the caverns. And upon seeing his dear sister, the glowing Ka Sngi who filled the world with Her brilliant beauty, instead of the brotherly devotion he should have felt in his heart, it was his body that gave him greatest concern—as he looked upon the lovely Ka Sngi with thoughts of lust and desire.

No sooner did he greet Her in the heavens, than he spoke of his desire for Her. He danced about, trying to tempt Her with his own glowing beauty. He bragged of all that he had seen in his travels, of the nights of abandon he had known, thinking this would win Her interest. And seeing that She did not respond, he then compared Her to all others he had met, telling Ka Sngi that no one in heaven, no one in the caverns beneath Earth, was as beautiful as She was in Her perfect radiance. Though his compliments were kind, Ka Sngi filled with astonishment as U Bnai then stated that Her beauty was equalled only by his own, and further added that She would be foolish to spurn the offer of his passions.

Ka Sngi was patient with Her brother, though She knew that what he said was filled with wrong thinking. With gentleness, She explained that he must not think of Her with passion, but only with brotherly concern. Despite Her reassurances of the sisterly love She felt, despite Her reassurances that he would someday find a better suited mate, U Bnai grew angry that his pleasure was being denied. So long had he done just as he pleased, he could not believe that he would not have his way, and determined that he would take whatever he desired, he then fell upon Ka Sngi in violent assault.

Rage filled the heart of the patient sister, for this insult was more than She would bear. So it was that She reached deep into Her own brilliant radiance and filled Her hand with the cooling ashes of Her fire, hurling these at U Bnai! As the dry grey ashes landed upon his face, the fire of U Bnai began to dim, smothering the light of the brother, as it smothered his wrong thinking passions. In shame, he left the presence of Ka Sngi, the scars left by the ashes scarring his arrogant vanity, so that from that day on he seldom appeared in the light of the day.

Many eons later, when Mother Earth grew old, Her three daughters looked down from the heavens and sorrowed when they saw their Mother lying still in death. In the deep grief they felt, they sought to show the respect that daughters give their mothers when they have finished with this life. Thus the daughters spoke together. Earth's body was vast. How could they perform the funeral rites that would free their Mother's soul from Her body?

Trying to decide how this might best be done, the three sisters agreed that Ka Sngi, the youngest, should perform the sacred rites. The Sun Goddess then sent down great waves of heat, trying to burn the body so that the soul could be free. The forests and meadows of Earth were soon scorched and grey but the body did not truly burn. After many days of trying, Ka Sngi returned to Her sisters, tired and discouraged. 'I have done all that I could, but still our Mother's body retains its shape of life and Her soul cannot depart.'

It was then that the second sister, the Goddess of Water, Ka Um, thought to make a flood. This would at least cover Earth's body so that it would not lie exposed. Ka Um then sent Her heaviest rains, pouring water from the heavens until the rivers and lakes overflowed their banks and the ocean fell in great tides upon Earth. The body of Earth lay deep beneath the flood. But when the waters began to slowly drain away, Ka Um returned to Her sisters, tired and discouraged. 'I have done all that I could, but still our Mother's body retains its shape of life and Her soul cannot depart.'

The eldest of the three, Goddess of Fire, Ka Ding, then understood that it must be Her task to free Her Mother's soul. With Her mighty powers, She burned the scorched forest until the intensity of Her heat caused Earth's body to burst into flame, to boil as heaving lakes of lava, so that great blisters formed into mountains, leaving deep valleys between. When the waters that remained from Ka Um's flood flowed into the valleys and formed rivers where they had not been before, Ka Ding knew that She had finally performed the sacred rites. It was in this way that Earth's body was changed enough to free the soul within Her.

RANGADA

This is another little known account of a mortal woman, this one from the great epic work known as the *Mahabharata*. Although Hindu tradition suggests that this 90,000 stanza work is from about 3000 B.C., most scholars of Indian literature date it to about 900 B.C., some to as late as 300 B.C.

High upon her horse she rode, courage shining clearly in the gleaming darkness of her eyes. Her hunting arrows sent straighter than any of the village, her fearlessness in driving off an enemy imitated but never equalled by those who followed her, Rangada led her people through hunt and battle.

Knowing little of modesty and coy behavior, Rangada spoke easily of what was on her mind. Thus when she found the youth Arjuna sleeping in the woods beneath a tree, she dismounted from her horse and walked closer to see the lovely lad who wakened from the sound of the forest leaves that crackled beneath her feet. In fear, he reached for his arrows, until Rangada spoke of her enjoyment of his beauty, explaining that she had drawn close only to better admire each fine feature of his face and the structure of his lean brown body, saying that for him she could feel love and that she would enjoy knowing his body in this way.

Arjuna, confused by her open speech, spoke quickly of his vow of celibacy, that which he had taken not many days before, and meant to keep throughout one year. But he then added to this reason for refusal that even should he desire to break his vow, he would surely not do so with a woman so outspoken, one whose quiver of arrows told of a life that he did not regard as womanly, at least not as he believed a woman should be.

Hurt deeply by the words he spoke, confused in heart and mind yet still filled with wanting to know Arjuna better, Rangada put away her hunting clothes, discarded her bow and arrows. In their stead, she wrapped herself with silks, slid bangle bracelets upon her arms, slipped bangle bracelets upon her ankles, hung golden loops upon her ears, rubbed sweet smelling oils upon her cinnamon skin—and made her way to the tent of Arjuna. Entering without a word, as Arjuna sat in holy meditation, Rangada lay down upon his mat, so that when his eyes did open she beckoned him to come and lie beside her.

So it happened that Arjuna broke his vow of celibacy, for though she said her name was Malha, Arjuna thought that the woman who had appeared so mysteriously in his tent was the nymph or Goddess, woman as perfect as woman can be. In the months that then passed, Malha and Arjuna wandered joyfully along the banks of rippling mountain streams, made love on the soft ferns of the forest, as Arjuna hunted for what food was needed and Malha prepared it to suit his taste.

Thirteen moons had grown large and disappeared when a group of villagers riding by Arjuna's tent stopped to ask Arjuna if he had seen their leader. They spoke of a woman just twenty-two years, a woman of most perfect aim, a woman whose body blended perfectly with the rhythm of her horse's gallop, a woman whose heart was brave, whose courage any man would want to follow. The villagers then told Arjuna of how their homes had been attacked and how though they had battled fiercely, they could not drive the invaders from the land. Again they spoke of their leader Rangada, agreeing upon her brilliance in both hunt and battle, explaining their days of constant troubles since her disappearance. Arjuna, thinking to help them in their plight, knowing of his own prowess in battle, offered to ride with them. As he waited for their answer, he thought of the brave woman leader, imagining the pleasures of riding alongside such a remarkable woman.

Within the darkness of the tent, Rangada heard the speaking and recognized the voices of her comrades of the past. Unable to remain quietly inside, as she heard the reports of their troubles, she came forth to greet her friends, to offer her help—daring Arjuna's wrath at the game she had played as Malha. Cries of joy greeted Rangada's appearance, each village comrade reaching out to grasp the hand of the leader who had so long been missing. Some fell upon their knees with gratitude that she had finally been found, but none was more astonished than Arjuna.

Even as Arjuna saw his gentle Malha mount a great black steed, her arms strong enough to calm its excitement, her legs strong enough to soothe its great body, still he did not trust his eyes. But when from her seat high upon its back, Rangada invited Arjuna to join them in the battle, he mounted the horse by her side, ever puzzled by the feelings of unexpected joy that came from riding alongside Rangada Malha.

USHAS

The name of Ushas, and her identification with the dawn, occur in the *Rg Veda*. Her image is definitely of Indo-European origin, to be regarded as much the same deity as Eos of Greece and Aurora of Rome. In accordance with most of the female deities of the Vedic writings, She is young, lovely and somewhat nymphlike. The association of Ushas with the dawn led to references in later texts that call upon Ushas to arrive as the dawn of spiritual awakening.

Holy Spirit of the morning light,
Her golden glow rises in the eastern sky
as Her chariot drawn by seven cinnamon heifers
passes through the celestial gates,
followed by one hundred golden chariots.
Her gauzy veils of many colours,
each embroidered with threads of gold,
float behind Her in the gentle breeze,
revealing the smile upon Her face.
Riding upon Her path in the heavens,
She arrives as the dawning of the day.

Sun before the sun,
as old as the time
when the sun first rose
on the first morning,
Ushas is forever young,
causing some to wish
that She would not arrive each day,
for Her eternal youth only serves to remind
that each time that She appears,
the rest of us grow older.

Yet those who embrace
the joys of knowing many dawns,
call upon Her to bring the light of dawn
into the inner night of the mind,
asking that She shed Her rays of morning light
not only to awaken each body,
but to awaken each mind.

# of sea and star and serpent

-- SUMERIAN

umer, the most ancient literate civilization on record, left a legacy of Goddess imagery and reverence that gleams with the rich patina of five thousand years. As Creator of heaven and earth, as giver of the laws of life, the concept of writing, methods of agriculture and much more, images of Goddess reverence in Sumer allow us to glimpse into the dawn of civilization.

After several millenia of Goddess worshipping Neolithic cultures in the Near East, such as those of Jericho, Catal Huyuk, Hacilar, and the Hassuna and Halaf periods, a culture began to develop along the southern banks of the Tigris and Euphrates Rivers. This culture, known as Sumerian, appears to have been the first in the world to have developed a system of writing. The Sumerian culture is associated with a slightly earlier culture known as Ubaidian, formed by peoples who had entered Mesopotamia shortly before the Sumerian period. Some of the people of the Ubaidian culture are known to have settled at the site of Eridu, close to the Persian Gulf. Although Ubaidians are most often credited with initiating Sumerian development, lesser known cultures in the Eridu area probably played a part in the initiation of this ancient civilization. None of the evidence has so far provided scholars with knowledge of the racial or linguistic identity of the ancient Sumerians.

The Sumerian language confuses the identification of the Sumerian peoples even further, in that their language was neither

Semitic nor Indo-European, the two major language groups of the area. One of the foremost scholars of Sumerian culture, Professor S.N. Kramer, described the Sumerian Language as ". . .reminiscent to some extent of the Ural-Altaic languages." These languages are best known among groups of northern Siberia and among the Finns, the Turks and other north Asian groups (see Japanese section). One must be careful not to draw conclusions from such a statement, but consideration of this possible link certainly suggests the need for further research.

Thus the racial identity of the Sumerians is still quite open to question, but there is no question that from about 3500 B.C. onwards, Sumer was well into an astonishing cultural flowering. The development of the culture reached a high point in the Jemdet Nasr period (about 3200 B.C.) with the invention of writing. From 3200 B.C. until shortly before 2000 B.C., writing appears to have been used primarily for keeping temple records of land assignments and the gathering and distribution of crops and livestock. One early law code (Urukagina) is dated to about 2300 B.C. But except for a few fragments and the temple records, most of the epic poetry, law codes, hymns and ritual texts of Sumer are from slightly before 2000 B.C. and afterwards. The Sumerian system of writing, wedge shaped marks (cuneiform) pressed into clay tablets while they were still damp, evolved from the initial use of pictorial symbols to those of an increasingly abstract nature. This major contribution to history was then adopted by the Semitic Akkadians, and through the Phoenicians of Canaan was eventually passed on to the Greeks, the alphabet symbols undergoing considerable changes and development throughout the many centuries in which this occurred.

It is vital to realize that our current knowledge of the Sumerians is based upon the chance fortune of what has so far been discovered and the condition in which it has been found. The artifacts that provide us with information about Sumerian life and religious beliefs are those that were in use from about 3200 to 1700 B.C. Excavations are continually adding to our body of knowledge about the Sumerian people. As this occurs over many decades, information is often found that confirms or contradicts scholarly theories based upon the earlier evidence. It is for this reason that I have chosen to present information that is known from specific tablets and artifacts, pointing out some hopefully interesting connections, but avoiding overly generalized analyses about what we simply do not yet know. It is important, however, to realize that what is known today about a particular Goddess image is not necessarily, or even likely, the totality of that image as it was known in the past. It is information that we know with some certainty today.

The evidence of Mesopotamia reveals that there was a close relationship between the Sumerians and the Semites who were settled slightly further to the north. This is attested by 2400 B.C. but may have existed long before that time. Many rulers of Sumer had Semitic names and at several sites evidence of Sumerian and early Semitic culture have been found side by side. One scholar even went so far as to suggest that the entire Sumerian culture was composed of Semitic people and that the Sumerian language was used only for purposes of writing, but the evidence seem to refute this hypothesis at almost every point.

It is true that the Sumerian Goddess Inanna is closely associated with the Semitic Goddess Ishtar (see Semitic section—Vol. I), Ishtar eventually replacing the name of Inanna at the great temple in Erech. But there are many differences in the imagery and symbolism of the Goddess as She appears under each of these names. Even within the Sumerian culture itself, many differences are to be noted between Goddess imagery and ritual as known in separate locations and various periods.

One location that invites further investigation is that of the city of Nippur, an extremely sacred centre of the Sumerians, and specifically connected to the bestowal of divine right to rulership. The name most often mentioned by scholars as the 'chief deity' of Nippur is Enlil, though it was his wife Ninlil who actually bestowed the divine right. Careful examination of the Sumerian account of Enlil's rape of Ninlil before their marriage, the name of Nanshebargunu given as the mother of Ninlil and as the Mother of Nippur, another text stating that the Goddess Nidaba (Goddess of Writing) was the mother of Ninlil, and the importance of the 'Laws of Nidaba' in Lagash where the Goddess was most often named as Nanshe—all exist as clues for a more careful exploration of the special sanctity of Nippur. Though Enlil's name was certainly important during the historical periods, the powers of the Goddess as Nanshebargunu, Nanshe, Nidaba or Ninlil may have preceded the importance of Enlil in Nippur.

We might also want to more carefully examine the legend of the attack upon the Goddess Ereshkigal by the war god Nergal, an account that deals with the way in which Ereshkigal lost the sole sovereignty of the Land of the Irkalla. This exploration should certainly include a careful consideration of the role of the male deity Enki (Ea) in his assistance to Nergal, as well as a study of the transformations and the continually increasing importance and power of Enki as he appears in the legends of Ninmah, Ninhursag, and Inanna.

While reading and rereading the translations of Sumerian epic poetry, it is difficult not to take notice of and to respond to the poetic use of metaphor and simile, as well as to the style of phrasing in which an idea is presented and then expanded upon. In the prayer of Enheduanna (from about 2300 B.C.), this ancient poet/priestess described her sad plight at being driven from the temple of Ningal in the city of Ur as that of being 'forced to flee the cote like a swallow'. The hymn, actually to Inanna, the daughter of Ningal, describes the wrath of Inanna as an 'attacking storm' and Inanna's voice as 'blowing louder than a howling storm. . .moaning louder than the evil winds'.

Another text, describing the destruction of the temple at Ur about 400 years later, is a lament for the Goddess Ningal. Here we can see the expansion of the message conveyed, as each new fact confirms and further explains the lines preceding it:

> Your city has been made into ruins,
> You are no longer its Mistress;
> Your righteous house has been given over to the pickaxe,
> You no longer inhabit it;
> Your people have been led to the slaughter,
> You are no longer their Queen. . .
> O Queen, your city weeps before you as its Mother.

It is not difficult to imagine Sumerian poems or hymns being recited aloud, this form of expanded repetition emphasizing and clarifying what is being said. A somewhat similar style of phrasing also occurs in Semitic literature, especially noticeable in the epics of Ugarit. It may well be that these written texts followed a long tradition of oral recitation. The poetic imagery found all throughout the Sumerian texts reveals a sophistication of thought and expression no less developed that any we have found since the days of the Sumerian people.

NAMMU

Nammu is probably the earliest recorded name of a universe creating deity so far discovered anywhere on earth. She is described in a few extremely ancient fragments as 'the mother who gave birth to heaven and earth'. The ideogram symbol used for Her name is identical to the sign used to designate the ocean. Ama or Amu is the Sumerian word for mother, and it is possible that the Sumerian *Nin* once preceded this Goddess name as it does so many others. Nammu is not only credited with being the Mother of all Deities, but also as the one who first decided that human beings should be made, an act then carried out by Her daughter Ninmah. Descriptions of the Sumerian paradise known as Dilmun, as an idyllic ancient homeland, are believed to have influenced other Near and Middle Eastern cultures and may be the source of the Hebrew account of Eden.

Ama Tu An Ki—
Mother who gave birth
to heaven and earth,
Primordial Creator of the Universe
who oversees the fashioning of life
and to each decrees their fate,
Oldest of the Old,
ancient, even among Sumerians.
Mother Primeval Sea left memories
in the land of the two rivers—
that it was She who had created all above,
that it was She who had created all below.

Memories of far off Dilmun island,
paradise where death and sickness were unknown,
perfect land where skies were always clear and blue,
where trees were thick in the orchard
and each heavy with its perfect fruit,
lingered as knowledge of the ancient homeland,
island where Sumerians had once lived,
island first created by Nammu.

NINA

Nina (Nana) also appears as a very ancient name of the Goddess in Sumer. She is most often represented as a serpent tailed or fish tailed woman, these images perhaps associated with Nammu as the Primeval Sea. The oldest artifacts identifying Nina are from the settlement at Eridu, close to the point at which the Tigris and Euphrates reach the Persian Gulf. Evidence of offerings of fish were found upon the ancient altars of Eridu, though in historical periods this city was associated with the male deity Enki. The prefix *Nin* precedes many Goddess names and some have translated it as Goddess or Lady (in its original sense as the female counterpart of Lord). There is a male deity known as Ninurta, described as a son of Ninmah but *urta* may mean ancient mother and may once have been a Goddess name itself. Since the name Nina is the most basic form of the title Nin, I have taken the liberty of including many other Sumerian Goddess names and aspects in this piece, but it should be understood that these names and the statements associated with them do appear as separate from Nina in the Sumerian tablets. It is generally thought that each of these Goddess names was originally known as that of the Mother Goddess in a specific town or community, and that later identification by specific aspects or activities in an assembly of deities may be the result of the continual centralizing of government and a subsequently more centralized theology.

From the deep waters of the Goddess Sea came the Holy One of many names, Ama Gal Dingir, Mother Great Goddess, Her mighty powers known among the people of ancient Sumer.

When they spoke of Her as She who watched over Nammu's isle of Dilmun—they said that She was Nin Sikil. When they called upon Her to tend them in their times of illness, to provide healing herbs and the magic words of cure—they said that She was Ninkarrak, Gula or Bau. When gratitude was offered for the beer and the wine that She had given for their pleasure and the libations at the holy rites—they said that She was Ninkasi. When they spoke of Her as Wild Cow of the Cattle Folds, High Priestess who sat upon the throne, offering sagacious counsel, interpreting the dreams of the people—they said that She was Ninsun or Ninsunna. When they spoke of Her as the birthgiving Mother, the one who wept at the time of the great flood, the one to whom all those who had drowned returned to at their death, the one whose temple graced the wide plains of Khafajah—they said that She was Ninti or Nintu.

When they knew Her as The Lady of the city of Lagash, the one who gave the barley of the fields so that the people could eat to satisfaction, or when She was approached in Her holy shrine and asked to untangle the threads of the images of dreams so that all could understand what had been told to them when their eyes were closed with sleep, knowing Her as The Judge of Humankind on the last day of each year, She who asked if they had comforted the orphan, She who asked if they had cared for the elderly and ill, She who asked if they had given shelter to the homeless, She who asked if they had given food to any who were hungry—they said that Her name was Nanshe.

When they spoke of who it was that formed the people of the earth with the guiding help of Nammu, and who it was that directed brother/husband Enki to feed the people She had made, and who it was that watched as Enki attempted to make people of his own and thus produced such a feeble being that it could not walk and could not talk and could not even reach its hand out to take the bread that had been offered, and who it was that seeing this cursed Enki for the sorrow he had brought by trying to fashion human life when it was not his natural work to do—they said that Her name was Ninmah.

When they looked upon Her as the holy mountain that rose from the primeval waters, the Wild Cow that came at the beginning and shattered the very air with Her presence as Regent of Earth and Heaven, and when they stood before Her shrine at Al Ubaid where the winged lioness guarded from above while images of Her sacred herd of cattle were marked in ivory on Her blue mosaic wall, and when they remembered that it was She who first gave birth to the healing plants that Enki ate in greed as soon as She had birthed them, and when they remembered who it was that then placed the gravely ill Enki by Her sacred vulva until She brought forth eight deities of healing, each born without any pain of labour, so that the greedy Enki was soon cured of his illness— they said that Her name was Ninhursag.

When they spoke of The Mother in the city of Nippur, She who owned the divine Dukug, the grain chamber of the heavens, and of the time She gave the gift of the Dukug, thus teaching the growing of the grain, how to sow, how to harvest, while in Her Tummal shrine on earth, She received the lad that She had chosen as the shepherd, and when they remembered that it was She who gave birth to the moon in the darkness of the Netherworld; and yet cannot forget the anger of the memory of Her rape by Enlil who then sat upon the throne of Nippur's First Mother, Nanshebargunu—they said that Her name was Ninlil.

When they gazed into the night time sky over the cities of Harran and Ur and saw the glowing circle of Her in the moon, and heard Her called upon by women who knew the power of Her light, and when they knew of the names of those who served as High Priestess at Her ever gifted altar as Enheduanna and Eannatum, those who had once lived in the cloistered gigparu rectory of the temple, and when they sang the songs of lamentation of the destruction of the city and called upon Her as The Mother and Queen of Ur, She who held the sovereignty while husband Nannar was Her ishib priest, and they cried because She could no longer watch over Ur and because Enheduanna who had once interpreted Her messages was no longer able to convey Her wishes—they said that Her name was Ningal or Nikkal.

Yet when they stood where the two rivers met and poured into the wide gulf that led into the sea, and knew Her at the settlement of Eridu as The Oldest One, Serpent Goddess of the Oracles, Mistress of Unfathomable Decrees, Interpreter of Dreams, Prophetess of Deities, She who assigned the destinies of lives while swimming as a fish, Her tail opalescent in the waters, the sacred sign that spelled Her name the same as the sign of the city of Nineveh—they spoke of Her as Nana or Nina and to Her they directed these prayers so many thousands of years ago:

Hear O ye regions, the praise of Queen Nana,
Magnify the Creatress, Exalt the Dignified,
Hold high the Glorious One,
Draw close to The Mighty Lady

O Nina, Lady of the Holy Rites,
Lady of precious divine decree,
Lady who decides the fates,
Thy word is reliable,
it excels above all else,
Prophetess of Deities art Thou,
Sovereign of the lands art Thou.

NIDABA

In the artifacts of the Goddess Nidaba, She is often symbolized as serpent or woman with a serpent tail. At the towns of Nippur, Lagash, Erech and Umma, She was regarded as the tutelary deity of writing, preceding any male deities to whom this important cultural contribution was later credited. The oldest evidence of writing so far discovered—and believed to be the earliest on earth—was found at the temple of Erech and dates back to the Jemdet Nasr period (about 3200 B.C.). Throughout the historical periods this temple was consecrated to the Goddess Inanna. This earliest form of written language, once deciphered and translated, turned out to be records of land assignments by the temple. Since later Sumerian documents explained that the group of priestesses known as the Naditu were in charge of this aspect of temple activities, it appears quite likely that it was the Naditu who first developed a method of recording their accounts, thus the very beginnings of the ability to record ideas in written form. Nidaba's name also appears as the author of the sacred laws of Lagash, those by which the Goddess Nanshe judged humankind each New Year. The images of Nidaba, and the woman scribe Belit Sheri who recorded the deeds of the dead, offer interesting parallels to the images of Maat and Seshat of Egypt (see Egyptian section).

Serpent Goddess of Wisdom, Divine Serpent Lady of Life, Basmu Usum—Holy Cobra, She who made Her way through the reeds of the marshes of Sumer even before it was called by that name and from the reeds that She knew so well, She created the stylus to press into the dampness of the soft flattened clay, giving one of the most precious gifts, that of taking what is in our mortal minds and preserving for those yet to come, ideas that might once have been forgotten—yet now remain as long as clay that has been baked in fire's oven.

Most Ancient Scribe, not only did She give the stylus but Her decrees of wisdom's ways, for those who were filled with the eternal presence of Her being marked down for all posterity what She taught in the beginning. Most Learned One of the Holy Chamber, born in the ib room of Goddess temple, yet at the same time living in the starry skies, Her seven arms holding the seven tablets, She is the designer of the fifty decrees of righteousness, Her laws for living written as arrangements of the stars upon Her heavenly tablets of the darkest blue of lapis stone.

Holy Nidaba, was it not She who taught the knowledge of the written word to Belit Sheri and then appointed Her as scribe to

[handwritten marginalia: STYLUS = PRESERVING IDEAS; LAW GIVER]

41

mark down the deeds of all who live—upon the leaves of the Tree of Life? It was She who arranged the patterns of the stars so that people may choose their paths between them, thinking always of Her wisdom, calling upon Her in times of indecision, in contemplation of the messages of sleep, asking always for Her guidance in best following Her ways.

Holy One of the Reed, Holy One of Wisdom—is there a knowing mortal upon this earth who can write a line, a phrase, a word, and remember Her ancient sacred being without thoughts of gratitude?

INANNA

Inanna was probably the most widely known Goddess name among the Sumerians in the later periods of Sumer. As Erech became the centre of Sumerian culture and government, Inanna's increasingly popularized image assimilated many of the aspects and rituals known under other Goddess names in various towns and communities. The name of Inanna, often written as Innin, may be related to the ancient Goddess name Nina. As Nina was symbolized by a serpent, so Inanna's name was often accompanied by a serpent coiling about a staff. The description of Inanna as the daughter of Ninmah or Ningal (depending upon the location of the text), also suggests the rise in importance of Inanna as Sumerian theological structures were changing. It is interesting to note that whereas Enki plays the role of son or troublesome husband in the legends of Nammu, Ninmah and Ninhursag, he is given a much greater stature in the legends of Inanna. The name of Inanna's assistant Ninshuber may reveal a change of gender over the years, as other Sumerian documents include the line Ninshuber Amamu, i.e. Ninshuber is my mother.

GRANDMOTHER

3RD GENERATION

MOTHER

DAUGHTER

From the ancient family of Creator Goddess Nammu, from Nammu's daughter known as Ningal or Ninmah, came the Daughter Goddess Inanna. Her Goddess powers lessened as Mesopotamian centuries passed, yet still She was called upon as Mistress of the Heavens, Sovereign Lady of the Land, Queen of the Assembly of Deities. But Inanna was spoken of as the daughter of Anu, or the daughter of Nannar, or the daughter of Enki, said to fix destinies with the help of Enlil, said to have received Her right to choose who would sit upon the royal throne from Enki. Though Nammu had created heaven and earth and Ninmah had created people, new tribes moving to the land of the two rivers made less of the nature of the Goddess, viewing Her as Daughter more than Mother, explaining Her still remembered powers as those that had been given to Her by men.

Yet the most ancient image of Creator Mother lingered in some Sumerian hearts for Inanna was still said to hold 'full power of judgement and decision and the control of the law of heaven and earth'. Her Goddess essence was called upon in the earthly form of Her High Priestess, to regulate the divine order, to fix destinies at the time of each new moon, and deepest reverence was paid to Her even by the deities of the Great Assembly of Heaven, as She announced the judgements of the land. Mortals looked upon Her holy light as the morning star that heralds each day, as the evening star that announces the arrival of each night, as the sacred planet Venus—Inanna watching over all.

It was said that Inanna's Eye was Ama Usum Gal Ana, Mother Serpent Great of Heaven, even as She was known as Lioness in Battle, lions adoring Her Goddess being carved upon a mace head at Khafajah, while Inanna sat upon Her lion throne or stood upon the lion's back, even as heifer horns adorned Her holy head in the ancient settlement of Erech. Those who spoke of moonlike Ningal as Inanna's Mother, said that Utu was the sun and now Her brother, yet many still claimed that She was The Mighty Queen, 'designer of all heaven and earth, able to make the mountains quiver, able to shake the very heavens, able to destroy the indestructible, able to make perish the unperishable.'

Some Sumerians spoke of Her tender love and of the time that She had favoured Agade, bringing peace and prosperity to that town through Her ever watchful guidance. Thus the tablets spoke of Her sagacious counsel given through Agade's elderly women and men who called upon Her as Majestic Queen, She whose decrees are supreme, Divine Mother who reveals the laws—while Her ever present symbols of the gatepost knot and loop were tied upon each storehouse filled with wheat and barley, speaking silently of the food that She gave, and of Her gift of the knowledge of the growing—as those in Nippur had spoken of Ninlil.

ATTRIBUTES
GATEPOST LOOP
8-POINTED STAR
EYE

Along the waters of the Tigris and Euphrates and the flowing Tigris finger of Diyala, each pouring into the wide and waiting mouth of the Persian Gulf, shrines and temples to Inanna were set as rising jewels upon the desert sands. At Kish and Khafajah, at Nippur and Lagash, at Agrab and Agade, Inanna's eight petalled star glistened alongside Her gatepost loop, while at the temple at Tell Brak set deep into the Khabur Valley, even before the time of the building of the pyramids of Gizeh, symbols of the Goddess Eye were left among a multitude of beads, and eight petalled rosettes glowed with the golden light of the evening star.

Of all the towns and villages that called upon Her name and built great shrines and temples to house the essence of Her divinity, none could compare with the temple of E Anna that stood on the ancient sacred grounds of the city of Erech. Close by the waters of the Euphrates, for centuries Her worshippers had erected the new upon the old, most ancient foundations beneath the newer grandeur of red and black and white mosaic pattern, carefully formed from the tiny bases of terra cotta cones. Until, with the ever growing cluster of courtyards and buildings, they formed the great E Anna, Inanna's House of Heaven, center of protecting guidance, home of the Great Goddess who watched over all from Eshnunna to Eridu.

Great were the powers of she who was the Entu, Lady who is a Deity, living in the sacred gigparu apartments as High Priestess to Inanna, incarnation upon the earth of Her heavenly being above, presiding over temple lands, over communities of people, dispensing land and food to all. The orphan, the elderly, the weak, were each cared for with as much concern and tenderness as those who could work the land of Erech and bring the fruits of their labours to the storehouse of the temple. Priestesses carried out the Entu's work, Naditu women living together in their gagu temple home, watching over the fields and fisheries, the poultry, the cattle and the orchards, recording what had been brought in, recording what had been given out, thus helping the people of Inanna—as the Entu governed wisely as the mother of the city.

Deep beneath earth's blanket, that which covered the sanctified E Anna for over five thousand years, lay the lowest level of the Goddess shrine at Erech, most ancient temple that housed the first markings recording the assignments of the land, the apportioning of the food, the allotments of the fish, the cattle, the wheat, the fruit, that which had been gathered and distributed by the temple offices. Ancient marks of written language pressed into the once soft clay by priestesses, those who collected and distributed all that was needed by the people of Erech, bestowed upon the memory of human mind the precious gift of written reminder, milestone of cultural growth—the pragmatic genius of the women of E Anna marked forever on the passing stream of time, indelible as the brilliant gift of the Sumerian Goddess.

Lying not far from the ancient tablets, tall as a child of four years, was the alabaster vase whose ringed carvings preserved images of E Anna ritual, Goddess or High Priestess seated upon the throne, horned as the heifer of heaven, approached by naked rotund men who brought their offerings of wheat and fruit, of fish and animals, to lay before the holy feet of She who sat upon the throne, guiding the community of Erech, over five thousand years ago.

At the time of the New Year, the priestess of Inanna prepared for the yearly sacred mating ritual from times most ancient even then, each year the High Priestess choosing for her bed the one she would appoint as shepherd, a new lad for the year, yet always spoken of as Damuzi, true son, consort of the Goddess. The priestess of Inanna made ready, wrapping her breechcloth and robes about her body freshly bathed, making her face to glow as amber, placing the kohl upon her eyes, inviting the new Damuzi to prove himself upon her bed, to test his fitness as the year's new shepherd.

The chosen Damuzi appeared before her, promising to perform Inanna's holy rites, promising to accomplish the divine pattern, stating that he had brought the presents to the sacred house of Inanna, declaring that he would follow carefully the ancient Goddess rites of the New Moon. The priestess of Inanna, though pleased with all the offerings and his promised dedication to Inanna, reminded the lad that he had not yet proved his worth, announcing to the gathered congregation:

> When on my bed he has shown his love,
> when he has given pleasure to my loins,
> when I have given pleasure to his,
> then shall I show my kindness to Damuzi,
> then shall I arrange his destiny,
> only then shall I appoint him to be shepherd
> of the flocks of my land.

Thus on the day of this holy ritual, on the day of the year's end, a bed was set for the High Priestess of Inanna, so that she might test the new Damuzi. Descending from the wide steps of the temple, she led the new Damuzi to her bed, assuring him that the fruits he brought were sweet, that his herbs and plants were tasty, and that his youthful beauty was as sweet as honey, promising that when she had enjoyed his beauty, her love would be more savoury than honey—for she would then choose him for Inanna's holy lap, appoint him as the year's new shepherd, present him with the crook and staff, touch him with the wand of shepherd-ship. So deep in Sumerian memory was the knowledge that the shepherd must be the lad who was chosen by the Goddess that later kings who sat upon Mesopotamian thrones spoke of them-selves as Damuzi, as the beloved of the holy Inanna, king—because they had been chosen for Her holy lap.

Within Inanna's holy house lived the priestesses in the mastaku quarters, immaculate, perfect, sacred nu-gig women who made love to those who came to pray, initiating those who would gain wisdom of the sanctity of life's creative process, of Inanna's gift to mortals, welcoming those who yearned to touch divinity, to understand the miracle of the creation of life, to be in contact with the essence of existence – through love sanctified within the sacred shrine, through communion with the holiest of women, the perfect earthly reflections of She who makes all life.

Though Erech had long been a mighty city, the first where written language saw the light of day, the first where the wheel of the potter had been made to circle round, where the High Priest-esses of Inanna had long sat upon the throne of guidance, there were those who had forgotten that Enki was but the son of Nam-mu, the First Mother who had created heaven and earth, and that Enki was the oftimes foolish husband of Ninmah or Ninhursag. Thus they told a story to explain the marvel of Erech's gains and the many gracious gifts of the Goddess to that town, claiming that its ever blossoming culture had been taken from Enki's home in Eridu, adding that Enki was a god of wisdom and that he was the father of the Goddess, of She who was still said to be Designer of all Heaven and Earth.

The tale they told was that Inanna had one day stepped into the Boat of Heaven and sailed south upon the wide Euphrates from Her home in Erech until She reached the watery abyss of

Enki's shrine in Eridu. Entering nervous Enki's home, She had been offered food and drink to appease Her possible wrath, yet it was not Inanna who grew drunk but nervous Enki who drank more than he served, and in his drunken state he had agreed to give all the gifts of culture, the precious one hundred Me's, to the mighty Goddess, so that She might take them back to Erech.

Arranging the one hundred Me's safely for the journey, back into the boat Inanna stepped. Hardly had She started north to Erech, when Enki changed his mind and sent a group of monsters of the sea to attack the Boat of Heaven of Inanna, to return the Me's to Eridu and Enki. With the help of loyal assistant Ninshuber, Inanna fought the monsters off, still piloting the boat along its course, all the while shouting angry curses at the god of Eridu for his sudden change of mind, for his daring to reclaim what he had freely given, and most of all for launching this attack upon the open waters without warning. So furiously did they defend the boat, that with Ninshuber's help, Inanna drove the monsters from their path and journeyed on towards Erech, finally docking safely at its shores.

Thus went the story that was told to explain why those of Erech spoke of the many gifts, the Me's that had been given by Inanna to Her people in the city of Erech: weaving and pottery, the sowing and harvesting of the grains, justice, truth and understanding, wisdom and the laws that guided people, eldership and the sexual rituals, the crook and the sceptre and the priestly office of Divine Lady. These gifts and many more did Inanna give to Erech—but the followers of Enki claimed that She had taken them from a drunken god of wisdom whose sagacity and decisions rang as hollow echoes in the bottom of an empty drinking jug, while they could not forget that She had brought them in Her Boat of Heaven.

Many were the tales about Inanna and Damuzi; many were the hymns of sadness sung upon Damuzi's death, mournful memories of the young lad's dying and how Inanna wept for Her son lover while the women of Inanna grieved in sympathy and lamentation:

> For the lover who slumbers,
> for the child who no longer
> brings happiness to the temple of E Anna,
> for holy Inanna who sorrows more deeply than any.

My child, the far removed,
my Damu, the far removed,
my lover who brought the plentiful food,
my lover who provided abundant drink,
my lover who is bound like the Tigris,
my lover who is captive like the Euphrates.

The mate of the Queen of Heaven no longer lives,
the keeper of the cattle stalls no longer lives,
in E Anna there is weeping,
the crying is for the plants,
for they no longer grow,
the crying is for the barley,
for it no longer grows,
the crying is for the flocks of sheep,
for no longer are the young lambs born,
the crying is for the herds of cattle,
for no longer are the young calves born,
the crying is for the great rivers,
for they no longer bring the floods.

Though the drought and famine of the land were reminders of Damuzi's death, Sumerians also remembered a time long before, when Inanna had descended into the Irkalla. Walking down the steps of the Land of No Return, arriving in the domain of the Land of the Dead, Inanna had found Herself a captive and had been freed only with Her promise that She would supply a life —in substitution for Her own. So it came to pass that Inanna once again ascended into heaven, searching for a substitute to send to the Irkalla in Her stead, accompanied and guarded by a host of Gallas, ghastly heartless demons who turned life into death.

Seeing the loyal Ninshuber waiting for his Mistress to return, the Gallas were about to take him as the substitute until Inanna stayed their pale white hands, telling of his constant, faithful service and declaring that Ninshuber was not to be Her choice as substitute. Approaching the city of Umma, the Gallas spied the god named Shara and once again stepped forward to claim him as the substitute, but Shara bowed low in the dust at Inanna's holy feet and for this act of reverence and respect, Inanna turned the Gallas from this humble god—thus sparing him from being taken to the Land of No Return. Approaching the city of Badtibera, the Gallas spied the god Latarrek and once again stepped forward to claim him as the substitute, but Latarrek bowed low in the dust at Inanna's holy feet and for this act of reverence and respect, Inanna turned the Gallas from this humble god—thus sparing him from being taken to the Land of No Return.

Finally arriving at the district of Kullab, a neighborhood upon the grounds of Erech where Inanna's temple glistened in the sunlight, Inanna was shocked to see Damuzi, the son She had appointed as the shepherd, the lover She had appointed as the keeper of the goat stalls—for no longer was he dressed in shepherd's clothes. Dressed in royal robes, he was sitting high upon Inanna's throne, and more astonishing, Inanna saw that he was rejoicing at Her disappearance, happily claiming Her position of Sovereign and Ruler of the Lands of Erech. There he sat, joyfully celebrating Her long absence, the days that She had spent in the Irkalla, hoping that She would never return.

Infuriated at his heartlessness, at his pleasure in sitting upon Her throne, while shedding not a tear at Her disappearance, or at the possibility of Her death in the Irkalla, his thoughts only upon the crook of sovereignty and the power that he had gained upon Her absence—Inanna looked upon him with the Eye of Death. Thus the Gallas claimed Damuzi as the substitute, dragging him off to the Irkalla, to the Land of No Return, for allowing his ambition to cause him to forget all love and loyalty to his mother, his mate, his Goddess.

So it came to pass that each year, at the time of remembering Damuzi's death, when the rivers grew low in the dryness of the summer, the story of how Damuzi died was told. And though Inanna grieved for the loss of son and lover, Her heart was for the welfare of the people, those who were Hers to protect and guide. Thus She banished even Her own son when he had rejoiced at taking the ancient Mother's place upon the throne, for despite the many changes in the nature of Inanna, many still remembered Her wisdom and Her guidance as those that had once been given by Her ancient Grandmother Nammu, She who gave birth to heaven and earth.

ERESHKIGAL

Although the Goddess who once held the sole sovereignty of the Irkalla, the Land of the Dead, is at times described as sister to Inanna, Ereshkigal appears to be a quite separate and perhaps more ancient deity. The legend included here was found on tablets at El Amarna in Egypt and dates to about 1400 B.C. But Ereshkigal's name appears on some of the oldest writings of Sumer. The translation of *kigal* is Great Earth, but the meaning of *Eresh* is uncertain. In this particular myth I have not only told the story of Nergal's attack upon Ereshkigal, as described on the El Amarna tablets, but also tried my hand at the unique style of Sumerian writing that made its way into my own sentence structure after so many readings of this and other Sumerian legends. It should be noted that Ea, the male deity who assists Nergal in this tragic story, was the Babylonian name for the Sumerian Enki.

Great was the feast
planned by the Annunaki,
joyous were the festivities
being arranged by this assembly of deities,
plentiful was the barley beer,
abundant was the khubuz bread.
Wine from the date, wine from the grape,
these flowed like a flooding river.
Quince and fig, pomegranate and apricot,
all of these were set beside
the overflowing baskets of fresh fish
and the mountainous platters of roasted goat.
All of the deities of the Annunaki were invited,
even the lesser deities of the Igigi
were asked to attend—
never before had such a banquet been made,
not even in heaven.

Far from the preparations of the heavenly feast,
She who was once known as the Birth Giving Mother,
She who was now Ruler of the Underworld,
She who was the Mistress of the Land of No Return,
She who was the Sovereign of the dark Irkalla,
Queen Ereshkigal—sat upon Her throne,
presiding over Her domain
of those who had passed from the living.

By Her side was the woman Belit Seri,
sacred scribe of the records of the dead,
She who wrote each human deed
upon the leaves of the Tree of Life.
By Her side was the righteous Nungal,
She who judged the essence of each life,
daughter of the Queen of Souls, Ereshkigal.

So busy was Ereshkigal
when the messenger of the Annunaki arrived,
when Kika had descended the steps of heaven,
and passed through the seven gates of Irkalla,
when Kika told Ereshkigal of the coming party—
that great was Her sadness when She had to refuse
the tempting invitation.
Too demanding were Her duties—
chaos would creep into the Netherworld
without Her constant presence.

Thus She chose Namtar,
he who followed Her every word,
Her most loyal assistant,
to ascend the steps of heaven,
to attend the great Annunaki banquet in Her stead,
there to join the feast as Her ambassador
and upon leaving, to bring the portion of Ereshkigal
back to the Land of No Return—
Ereshkigal's share would be brought to Her by Namtar.

When the proper time had come,
when the banquet was about to be given,
Namtar made his way through the seven gates of Irkalla,
one by one, he ascended the steps to heaven
and so awesome was the respect for Ereshkigal,
so great the fear and wonder
at Her Queendom of Dead Souls,
that each deity stood and bowed low when Namtar arrived,
for who in the Annunaki,
for who in the Igigi,
was not humble in the presence
of even a messenger of Ereshkigal?
Though only Her assistant,
Namtar was treated with esteem and honour.

51

Thus each deity paid respect to the Mistress of the Dead,
that is, all except one,
a young god, a warrior god,
a god that revelled in destructive storms
and stirred up pestilence and disease.
It was Nergal who would not stand.
It was Nergal who would not bow down.

Upon Namtar's return to Irkalla
the story of Nergal was told.
He described the astonishment
on the faces of the other deities at the feast
at the rudeness of the young god.
Namtar told how some had shouted 'ignoramus',
how others had pressed Nergal to courtesy,
but how none of these had prevailed.
Nergal had remained seated
while all the others stood and bowed
to the ambassador of Queen Ereshkigal.
'Can he be so young or so foolish
that he is ignorant
of the powers of the Mistress of Irkalla?
He shall see the Land of the Dead for himself.
He shall know that I alone
rule this mighty Queendom.
Namtar, bring him to me
so that he may extend his apologies.'

A second time Namtar ascended the steps of heaven.
A second time he entered the realm of the Annunaki.
There he announced the words of his Mistress,
that Nergal must descend to dark Irkalla
to offer his apologies to Ereshkigal.
Not a deity defended the young god's rudeness,
for all were in great awe of the Sovereign of the Dead
but Ea took Nergal aside and gave him warning,
he who thought to undermine
the powers of Ereshkigal
gave advice to the god of war and destruction,
'Refuse any bread that might be offered,
refuse any meat that might be given,
refuse any drink that might be served,

refuse any seat that might be set for you,
refuse any bathing water poured,
and most important,
refuse to be taken to the couch of the Goddess,
should She desire your body.'
Ea warned that if he accepted any of these,
Nergal might be forced to stay in Irkalla.

Thus Nergal descended to the Land of the Dead.
Nergal followed Namtar to the Land of No Return.
Down the long staircase of heaven did he follow him.
Through the seven gates of the Netherworld
did Namtar lead the god of war and disease
until they stood before the mighty Ereshkigal,
stood before the throne of the Mistress of the Dead.
All warnings flew from Nergal's mind,
so powerful and magnificent was Her being.
Mother of Mothers.
Was there a woman in heaven or on earth
who could compare with Ereshkigal?
Was there any whose strength was as mighty,
any who possessed greater wisdom of existence,
any as filled with the eons of experience,
any who through knowing death so well
better understood the essence of Life?
Overwhelmed by Her presence,
Nergal fell to his knees
and kissed the ground before Her,
and as docile as a young lamb,
he soon followed Her to Her couch of pleasures.

So long alone had She been through all eternity,
so busy with Her work had She been kept,
that the Mistress of the Netherworld
kept Nergal on Her couch of pleasures
for six full days,
kept Nergal on Her couch of pleasures
for six full nights.
But on the seventh,
Nergal asked permission to return to heaven,
requested that he might go home,
to assure the others of his well-being,
promising that he would soon return.

Though not pleased at the thought
of his absence from Her couch of pleasures,
Ereshkigal agreed to his departure.

Once returned to heaven,
once reappearing at the abode of the Anunnaki,
Nergal was again taken aside by Ea.
He who had warned Nergal before
now spoke again, saying
that though Ereshkigal might be difficult to resist,
should Nergal become Her lover
would he not fear for his other pleasures,
his desire to make great and bloody wars,
his delight in dealing out disease and pestilence,
his satisfaction in stirring up turbulence and storm?
Surely if he returned to this powerful Goddess
and became the lover of the Mistress of the Dead,
She would keep him on Her couch of pleasures
and there he would be forced to spend his life,
foregoing all his former pleasures.

Nergal then thought anxious thoughts,
Nergal feared the truth of what Ea had said
but just as he was thinking upon
the breaking of his word to Ereshkigal,
Namtar arrived in heaven,
the messenger of Ereshkigal
ascended heaven's steps yet a third time
and soon conveyed the words of his Mistress
that Nergal was now Hers,
that Nergal must be returned
to the Land of the Dead,
that Nergal must be sent back
to the Ruler of the Irkalla.

But Ea thought to defeat the mighty Queen,
took sides with Nergal against Ereshkigal,
by arming him with fourteen warrior demons,
by instructing him to make a sword
of the mesu, hashurru and supalu trees,
by supplying him with false tokens
for the seven gates of Irkalla,

Was there any whose strength was as mighty?

so that Nergal would not be naked and unarmed
when he arrived before Her throne,
as were the others who entered the Land of the Dead.
The god of the Anunnaki, Ea,
encouraged Nergal
to defy the powers of the Queen of the Irkalla.

Nergal followed Namtar down the steps of heaven,
as if accepting the word of Ereshkigal,
as if concerned about Her loneliness,
but at each gate of the seven
he passed out the false tokens of Ea,
at each gate of the seven
two of the warrior demons he planted,
so that when Nergal entered into Her presence
he was in a mind for war.
He stood before The Mighty One,
he stood before the Queen of the Nether world,
but once again he felt Her magnificence,
once again he desired to lie with Her
upon Her couch of pleasures,
and in the confusion of his desires
he wondered if he could have both—
Queen Ereshkigal
and the freedom to do all that he wished?
Surely not as long as Irkalla was Hers to rule.
Surely not as long as She held such power.
Surely not as long as She truly did not need him,
but only desired to have him
for the pleasures of Her couch.

The mind of the god of bloody war,
the mind of the god of disease and pestilence,
the mind of the god of destructive turbulence and storm,
soon thought of a plan
that was most comfortable to his mixed desires.
He thought of marriage—
and roughly grasping the hair of Ereshkigal's head,
he pulled Her from Her throne
and threw Her hard upon the ground,
threatening to cut off Her head—
unless She agreed to be his wife.

He demanded that he should sit upon the throne
and that She should sit beside him.
He demanded that in his hands,
She must place the Tablets of Destiny,
that which had been Hers alone.
He demanded that he be master
of the land of the Irkalla
and that She be his dutiful consort.
Lying upon the cold stone floor,
seeing the warrior demons fending off all aid,
seeing the sword of mesu, hashurru and supalu
close upon Her throat,
Ereshkigal realized the alternative
would be Her violent death—
and thus She agreed to the proposal.

The records of Assyria and Egypt
tell us this is how
Nergal took control of the Land of No Return
from the ancient Sumerian Ereshkigal.
They tell us that upon Her acceptance,
upon Her agreeing to his 'proposal of marriage',
he then kissed Her.
They do not say how She felt.
They tell us that he then wiped away Her tears.
They do not tell us what was on Her mind.

Yet one small prayer,
more ancient even than the stories of Nergal,
remind us of the omnipotence
that Ereshkigal once knew,
remind us of a time
when death was but a part of life,
a return to the Great Mother:

"I will praise the Queen of Humankind,
I will praise Ereshkigal,
Queen of Humankind.
Among all the many deities,
Ereshkigal is merciful."

she who makes the universe spin round

— EGYPTIAN (handwritten annotation)

The magic powers of the uraeus serpent that emerges as the Third Eye, the broad winged vulture who protects in death, and the nurturing cow upon whose belly the stars of heaven shine—remain as symbols of the Goddess from the lands that lie along the Egyptian Nile.

Small clay statues created by the people of the neolithic cultures of the Badarian, Tasian, Gerzean and Amratian periods have been unearthed at numerous sites of pre-dynastic Egypt. The similarity of these statues, formed between 4000 to 3000 B.C., to those of the following dynastic periods, reveal that they were images of the Goddess in those earliest periods of developing Egyptian culture.

At about 3000 B.C., Upper Egypt (the south) and Lower Egypt (the Delta area) were brought together under a centralized government. Primarily accomplished through martial conquest, this amalgamation of The Two Lands is most often associated with the arrival in Egypt of a group known as the Shemsu Hor, people of Horus. Before the consolidation of these two areas, which differed both culturally and topographically, each was symbolized by an important Goddess figure. Upper Egypt was known as the land of Nekhebt, whose image was the wide winged vulture, while Lower Egypt was the land of Ua Zit, the Cobra Goddess whose image was retained in the sacred Uraeus head dress. Despite all political events, Goddess reverence remained

UPPER EGYPT 3000 B.C. Lower EGYPT
SOUTH NORTH
NEKHEBT UA ZIT
WIDE-WINGED VULTURE COBRA GODDESS

deeply ingrained in the hearts and minds of the people of ancient Egypt.

For the three millenia generally referred to as the time of ancient Egypt (3000 B.C. until the Roman period), the culture of Egypt was relatively self contained. Yet there were contacts, some through war, most through trade, between Egypt and the nations of Crete, Cyprus, Canaan, Anatolia and Sumer. Certain images and theological concepts of Egypt invite comparison with those of these other ancient cultures. Although there is no evidence of direct contact between Egypt and India, artifacts do reveal trade connections between Egypt and Sumer, and between Sumer and the west Kulli area of India. The appearance of the serpent, the lotus and the cow as sacred symbols of the Goddess in both Egypt and India may provide the start of an interesting study, one which should not fail to take the presence of Australoid people both in Arabia and in India into consideration.

Egypt's relationships with its neighbors to the south and west are more obvious, Egyptian references to the Goddess in Nubia and Libya confirming these connections. yet little research has been done on these relationships, despite specific references to the Egyptian Goddess Hathor as a lioness in Nubia. In any study of these relationships, it is of paramount importance to examine the passages in Herodotus which reveal that *all* of Africa (with the exception of Egypt) was once referred to as Libya (see African section—Vol. I). Egyptian references to the Goddess as The Fiery One, the Cobra or the Heavenly Cow invite interesting comparisons to beliefs that still exist in Zaire. Accounts of the Alur people include images of a divine celestial cow that provides the rain, while Nkundo lore includes a description of the magical serpent Indombe who, when angered, emanates a blazing heat and light from Her body. Egyptian ideas about the site of Creation as a flaming island in the waters may reflect images not unlike the still fiery lava pit of Mt. Nyiragongo in Zaire, as it once stood in the waters that extended from Lake Kivu. Geologists have found that the present land mass north of Lake Kivu, the site of the flaming volcano Nyiragongo, was part of a vast lake during periods of human habitation.

The religious ideologies of ancient Egypt are complex. Contradictory accounts of Creation, each from a different area, reveal that each one claimed the status of prime mover for their own local deity. As a result of this complexity and multiplicity of

Egyptian materials, many contemporary texts on Egyptian beliefs may be misleading in that large bodies of information may be completely ignored or mentioned so briefly that they are overlooked or assumed to be of little importance.

Although most scholars describe Amun, the ram or goose deity of the town of Thebes, as male, they often neglect to mention that several early documents refer to Amun as father and *mother*. The most oft ignored body of evidence is that which was found in the town of Khemmenu (Hermopolis). In the Khemmenu material, the female Nuneit and the male Nun who were both regarded as the Primeval Sea, were described as the first deities to exist. The more familiar but later accounts from Thebes reveal the influence of the Khemmenu beliefs, but cite Amun as the prime mover, thus lessening the importance of Nuneit. Some contemporary studies mention Nun only, explaining that he was regarded as the one who made the Nile rise. These same studies neglect to mention that, according to the Khemmenu material, it was Nuneit who first created the Nile. Another difference in the Theban and Khemmenu accounts is the role of the female Amunet. The Khemmenu texts specifically state that Amunet alone attended the great Cosmic Egg, the egg from which the sun god Ra was said to have been born. Since, in other texts, Ra is most often described as the son of the Goddess whose body was the heavens, Nut or Net, the reference to Amunet in this context may be extremely significant. Not only is the figure of Amunet absent in the majority of studies of Egyptian culture, but many scholars state that the Cosmic Egg was laid by the male Amun, who, strangely enough, is identified as a goose, rather than a gander. It is interesting to note that the hieroglyph for the Cosmic Egg was the same sign that was used to designate an embryo in a woman's womb.

Another area in which subjective choice of material distorts the reader's understanding of Egyptian beliefs is the general emphasis on the male Thoth, and the exclusion of material concerning the Goddess Seshat (Sefchet). In very early dynastic writings, Seshat was described as the Goddess of Writing and the Ruler of Books. Yet nearly all contemporary studies discuss Thoth as the singular deity associated with the scribal arts, while passages concerning Seshat, and the fact that they were earlier than those concerning Thoth, are simply ignored.

One rather astonishing practice of many scholars of Egyptian religion is the stated perception of *Maat* as an abstract principle, rather than as a deity. Numerous images of the Goddess Maat show Her in the form of a woman. The many verbal references to Her as the manifestation of truth, justice, moral law, and cosmic balance give us some idea of the extreme importance of Her image, but these attributes do not define Her as any more or less of an abstraction than Jehovah, Allah or Brahma.

Should the reader feel that the above perhaps reveals the limitations of space, rather than a male-oriented bias among many scholars, we must still confront the most oft used translation for the word *roemt* whose sign includes specific images of a woman and a man, the word that a few scholars have translated as 'people' or 'humankind', but most have translated as 'man' or 'men'.

Aside from these problems of bias, upon reading the vast body of literature on ancient Egypt, most especially the direct translations of specific documents, an endless wealth of material on Goddess images in Egypt may be discovered. From birth to death, and even after death, the Goddess was perceived as a sacred essence that played a vital part in the life of every Egyptian. From the time of the nameless statues of the prehistoric period until the time that the temples of the Goddess Isis were closed by the Emperor Justinian in the fifth century A.D., Goddess reverence in Egypt provided images of womanhood that may rise to the surface of our woman mirrors of today.

UA ZIT

The image of the Cobra Goddess Ua Zit, who was revered on the Nile Delta of pre-dynastic Egypt, was retained for three thousand years as the Uraeus serpent, The Eye, ever present on the foreheads of other Egyptian deities and royalty. The ancient Ua Zit may well be the origin of the serpent imagery so closely associated with Goddess reverence on Crete. Ua Zit was also associated with images of Au Set (Isis) who was linked to the star known as Set, Sept and Sothis in Egypt (Sirius in Greece). The name and concept of Ua Zit may have been connected to the Sumerian belief in *Ama Usum Gal Ana,* Great Mother Serpent of Heaven—*zit* or *zet,* the Egyptian word for serpent; *usum,* the Sumerian word for serpent. The image of Ua Zit may also have survived in the Arabian Goddess Al Uzza who was regarded as either Venus or Sirius. The most sacred centre of the worship of Ua Zit was the Delta town of Per Uto (the Greek Buto) that is thought to lie beneath modern day Dessuk. Buto was regarded as one of the most important oracle sites of Egypt at the time of Classical Greece. Although the Greeks spoke of the Cobra Goddess as Buto, they dedicated the Buto shrine to the Goddess Lato, mother of the sun and the moon. The placement of the Ua Zit Cobra on the forehead, invites comparison of this image to the Indian concept of the Shakti Kundalini serpent rising to the Ajna Chakra (see Indian section).

Deep beneath the ever accumulating silt
of the Delta lands of the mighty Nile
lies the holy place of the ancient Cobra,
Goddess known as Ua Zit, Ua Zet, Uatchet, Wazit,
Wadjet, Uadt, Udot, Edo, Edjo, Uto,
Uterus womb that rose between the reeds
on the secret Khemmis isle that floated
on the lotus marshes of the Delta,
great Zet serpent of the wadi canals,
who took the holy Au Set in as daughter,
who protected holy Au Set in childbirth,
who protected the child that Isis bore.

Ua Zit spread Her cobra hood
at the Buto site of oracles
where the future was foretold,
so that Buto gained renown throughout the world.

Ua Zit wound Her serpent body
about the royal sceptre of cosmic sovereignty,
as She coiled about the sacred lotus,
as She twisted about the waz reed of the Delta,
the reed of the marshes
taken to form the first stylus of Egypt,
the pen that marked both idea and event
upon papyri, bone and clay.

Uniting with Her sister Nekhebt,
to create the power of all Egypt,
as Isis united with Her sister Nebt Het, Nepthys,
Ua Zit emerged from holy forehead
as the Third Eye, the Eye of Wisdom,
as the venom that She spit forth
with fiery red tongue
gave Her the name of The Lady of Spells,
The Lady of Flame,
The Lady of the Flaming Waters,
The Lady who shed Her skin
to be born again and again and again,
for Ua Zit had existed before Egypt was born,
had existed before the Creation.

MAAT

Although Maat is most often described by contemporary scholars as an abstract concept, images of Maat in both murals and sculptures depict Her as a woman, the ostrich feather upon Her head, a sceptre in one hand, the life symbol of the ankh in the other. Somewhat like Huruing Wuhti of Hopi beliefs, Maat is at times depicted as twin sisters, though a singular Maat is the more general image. Egyptian texts refer to Maat as The Eye, much like Ua Zit, but Maat is associated with the heart as the place where moral judgements were made. The name and images of Maat occur in many Egyptian writings, most significantly in the various versions of the Egyptian Book of the Dead. The ostrich symbolism associated with Maat, alongside references to Maat's role in the Creation, suggest that any study on the concept of the Cosmic Egg should include a more careful examination of how the image of Maat may have been connected to this primeval event. It may be of interest to note that discs of ostrich eggshell have been discovered in the burials of pre-dynastic cultures, while the hieroglyph for the *Ba,* soul, is almost identical with the sign that designates the ostrich. The imagery and concepts associated with Maat may be the foundations for later Greek images of the Goddess Themis who holds the Scales of Justice, and perhaps the early Greek Goddess of Wisdom, Metis.

The Eye of Heaven,
Sister twins who judge what is right,
Ever present Maat,
Guardian of the justice and truth of the universe,
Guardian of the rhythm and order of the cosmos,
Sovereign of the Council of Maat
where the assembly of deities, the great Ennead,
rule by Maat's decrees.

Great is Maat
who gave the unalterable laws of life,
who insisted upon truth and kindness,
who took the ostrich feather
that She wore upon Her head
and placed it in the balance,
to test the weight of each heart
that lay in the other bowl of the sacred scales,
the heart of each who died
to be weighed against the lightness of Maat's feather,
as Maat tied a cloth about Her eyes
so that no prejudice
might fault Her word.

Heavy is the heart
that has not given bread to the hungry,
that has not given water to the thirsty,
that has not given clothing to the naked,
that has not given a boat to the shipwrecked.
Light is the heart
that has lived a life of good deeds,
as it lies in the bowl of the balance
in the Hall of Double Maat
where Maat announced the judgement
to be recorded on the leaves
of the Tree of Life.

In hopes of achieving the Maa Kheru,
the true voice, the light heart
light as the first day
when it was given by the mother,
the reverent submerged themselves in the waters
that were the Pool of Maat,
the place where the Flame was buried,
where the crystal tablet was transformed into water,
the place where the sceptre of flint
lies upon the shore,
flint known as the Giver of Breath,
flint scythe that reaps what has been sown.
as the soul reaps the deeds of its heart,
as it balances against all that Maat decreed.

Maat watches as the Morning Star,
the Eye that sees each day begin;
Maat watches as the Evening Star,
the Eye that sees each day come to an end,
Her double light a constant reminder
of the Scales in the Hall of Double Maat.

THE LADY OF THE AMENTA

The *Amenta* of Egyptian texts is the heaven that could be attained by those who led lives of righteousness. According to the Egyptian Book of the Dead, the soul went through a period of arduous testing and judgement before it was allowed into the Amenta. Upon finally arriving, the soul was welcomed by the sight of the Lady of the Amenta who stood upon the summit of the heavenly mountain. The final hieroglyphs of the Book of the Dead associate the Goddess as Hathor, Methyer, Au Set and Maat with the concept of the Lady of the Amenta. *Amn, Amen* or *Amun* literally means hidden in the sense of invisible or secret. What appears to be a multiplicity of names and images of the Lady of the Amenta may have been understood to convey the multi-faceted nature of the Goddess who was hidden by the profusion of names and traits, yet inherent in all. References to the role of Amunt (Amunet, Ament) in the Khemmenu accounts of Creation may be yet another aspect of the identity of the Lady of the Amenta.

I have chosen this particular account of the Goddess as the one in which the many other Goddess names and aspects are described. It should be understood that each of these names do appear as separate deities. Some are associated with a specific community or town and may have been drawn into theological structures that incorporated various beliefs, as populations came to live under increasingly centralized governments. Though a total synthesis may never have been made, to the extent of the perception of aspects of Devi in India, it should not be forgotten that the Goddess as Au Set (Isis) was known as 'Mother of One Thousand Names'.

It was the Lady of the Amenta who stood upon the holy mountain of heaven, waiting for those who had passed the rigours of the Hall of Double Maat, waiting for those who had recognized the Ladies of the Pylons of Testing, waiting for those whose hearts were light enough to allow their souls an everlasting peace.

They said that She was Au Set, and also Maat, while at the same time She was Hathor, and yet Meh Urit. Still She was Taurit, and at the same time She was the perfect face in the boat of one million years. Lady of the Amenta, might She also have been Amunet, She who existed on the Isle of Flame that rose out of the primeval waters and helped all life to come forth from the great Cosmic Egg? They said that She was Amn, invisible as the air that we breathe, yet as real as the breeze or the wind. And it was said at Khemmenu that it was Amunet who helped the Egg of Life to open, the Egg that some said had been laid by a serpent, the Egg that some said had come from the womb of a feathered bird.

They said that She was the Lady of One Million Ka, the Lady of all spirit bodies, the Great Magician, She who had come forth from the primeval waters, green as the frog that explored the bank of the river, remembered in Nubia and Sudan as She who attended each woman in birth, midwife as Amunet was midwife—but they gave Her name as Heqt or Hekit.

When Her work was apparent in the bountiful harvest and in the flow of abundant good fortune—they said that She was Renenti. When She blessed the future of each child that was born—they said that She was Meshkenti. When She filled the rivers and the lakes with the fish that satisfied all appetites—they said that She was Mehiti. When the waters of the river surged so full that they overflowed upon the land, helping the new crops to grow tall and full—they said that She was Merit.

When in the town of Bubastis, where lives were filled with joyous pleasure and graceful feline beauty, as the women and the men arrived in barges, clapping and singing, playing upon flute and sacred sistrum, where Her people honoured Her in festival, as Her catlike head sat upon Her womanly body while She protected the souls of cats that had died and had been wrapped in the linen of the afterworld—they said that She was Bast. When She roared as the powerful Lioness who excelled in the hunt, and was known for Her strength in rage as She aimed Her perfect arrows from Her bow, conquering all enemies that challenged the safety of Her town of Memphis—they said that She was The Powerful Mother Sekhmet.

When She appeared as the kindly, mothering cow whose udders provided the milk of good fortune—they said that She was Methyer or Meh Urit. When She was known as the oldest of the old, the Mother who gave birth to all other dieties as She took the form of a Hippo who roared wildly as She cooled Her body in the waters filled with brown earth—they said that She was Ta Urt or Taurit. When She appeared as the ancient vulture who was once known as Nekhebt, and made Her home in Thebes where She gave birth to the Moon, Khonsu, and as the Mistress of Heaven She possessed nine mighty bows, and was known by the picture of the wide winged vulture that was the very word for mother—they said that She was Mat or Mut.

When She appeared as the silent serpent who slid among the tombs in the moonlight, Her womanly head upon reptilian body —they said that She was Mertsegret. When She was known by the sign of the many legged scorpion—they said that She was Serkhit. When She appeared as the two holy ones who came forth from the Sudan, one as the Lady of Life, the other as the Serpent of Rebirth—they said that She was Ankhet and Satet.

Yet even without a name, the Goddess of ancient Tamera, the land that we now know as Egypt, came forward in the testing of each soul so that the dead one of the still heart recognized and acknowledged each: first, The Lady of Terrors, the Sovereign Mistress of Destruction who protected those who travelled on the right paths; second, the Lady of Heaven, Mistress of the World, who devoured with fire and was greater than all humankind; third, The Lady of the Altar, the beloved of every other deity, She to whom all offerings were made; fourth, The Lady of Knives, Mistress of the World, She who protected the needy from their foes; fifth, The Lady of Breath, She whose presence could not be known; sixth, The Lady of Light, The Mighty One, the one whose height and breadth were beyond knowing; seventh, The Lady of the Linen, who wrapped the bands about the one who had died; eighth, The Lady of the Tongues of Flame; ninth, The Lady that is Highest Chief, Lady of Power who was robed in emeralds; tenth, The Lady of the Great Voice, She who might terrify all others, but feared none; eleventh, The Lady Who Burned all Evil; twelfth, The Lady of Splendour as brilliant as fire; thirteenth, Au Set, She who blazed as the light that made the Nile waters rise and overflow, as She reached out to all; fourteenth, The Lady of the Knife who danced in blood on the Day of Judgement; fifteenth, The Lady who trapped all evil in its own lair; sixteenth, The Lady of the Rain Storm; seventeenth, The Lady of the Knife and the Ankham Lotus of rebirth; eighteenth, The Lady of the Temple who purified all sinners; twentieth, The Lady of the Deep who gives drink to the thirsty; twenty-first, The Lady who is the Knife known as the Giver of Breath.

Thus when the heart, that was first given by the mother, recognized and acknowledged each of the many natures, and after many years of life the heart was found to be as light as the feather of Maat, the soul was free to enter into heaven, there to look upon the Holy Hidden Mother—the Lady of the Amenta.

SESHAT

Seshat (Sefchet), appears in Egyptian documents as early as the First to the Third Dynasties. In them, She is referred to as the Goddess of Writing and Ruler of Books. Although Seshat's attributes are reminiscent of the Sumerian Nidaba, Seshat might also be compared to the Sumerian Belit Sheri, both Seshat and Belit Sheri depicted as scribes who record the deeds of the dead upon the leaves of the Tree of Life (see Sumerian section). In some references, Seshat was associated with the more familiar male deity of the scribal arts, Thoth. This relationship may be of interest in that other documents link Thoth with the Goddess Maat—in this same activity of the judgement and recording of the deeds of the dead.

Sacred Seshat, Holy Sefchet,
It was She who designed the hieroglyphs
so that words could be recorded,
She who invented numbers,
so that the barrels of barley could be measured,
so that even the stars of heaven
could be counted.
Divine Architect of the first temples,
it was Seshat who first stretched the cord
to decide upon the width and length,
to decide upon the placement,
of ancient Egypt's shrines.

Sacred Seshat, Holy Sefchet,
Divine Inventor of the scroll of papyri,
the sheet of tchama,
held the ink palette
that She so wondrously devised
in one perfect hand,
held the reed stylus pen
that She so wondrously devised,
in the other.

What is equal to the wonderment of Her work,
for it is Seshat who stood before the Tree of Life
in the great Hall of Double Maat,
marking down for all eternity
that which was done in each life,
writing upon the multitude of tiny leaves
that grew from the branches of the holiest of trees,
recording for memory eternal
the sum total of each life,
recording them no worse than they had been—
and no better.

Sage were Her words of advice:
Enjoy your life,
before the heart that your mother gave you lies still.
Death arrives sooner than expected,
and all the grief and mourning
will not bring the still heart back to life.
Earthly treasures will be left behind,
possessions decay with time,
but your daily deeds, both good and bad,
are truly what you own forever.
Give bread to those who have no field
and a good name is yours for eternity.

HATHOR

The cow of the heavens, known as Neit, Methyer or Meh Urit, was best known by the name of Hathor. There is no question that this last name was one assigned by the worshippers of Horus, since Hat Hor literally means House of Horus. But images and concepts of the holy heifer seem to have preceded this name. Some texts describe Hathor as the wild cow upon the primeval hill that emerged from the waters. In the Book of the Dead, this image was also known as Meh Urt. Hathor's association with the lioness of Nubia and Her title as the Lady of Punt suggest that reverence for the celestial cow may have come to pre-dynastic Egypt from groups that had lived on the more southerly stretches of the Nile in Sudan. It is interesting to note the image of the celestial cow that still exists among the Alur people of Zaire, as well as the fact that the Dinka people of Sudan long revered lions as their totemic ancestors. As the Cow that is the heavens, and as the Lady of the Sycamore, Hathor is closely linked with images of Neit. The uraeus cobra so often shown on the forehead of Hathor also links Her to the Goddess Ua Zit.

Wild Ox, Fierce Lioness, Gentle Cow of Heaven, like ancient Neit, Hathor is the sacred cow who provides the milk of life. Was She not known since the days of those who first came to dwell along the Nile's fertile banks when the land was new, those who drew Her image on the rocks of Naquada and at the settlements of Girzeh some seven thousand years ago?

Like ancient Neit, She nestled in the foliage of the Great Sycamore, waiting to welcome the souls of those who would no longer live on earth, ready to supply them with food and with drink, Her ripening figs that grew upon the Sycamore known as the food of eternity. Lady of the Sycamore, Living Body of Hathor upon Earth, this holiest of trees is blessed by the Goddess who sits within its branches. Many are the natures of Her mysteries, for some say that She is Seven Hathors, as Au Set is the seven stars that shine in Sothic constellation.

Yet who, in all the great lands of Egypt, ancient Tamera, did not learn when but a child that it was Hathor who first taught the sweet sound of song, the graceful movement of the dance that follows the rhythm of the jingling of the sistrum rattle that bears Her image? And who did not learn that it was Hathor who first taught the mining of the malachite, the sacred blue green stone that lay in the earth, though some say it fell as powder from the emerald stars that glistened upon the vastness of Her belly? And

who did not learn that it was Hathor who taught of love and first
explained to mortals the way in which new life was made, and
gave lovers to the lonely.

She was the Mother who gave happiness; She was the Mother
who gave joy; She was the Mother who exulted in all that was
good. From the chambers of Her temples, they carried Her image
each morning, setting it upon the sunlit terraces, so that She might
look upon the dawn. Her name was called upon from Byblos to
Somali, from Nubia to Sinai, from Edfu to Ombos, from Deir el
Bahri to Thebes, from Heliopolis to Denderah, still She was
known as The Lady of Punt, the land of cone roofed huts that
could be sailed to by following the ocean coastline to the south,
the Land of Ebony and Ivory.

Ancient priestesses stood before Her altars, women known as
Sepi and Nisedger Kai, Matmuti and Demiosnai. They called
upon the ancient cow of heaven as Lady of the Stars, the One who
Shines as Gold, Mistress of the Desert, Lady of Heaven,
Sovereign of Imaau, Hathor who gives the breath of life to the
nostrils with Her sacred ankh symbol, Hathor who heals with Her
celestial milk that soothes the torn body, Hathor who sends the
wind for the sails so that the boats may glide along the waters,
Hathor who appears as the Sacred Seven who come to the birth of
each infant to prophesy the destiny that each will come to know.

Each year, the joyous Feast of Hathor was celebrated with
the sweet music of the sistrum, as all of Egypt danced to please the
Goddess. But most important at this greatest feast of the year was
the drinking of the red barley beer, the beer that flowed like the
river when it overflowed, dizzying the mind until it forgot all else
but thoughts of the power and the wisdom of the Goddess. Two
stories were told to explain the reason for this day, both relating
why it was the first day of the New Year, and why it was dedicated
to Hathor. The Book of the Cow of Heaven told of the sun god
Ra calling to Hathor for help. Calling upon Her as his Eye, he
told Her of the men who had gone to the mountains, there to plot
a conspiracy against him in his weakened period of great age. As
he begged for Her protection, She took the form of the angry
lioness Sekhmet, and in this form She went forth to slay his
enemies. Easily conquering those who had plotted the harm to
Ra, Sekhmet Hathor began to enjoy the taste of blood. Now even
more afraid, for Sekhmet Hathor did not stop and it seemed that
She might destroy all humankind, Ra mixed the red ochre of the

ground into great vats of barley beer and poured this on the ground so that it might appear as blood. Sekhmet Hathor began to drink and drink and drink, until She grew so drunk that She returned to Her gentle form of Hathor. According to the people of Ra's Heliopolis, this is why red beer flowed like water at the Festival of Hathor.

But a second tale was told by those in Denderah, where images of Hathor stood tall about the temple, as the joyous day of the New Year, the Feast of Hathor, was celebrated in the Nile town not far from the most ancient rocks of Naquada. Here they said that Hathor had grown angry, and threatened to destroy the universe that She had created. Roaring with fury, Hathor threatened to wash the very earth back into the primordial sea and to return to Her ancient form of the great serpent. In Her rage, She took the form of the lioness and made Her way back to the land of Nubia. In Hathor's absence, grief and chaos came to the land of Egypt. The land of the Nile knew only confusion and disorder. So desperate was the situation that Hathor's brothers, Shu and Thoth, also took the forms of lions and followed Hathor into the land of Nubia. After many months of searching for the Powerful One, they came across Her sitting upon the Mountain of the Sunrise.

Tragic tale after tragic tale came forth from the brothers, each ending in words of persuasion, asking, begging, pleading for Hathor to return to Egypt. Hathor filled with compassion for the people that She loved. Though Her heart was filled with reservations, Hathor once again returned to Egypt, bringing peace and harmony back to the land of the overflowing Nile. So it was that as the river began to swell, as the constellation of Sothis rose with the morning sun, Egyptians celebrated the Feast of Hathor, knowing a new and better year was coming, honouring the Great Mother of Heaven with song and dance, and beer that flowed as water. Hathor had returned and with Her came the goodness of life.

NEIT

Even upon a casual reading of Egyptian documents, one will find a multitude of references to the Goddess in Egypt as Nut, Net, Nit, Neit and Neith. Although many scholars discuss the first three names as those of one Goddess, and the last two as another, both Neith and Nut were described as emerging from the primeval floodwaters and as The Mistress of Heaven. Later texts do generally identify the name Neith with the worship of the Goddess in the town of Sais, while the names Nut, Net or Nit are most generally used when referring to the Goddess as the divine woman or heavenly cow who *is* the heavens. To some extent, this confusion results from the lack of vowels in Egyptian hieroglyphs, many scholars making educated guesses and inserting vowels to ease the pronunciation. All the above names may be related to the Egyptian word meaning deity, *neter*. A good part of the material included in this account is drawn from the early *Pyramid Texts* of Unas, Pepi and Teti.

Most ancient Mother,
Great Radiant One,
Lady of the Stars,
Mistress of the Celestial Ocean,
Highest Judge,
Fiery One who rose from the Primordial Floods,
It is Neit who reaches down from the heavens
to take the hand of each who dies,
taking them into Her arms
to place them as stars of the universe,
each to light Her perfect body
with an emerald light,
sowing mortals upon Her heavenly self,
as others sow the green plants of the fields.

Some say that She is Nuneit,
the primeval waters that once covered all earth;
some say that She is Tefneit,
Giver of the moisture and the sunlight;
Some say that She is the Lady of the Loom and Shuttle,
and Lady of the Arrow and the Bow,
the Lady whose image stood at the most ancient shrine
of Sais upon the Delta lands
the most sacred image marked:
I am all that has ever been,
I am all that is,
I am all that shall ever be,
yet never have mortal eyes
perceived me as I am.

Ascending from the primeval waters,
Her body became the vast heavens,
Her perfect toes and fingertips touching the earth
as She arched over it in cosmic beauty,
the tear from Her eye creating the Nile,
the stars glowing with emerald light
set into Her very body,
the single word 'beauty' marked as glyph
between Her sacred horns.

The earth nestles between Her thighs,
as daily She gives birth to the sun,
each evening accepting him back into Her body,
just as each mortal returns unto Her
when the span of life is over,
Her holy image painted on the ceilings of each tomb,
Her holy image painted inside the inner lid
of the wooden casket in which dead repose,
as She leans forth from Her celestial sycamore
to quench the thirst of afterlife.

Joyous was the festival of Lamps
when all Sais glowed with flames
in honour of Her mysteries,
each small dish of oil and salt,
with woven wick afloat,
burning brightly through the night
in memory of the great fire upon the waters,
in memory of the Fiery One,
The Great Magician Neith.

Though if Her anger was provoked
She might cause the sky to crash upon the ground,
still She was the Mother of All,
broad winged Goddess who protects from evil,
who defends the good with bow and arrow,
as She once defended those ancient priestesses
who took Her name:
Neit Hotep,
Meryet Neit,
Her Neit,
priestess queens who ruled when Egypt was young,
when only women served at Neit's altars,
each knowing throughout her life
that she would one day glisten as a star
upon the measureless body of the Mother of Heaven.

AU SET (ISIS)

Although the name of Isis is most often used to designate the most well known image of the Goddess in Egypt, the name Isis, literally Ancient Ancient, was the Greek interpretation of the name of the Goddess that Egyptians spoke of as Au Set or Au Sept. Au Set was identified with the star best known as Sirius; the Egyptian names for this star were Sothis, Sept and Set. The constellation Canis Major, which includes the very bright star Sirius, appeared on the horizon just before sunrise at the time of the year that the Nile began to swell (approximately mid June). This seven star constellation may account for the idea of the seven Hathors, so closely related to Au Set, as well as images of the seven headed serpent. The horns on images of Au Set were directly drawn from images of Hathor as the celestial cow, the sun disc between the horns explaining the role of the Goddess as the mother of the sun. Later ideas that Au Set or Isis was associated with the moon were not known in early Egypt which regarded the moon as the male Khonsu, son of the Lioness Sekhmet. Au Set was linked to the Goddess as Neit who was regarded as Au Set's mother, and also to the Goddess Ua Zit who was so closely associated with Au Set giving birth, the uraeus cobra nearly always shown on the forehead of images of Au Set. Au Set's connection to the seaport of Byblos in ancient Canaan (Lebanon) may be better understood by a reading of the Goddess as Ashtart (see Semitic section—Vol. I).

Sirius, Sothis, sacred star that was first known as Sept or Set, the seven lights of heaven known as Au Set, She arrived to herald the time of longest light and brought with Her the gift of the abundant soil, as She raised the waters of the Nile, the waters that She had created from the tear of Her eye. Thus She commanded the blessed months of the Sothic inundation to begin.

Many names had the wondrous Au Set: Mistress of the Cosmos, Ruler of the House of Life, Sovereign of all that is Miraculous, Almighty Lady of Wisdom, Mother From Whom All Life Arose, Primeval Lotus Nefertim, Establisher of Justice, Champion of Righteous Law, Giver of the Gift of Abundance, Inventor of Agriculture, Designer of the First Sail, Planter and Harvester of the First Flax, Inventor of the Loom, Source of the Healing Herbs, Owner of the Throne, Magistra of Fate, The One Who Separated Heaven and Earth, Roadmaker of the Paths through the Stars, Controller of the Wind and Thunder, Restorer of Life, She Who Makes the Universe Spin 'Round. What in heaven or on earth was not of Her making?

At the procession of the harvest, they remembered that it was beloved Au Set who first understood the ways of the seeds and the planting, bringing the abundance of the stalks of wheat and barley which were so proudly carried at Her sacred festivals, in honour and commemoration of what She so ingeniously discovered in the beginning. And from Mother Au Set came the knowledge of justice and the law of the heart, so that no one needed to fear insolence or violence, nor excessive punishment. For as Au Set dispensed justice to all people, She taught that they must dispense it to each other. Declaring that righteousness was more valuable than gold or silver, Her very name sanctified an oath of truth.

Through Her dedicated daughters who cared for Her many sacred shrines, She gave the medicines of healing, protecting women in childbirth, restoring sight to those who could not see, returning the use of a damaged arm or leg that would not move, delighting in helping those who called upon Her to regain their strength and health. Often, She visited even during the depths of sleep, gently brushing Her wings in healing incantation over ailing bodies until health came once again. It was Au Set who gave the recipes for birth and non-birth and explained the magic of the shepen seeds that soothed the constant crying of an infant. It was Au Set who gave the gift of knowing the future of the womb, explaining that if the seeds of barley grew quickly in the waste water of the fullbellied woman, she would surely be blessed with a daughter, while if the seeds of wheat grew first, it was a boy that would be born. It was Au Set who taught of the jasper and carnelian made into the image of Her holy tie, symbol once made of woven loop whose loose ends told of separation, while the loop above the knot revealed the oneness. It was Au Set who taught how to dip the sacred knot into the water of the ankham lotus flower of rebirth, and how to then press it into the wood of the sycamore fig, while reciting these words of incantation: Holy Blood of Au Set, Holy Splendour of Au Set, Holy Magic Power of Au Set, please protect the wearer of this amulet and halt those who would do this wearer harm.

Even in the time of the still heart, the time of being wrapped in bands of linen, when the sacred loop of Au Set was seen by those who judged, the wearer was rewarded with fertile acres in the Sehket Aaru of the Amenta. For wearing it announced the understanding that all people come forth on earth to do the will of their ka, and if the ka of the heart was as light as the feather of

79

Maat, Au Set would then breathe the air of divinity into the nostrils of the still heart, air more pure than any ever known, while the ever burning flame that blazed behind Her protected the body that remained on earth.

Though wiser than all people, though wiser than all deities or spirits, the followers of Ra said that there came a time when Au Set knew all—except the secret name of Ra. Though Ra was each day born from Mother Neit who had once held the holy Au Set in Her heavenly womb, still Au Set did not know this name and was determined to know of it. Thus Au Set formed a serpent made of the earth and of the spittle of the sun and when Ra walked across the serpent's path, Au Set's powers were so deep in the venom that Ra was paralyzed by the serpent's bite.

The jaw bones of Ra, they clattered. The limbs of Ra, they shook and trembled. Ra could not move, but finally he found his voice. "Never has there been such a pain.", he said. "There is a fire in my heart and water in my limbs." He called to all the holy ones but none knew how to help. Then Au Set appeared, She whose mouth held the breath of life, She whose magic banished pain, She whose word was capable of restoring life even to the still heart. Au Set appeared before Ra and offered to help, knowing full well Her plan and goal. Ra told Her of how a serpent came into his path and had bitten of his body. He told Her of the pain that he felt, hotter than fire, colder than water. He told Her that his vision was so badly blurred that he could not even see the sky. Tears streamed from his face. Perhaps with compassion, perhaps with guilt, Au Set carried out Her plan, telling Ra that if he would trust Her with his secret name, She would heal him of his pain.

But the name did not come easily from the tongue of Ra, for instead he began to boast of his royal ancestry, to describe his privileges and powers, rambling on and on about what he could do. Listening with patience, Au Set then reminded him that he had not yet told Her what She needed to know; Ra had not yet revealed his secret name. Despite his ancestry and powers, the pain of Ra was great. So it was that, reluctantly, he bid Au Set to enter into his heart where She would learn his secret name. And in this way, Au set gained this last knowledge; adding it to Her omnipotent wisdom, She began the cure.

Seeds of coriander She took, seeds of the khasit She took, the leaves of the saam She took, seeds of the shammis She took, juniper berries She took—and grinding these into a fine paste, mixing it with honey, She soothed the ointment upon the injured Ra. As She did so, She spoke the secret name that She alone had learned, until the pain of Ra disappeared. Some say that Au Set was not all wise until She learned the secret name of Ra, yet others say that She was wise enough to know how to discover it.

Another time so long remembered was when Au Set first discovered the planting of the seeds, receiving this knowledge at the very moment that She had placed offerings upon the holy altars of those who had engendered Her. Upon receiving this gift of the knowledge of renewable abundance, Au Set spoke of it to Her brother who was known by the name of Au Sar or Osiris. In his excitement at what Au Set had learned, Osiris ran off to tell all the others, only to be murdered by his jealous brother Seth who sealed the body of Osiris in a perfectly measured coffer and placed this box of wood on the river so that it floated out to the Great Sea.

When news of the murder reached the ears of Au Set, She set out to search for the body of Osiris, and thus began Her long journey. It was not until She reached the far off port of Byblos, on the northeastern edge of the Great Sea, that She found the temple pillar built of the wood of a tamarisk tree, its branches still entwined about the coffer that held the body of Osiris. Thus retrieving it from the Temple of Ashtart in Byblos, Au Set brought it back across the waters to the sacred site of Per Uto, planning to give it proper Egyptian burial.

It was there in the marshes of Per Uto that with the help of sister Nepthys, Au Set made the breath of life enter into the body of Osiris though his heart was still, the sisters patiently fanning the air with their great wings—until Au Set conceived a child within Her womb. It was in Per Uto that She stayed, consoled in Her grief by the holy Cobra Ua Zit, until the child Horus was born. Thus it was said that Ua Zit helped Au Set in Her childbirth among the reeds of Per Uto, safe upon the isle that floated in the marshy waters. But when Au Set left the safety of Per Uto, leaving the child to the caring wisdom of Ua Zit, Seth came again and stole the body of Osiris.

This time he cut the body into fourteen pieces which he scattered along the lands of the Nile, so that Osiris would not be honoured by burial place or tomb. But Au Set was determined to give Her brother proper burial, thus She made Her way in a barge among the marshes of the Nile, burying each part where She found it. Though the backbone of Osiris found peace at Busiris and the head came to lie at Abydos, never did Au Set find the fourteenth part, the childmaking organs of Osiris, while fishermen gave witness that this part had been fed to the oxyrhynchus fish of the Nile. So it happened that Au Set ruled upon the throne, ever holding the child Horus upon Her holy lap.

Great shrines and temples were built to honor Her magnificence, Her holy spirit living at Edfu and Bubastis, at Saqqara and at Memphis, at Busiris and at Pharos, at Philae and at Byblos, even as She lived in the heavens, shining as the astral Sothis. For over three thousand years Her ominipotence was known, spreading across the Great Sea to Sicily and Pompeii, to Palermo and Campania, and throughout the widespread lands of the Romans. But the Roman consuls sometimes thought to abuse Her sacred altars until Aurelius Caracalla defended Roman reverence to Her name, saying that She was one with mighty Ceres. Thus Romans erected a great temple to Isis, one that glistened on the Hill of Capitoline, not far from where the Tiber flowed.

The Roman festivals of Isis celebrated the joyous blossoming of springtime, as devotees moved along in sanctified procession, celestial sounds of pipe and flute patterning the rhythm of the white robed followers who called upon Her name. But there came a time of sadness when Justinian silenced the music in the streets, emptied the sacred houses of Her worship. Still many remembered the image of the Perfect Mother with the holy child upon Her lap, the woman whose body had been adorned with the stars of heaven, though Her mother essence gained yet another name, Maria.

ISIS (after Apuleius)

Altars to Isis have been discovered as far from Egypt as the banks of the River Thames in London, many of these dating to the Roman period. The worship of Isis was well known in the Roman Empire and the images and rituals from Egypt generally well accepted and familiar to the Roman population. This particular piece is based upon passages of the Wm. Adlington translation (1566) of the book written by the North African born

Ruler of the House of Life
from a tapestry by Jenny Stone

Roman writer Apuleius, originally entitled (like Ovid's) *Metamorphoses,* later popularized as *The Golden Ass.* The very specific imagery and speeches are included in the story of Apuleius' travels during which he finds himself trapped in the form of a donkey. His search for the help of the Goddess leads to the passages in which the following descriptions and statements occur.

Brilliant from the sea, She rose, flower garlands crowning Her abundant hair that fell upon Her perfect neck. Set upon Her forehead was the circlet of mirror, attended by a serpent on each side, as the sheaves of wheat that rose from the circle shone in the moonlight. Her cape as dark as the night gathered in folds beneath Her left arm, flowing over the shoulder of Her right, all but covering the linen that lay white upon Her golden body, the weave of finest linen adorned by the crocus of yellow, the rose of red and the flame of brightest orange. Stars glittered along the edges of the blackness of the cape; stars circled on the cape of night around a mid-month moon. And upon the lowest hem that fell upon Her perfect ankles, the ripest fruits and the brightest of flowers wreathed in abundant border.

Encircled by the fingers of Her right hand was the sistrum rattle adorned with the face of the mighty Hathor, its thin copper discs moving along upon narrow rods in bell like tones. Encircled in the fingers of Her left hand was the golden cup that formed the boat, its handle rising as uraeus cobra leading the fore. Her palm sandalled feet were scented with the finest incense and spices of Arabia, as Her voice resonated with these words:

> I am Nature, Mother of All,
> Ruler of the Elements, Progenitor of Worlds,
> Chief of All Deities,
> Mistress of the Living,
> Mistress of the Dead,
> The Sole Manifestation
> of all goddesses and gods.
> It is my will that controls
> the planets of the sky,
> the helpful winds of the sea,
> and the grievous silence of the dead.
> Though revealed by diverse customs and rites,
> and called upon by many names,
> my omnipotence is respected throughout the world.

To the Phrygians of Pessinus,
I am Mother of All Deities.
To the Athenians,
I am the wise and valiant Athena.
To those of the Cyprian Isle,
I am Aphrodite or Venus,
born of the foam of the Paphian coast.
To those of Crete who use the bow,
I am Dyktynna, Artemis or Diana.

To those of the island of Sicily,
I am called Persephone or Proserpina.
To the Eleusinians,
I am Mother Demeter, Mother Ceres,
or simply Mother of Wheat.
Some call upon me as Hera or Juno,
Bellona or Hecate.
But both of the Ethiopian peoples,
those who live in Egypt
and those who dwell further to the East,
understand my ancient wisdom
more than any others,
for they know the ceremonies that are dear to me
and call me by my true name—
Almighty Isis.

Upon seeing Her perfect image, upon hearing Her perfect voice, Lucius Apuleius began to pray: O Holy Blessed Lady, constant comfort to humankind whose beneficence and kindness nourish us all, and whose care for those in trouble is as a loving mother who cares for all her children—you are there when we call, stretching out your hand to put aside that which is harmful to us, untangling the web of fate in which we may be caught, even stopping the stars if they form a harmful pattern. All other deities, whether bountiful or merciless, do reverence to Thee. It is Isis who rules the world, stamping out the powers of evil, arranging the stars to give us answers, causing the seasons to come and go, commanding the winds to move ships, giving the clouds to water the growing seeds so that we may have food. If I had one thousand mouths and one thousand tongues within each, still I could not do justice to your Majesty. Yet I will forever remember your help in my time of need and keep your blessed image deep within my heart.

to walk the trail of beauty

-- American Indian

From the Athapascans to the Zuni, Native American accounts of mother as creator, earth as mother, woman as nature, woman as ancestral mother of tribe or clan, and woman as teacher of culture—emerge in a vast diversity of images and legends.

This diversity is quite understandable when one considers the immense number of different cultural groups that inhabited the continent of North America long before Euro-Caucasians arrived; scholars of linguistics have discovered some 550 different languages spoken by Native Americans. Yet integral to many of the accounts of origins and spiritual beliefs of Native American groups separated by thousands of miles is a sense of deep personal connection to earth and a oneness with the beings and processes of nature.

The people we today refer to as Native Americans are descendants of groups of people who entered the North American continent in waves of migrations that occurred over many millenia. The most generally accepted route of these migrations is that of the land bridge that once stretched across the Bering Strait, connecting the Chukchi Peninsula of Siberia with Alaska. Although there is a great deal of scholarly debate about the earliest dates of these migrations, and some would state a cautious 10,000 B.C., many others claim that they began some 40,000 years ago. Whatever the dates, the racial links between Native American peoples and the Proto-Mongolian groups of Asia are noted with almost universal agreement.

87

One of the earliest recognizable cultures of North America is the Sandia of New Mexico, arguments on the dating of this culture ranging from 25,000 to 10,000 B.C. Following the Sandia were the Clovis, the Folsom, and the Cochise cultures among others, each revealing specific stages of Native American development. Although cave dwelling is not generally associated with Native American groups, very early sites such as Danger Cave in Utah, Gypsum Cave in Arizona, and Bat Cave in New Mexico reveal that some Native American peoples did make use of caves as habitations. These particular cave sites occur in the southwest U.S., but this does not imply that caves in other areas of North America may not have been used in a similar manner. The name Cherokee, derived from *Chiluk-ki,* literally means cave dwellers. The knowledge of cave habitations in the southwest is especially interesting in that cave dwellings of the southwest may be connected to Pueblo concepts of the Womb of Mother Earth. The generally round, often subterranean, Pueblo shrines of rituals and ceremonies, the *kiva,* contains a central opening in the ground, a hole known as a *Sipapu* or *Sipapuni.* This opening in the kiva is regarded as the Womb of Mother Earth and symbolic of the Place of Emergence, the sacred site at which Pueblo people came forth into the Fourth World, the world in which we now live. The transfer of humanmade substitutes for ritual caves, such as the crescent trench for Kunapipi in Australia and the Inna shrine of the Cuna in Panama (see Vol. I), suggests that a further exploration of possible links between the significance of the kiva and the use of caves might result in some interesting studies.

The pueblo dwellings built by Native Americans are admirable feats of structural engineering, often containing hundreds of rooms built on high rocky cliffs (such as Mesa Verde in Colorado) or set deep into massive caves (such as Betatakin in Arizona). The pueblos were constructed by a group of people known as the Anasazi, The Ancient Ones, members of a culture that flourished from about 300 A.D. to about 1300 A.D. The Pueblo people of today, primarily the Hopi and Zuni (the sources of the accounts of Huruing Wuhti and Spider Woman that are included in this section), have retained beliefs and customs that may survive from the Anasazi period.

Other clues to early Native American cultures were left by what is known as the Hohokam culture, literally 'Those Who Have Vanished'. Sites near Phoenix, Arizona reveal a well developed network of irrigation reservoirs and canals built by the Hohokam people some two thousand years ago. Several aspects of the Hohokam culture suggest that it was deeply influenced or even initiated by groups of Native Americans that had moved north from Mexico during the early Classic Period of that area. Connections between Native Americans of North and South America may be further noted in the Uto-Aztecan languages. These languages, known among the Comanche, Utes, and to some extent the Hopi of North America, also include the Nahuatl language of the Aztecs. The Corn Mother of the Hopi and Chicomecoatl of Mexico (see Vol. I) may be more closely linked than the apparent association of the Goddess with maize as an important food.

The great Mound Builders of the area that is now Ohio, Kentucky and West Virginia created earthworks that rise as high as seventy feet and often stretch for miles. These burial mounds are attributed to the Adena and successive Hopewell culture, the Hopewell extending as far as the areas known as Minnesota, Florida and New York. Objects found in these mounds reveal an early Native American knowledge of working with copper and quarrying stone, and a mobility or trade network that allowed the Mound Builders to acquire stone from Wisconsin, mica from the Appalachians and obsidian from the Rocky Mountains. The culture of the Mound Builders initially appeared at about 1000 B.C. and flourished for some 1500 years. Archaeological evidence suggests that the decline of this culture may have been the result of a widespread invasion or violent attack at about 500 A.D.

The Iroquois language reveals the connections between the Oneida, Onandaga, Cayuga, Seneca, Mohawk, Tuscarora, Huron and even the more southerly Cherokee. The League of Nations formed by the Iroquois who lived in the area of the Great Lakes may well have been an important influence in the formulation of the concepts of U.S. democracy, concepts generally attributed to Classical Greece or Magna Carta England. Those stating this premise point out that ancient Greece was not truly a democracy since slavery existed, while England still supports a royal family. Those who disagree with the importance of Iroquois influence upon Euro-Caucasian ideas about democracy argue that the system of the Council of Sachems, the governing body of the Iroquois League, was not truly democratic either. The Iroquois *women* chose the sachems and had the power to remove them if they did not perform their duties satisfactorily. If many aspects of a democratic system were adopted upon observation of the Iroquois government, we may, in hindsight, conjecture upon the effects of the rejection of this particular aspect of the system. Another interesting aspect of Iroquois social structure was the control that Iroquois women had over the food supply, even the results of hunting. This particular area of control enabled the women to decide on whether or not to supply food to men preparing for war, the refusal to supply food staples cancelling many a battle. Incidentally, Iroquois women were also responsible for appointing the religious clergy, both genders represented equally among the Iroquois 'Keepers of the Faith'.

Another major group of Native Americans linked by their languages are the Athapascans (Athabascans). This grouping includes many of the tribes of Alaska, Canada and the northwest U.S. It also includes the Apache, Kiowa and Navajo of the southwest. The Athapascan peoples appear to have been relative late comers to North America and the fact that Athapascan languages are tonal has caused some scholars to compare it with Chinese. Accounts of Changing Woman and Asintmah, included in this section, are both of Athapascan origin, though Changing Woman is spoken of by the Navajo of the southwest, while the account of Asintmah is told in western Canada. The accounts of origins of cultural knowledge, such as the legends of Pasowee of the Kiowa and Wild Pony of the Jicarilla Apache are also representative of Athapascan peoples.

One important aspect of spiritual beliefs that exist among many diverse Native American groups is the significance of dreams and visions. Cultural information, spiritual knowledge, and prophesies of the future, are often attributed to dreams or trance visions. The accounts of Pasowee and Wild Pony provide some idea of the part that dreams played in the receiving of wisdom. The respect for dreams as a source of useful information has been known in many cultures, including Sumer, Babylonia, Australia, Greece, China and Africa, thus the existence of this view of dreams is not unusual. Yet the degree to which Native American peoples have valued dreams as a vehicle of both cultural and spiritual wisdom should certainly be considered in any exploration of this most puzzling and fascinating experience of humankind.

The legends included in this section are but a small portion of the accounts and images of woman as sacred and/or heroic among the Native American peoples. Those interested in further research may find the following to be of interest. The Three Kadlu Sisters, known among the Inuit (Eskimo) of Baffin Island, are said to cause thunder and lightning by rubbing their bodies together. Sedna is known among the coastal Inuit as the Goddess of the Dead and as the Sovereign of the Ocean, ruler over the sea mammals and fish so vital to Inuit life. Along with the accounts of Huruing Wuhti and Spider Woman that are included in this section, the sacred rituals for the Deer Mothers and the Corn Mother are important in Pueblo spiritual beliefs. Buffalo Cow Woman is remembered as the Ancient Mother who gave the wisdom of the peace pipe to the Lakota (Sioux). The Cree people of the Algonquin speaking tribes (which also include Cheyenne, Blackfoot, Naskapi, Arapaho, Micmac, Penobscot, Chippewa and Ojibwa) speak of the Grandmother of People, Messak Kummik Okwi. This primal grandmother was understood to be in charge of all the food on earth, an image similar to that of mother as earth, explaining the Algonquin custom of placing a small portion of each meal upon the ground—to thank 'Our Grandmother'.

The changes in Native American cultures and customs caused by the continually increasing occupation of North America by Euro-Caucasians are obviously enormous. It has only been through the most dedicated and tenacious persistence that what we know of Native American beliefs has been retained. Yet despite all that has occurred to weaken or erase these ancient beliefs, the concept of earth or nature as Mother emerges into contemporary thought with a deep significance. Facing threats of partial or total destruction of the planet by radiation, pollution, toxic chemicals and the abuse of resources, a perception of earth as our Mother may well be one of the most viable paths towards preserving life. And those among us who heard the term 'trespassing' used to remove Native Americans from Alcatraz Island might well consider the irony and arrogance in Euro-Caucasians accusing Native Americans of trespassing on any part of North America, certainly this westernmost outpost of the lands regarded for thousands of years as Mother.

SPIDER WOMAN

Pueblo

Accounts of Spider Woman as Creator are known among many of the Pueblo people of the southwest of North America. One of the most detailed accounts of the Creation by Spider Woman is from Sia, a pueblo of the Keres. Although Sussistanako is the most often mentioned name of Spider Woman, She is also spoken of as Tsitsicinako and Kokyangwuti. Her daughters, Ut Set and Nau Ut Set, are also known as Itsictsiti and Nautsiti. The account presented here is an adaptation drawn from several sources, with special acknowledgement to the not yet published work of Judith Todd.

In the beginning there was nothing but Spider Woman, She who was called Sussistanako, Thinking Woman, Thought Woman. No other living creature, no bird or animal or fish yet lived. In the dark purple light that glowed at the Dawn of Being, Spider Woman spun a line from East to West. She spun a line from North to South. And then She sat by these threads that stretched to the four horizons, these strands that She had drawn across the universe, and sang in a voice that was exceptionally deep and sweet. As She sang, two daughters came forth: Ut Set, who became the mother of the Pueblo people, Nau Ut Set, who became the mother of all others.

Following the directions of Spider Woman, these two daughters formed the sun from white shell, red rock, turquoise and pearly abalone shell. When it was ready, they carried the sun to the top of the highest mountain and dropped it into the sky so that it would give light. But when they saw that it was still dark at night, they then formed the moon, putting together pieces of dark black stone, yellow stone, red rock and turquoise. Still things were not quite right, for when the moon travelled far, there were many nights when they could not see. It was for this reason that with the help of Spider Woman, Ut Set and Nau Ut Set created the Star People, giving them sparkling clear crystal for eyes so that there would never be complete darkness again.

Once the lights of heaven were in place, Spider Woman used the clay of the earth, the red, the yellow, the white and the black clay, and with this She made people. Upon them She placed a covering of creative wisdom, that which She spun from Her own Spider being. To each, She attached a thread of Her web. It is for this reason that each person has a delicate thread of web con-

92

nected to Spider Woman, connected to the doorway at the top of the head. Those who do not know this, allow the door to close, but it is only when we keep the door open by chanting through it, that we may draw upon this link to the creative wisdom of Spider Woman.

Many forgot about the door. Many people grew cruel and corrupt. They forgot the ancient wisdom. Three times over people forgot and three times over they were washed away in great floods. But each time Spider Woman saved those who did remember, those who had kept the door at the top of their heads open. These were the people that She brought to the place of hollow reeds. Teaching them to use the reeds as boats, those whose doors were still open floated upon the waters until the time they might enter into the new world, the Fourth World. The floating was long. The waiting was long. The travelling was very far. And when it was over, they emerged into the new world, climbed up through the Sipapu hole that was the Womb of Mother Earth.

Ut Set provided them with corn, explaining that it was the milk of Her breasts. Nau Ut Set gave them prayer sticks and stones for grinding the corn. Spider Woman provided them with eagle feathers for their hair, so that they might travel safely forever after. But only those who remember to keep the door open, to draw upon the wisdom of Sussitanako, know which way to travel, for they can see and feel the thread that is part of the Web of Destiny that Spider Woman weaves.

HURUING WUHTI
Hopi

This legend of Creation from the Hopi people of southwestern North America presents a double image of Creator that is puzzling, yet perhaps related to the two daughters of Spider Woman. The mysteries involved in the idea of two separate deities with the same name, or two aspects of the same deity that dwell in separate locations, are certainly of interest, as is the belief that the creation of earth and life was accomplished by Sister Goddesses. It is also interesting to note that the Hopi account states that the first woman was created before the first man.

Sister Mothers of the World, as old as the time when all the universe was the Great Sea, Mother Huruing Wuhti lived in the House of the Ocean of the East, Mother Huruing Wuhti lived in the House of the Ocean of the West. So it was that they created the land in the waters between them, created the earth on which we live.

Soon they wondered if there was any life upon the earth. They met upon the bridge that was the great rainbow that stretched between them, the bridge that reached from east to west. And there on the rainbow bridge they created a tiny bird, a bird to fly over the earth to see if any life existed. When the bird returned, bringing the message that there was no life to be found, the Two Mothers, Huruing Wuhti, then together formed the animals and birds that now live on earth.

Pleased with what they had done, they then formed a woman. Naming her Tuwabontums, they placed her on the earth. When this was done they formed a man. Naming him Muingwu, they placed him on the earth. So it happened that Tuwabontums and Muingwu became the first parents of the Hopi people. It is for this reason that Hopi people remember the Mothers Huruing Wuhti as creators of the earth and the life upon it.

CHANGING WOMAN

NAVAJO

Although Changing Woman is regarded as an anthropomorphic figure, the beliefs and customs associated with Her allow us to understand that She is the processes of Nature. This Navajo concept of female deity may well be compared to the accounts of Nu Kwa and Mother Nature (Tao) (see Chinese Section-Vol. I). The extremely important Navajo concept of walking in the Trail of Beauty certainly brings the concept of Tao (The Way) to the mind of any student of spiritual thought.

Creator of the Navajo people, Changing Woman, Estsan Atlehi, is the Mother of All. She is the Holy Woman who brings each season, Mother Earth who is the seasons, Iyatiku who Brings All Life, Mother Nature in all that She unfolds.

Some say that She was born at the foot of the Mountain Around Which Moving Was Done, born on a bed of flowers, a delicate rainbow arching as coverlet over Her infant body. From Her body grew the four mountains of the compass points, the mountains that mark the East and West, the mountains that mark the North and South. This day of birth was a day of joy, a day of brilliance and thus the memory of it is kept in the ever joyous song of The Blessing Way. For if Changing Woman had not been born, She would not have rubbed the skin of Her perfect body—and in this way brought forth the Navajo people.

It is Changing Woman who teaches the flow of life, the restlessness of the sand as it flies with the wind, the wisdom of the ancient rocks that never leave their home, the pleasure of the tiny sapling that had risen through them. So it is into the House of Changing Woman that each young girl enters, as her blood begins to flow with the moon, as she passes into womanhood.

It is Changing Woman who teaches the cycles, the constant round of hot and cold, of birth and dying, of youth and aging, of seedling to corn, of corn to seedling kernel, of day to night, of night to day, of waxing moon to waning moon—and thus She gave the sacred songs that help to ease all in their passage. For is it not Changing Woman who each year sleeps beneath the blanket of snow as Grandmother who walks with a turquoise cane, but then each year awakes with the flowers of Spring, awakes as the young Mother of us all?

It is to Changing Woman that we look as we search for the wisdom of life. While some may believe that they can defy Changing Woman's patterns to make their own, wise people know that this cannot be done, for to try to change the ways of Changing Woman, is to destroy all life. But those who understand the ways of Changing Woman, forever walk The Trail of Beauty.

The Trail of Beauty = Tao

WHITE SHELL WOMAN

NAVAJO

This Navajo account of the birth of White Shell Woman, <u>Yolkai Estsan</u>, not only offers an explanation of how we came to have light on earth but strongly suggests the spiritual importance of both the birth and the event. The interpretation of the identity of White Shell Woman has been both as sister to Changing Woman and as an aspect of Changing Woman, rather than as a separate deity. The concept of double female or sister deity may be compared to Huruing Wuhti of the Hopi people and to Ut Set and Nau Ut Set of the Pueblo. It may also be of interest to compare this concept with that of the triple Goddess images as known among the Celts, Greeks and Scandinavians.

Yolkai Estsan, White Shell Woman,
uttered the cry of infancy,
made Her first sound of life,
as She lay at the foot of Mount Tacoli,
as She lay in a cradleboard
formed of two rainbows,
the thin red lines of the rising sun,
the fingers of dawn, touching Her tiny feet.

Four coverlets were wrapped about the baby girl,
each blanket woven of misty cloud,
one black, one yellow, one blue, one white,
four blankets trimmed with loops of lightning,
dawn's sunbeams woven carefully through each loop,
while over the small brown face
the arch of a rainbow could be seen.

Thus White Shell Woman came into the world,
on a day when the world
had long been sad and troubled,
had long been dark with cloud,
on a day when the light of dawn
touching the light of the rainbows
glowed in immense but silent promise.

Soon feeling the darkness,
Yolkai Estsan formed a circle,
shaping it of turquoise and white shells.
Over this She held a rock of crystal,
held it until a fire burst forth,
a blaze that grew so hot, so bright,
that with the help of the Holy People,
White Shell Woman pushed it further and further away,
higher and higher into the spaces of heaven.
So it happened that Yolkai Estsan,
She who had been born at the time of trouble,
She who had arrived attended by rainbows,
brought light to the Earth.

CREATOR OF THE SUN

ASINTMAH

WESTERN CANADA — ATHAPASCAN PEOPLE

The idea of Earth as Mother is one that is found in the religious beliefs of
many Native American groups. This account of Mother Earth and the
first woman of the world is from the Athapascan people of western
Canada. The Athapascan language is used by Native American peoples
who inhabit Alaska, western Canada and the northwestern United States.
It is this language that links the Kiowa, Apache and Navajo people to
these northwestern tribes, for despite the great migrations southwards,
the languages are still similar enough to reveal the connections.

When Mother Earth was very young, the mountains and the
rivers of Her proud body blossomed in the springtime of Her being. She was more than fair to look upon, but Her greatest beauty
of all was that part of Her that became the homeland of the northern Athapascan peoples.

It was here on this most perfect part of Earth that She
adorned Her body with caps of crystal snow and glistening ice
that melted when She grew warm. From this snow and ice came
streams of clear blue water, feathered with bubbling foam, racing
over granite boulders across Her beloved body that held the trees
whose tips grazed against the heavens.

It was on this most perfect part of Earth that Asintmah, first woman of the world, appeared at the foot of Mount Atiksa near the Athabasca River. The holy Asintmah walked among the forests that grew upon Earth, gathering branches that had been discarded by the trees, careful not to tear or wrench away any that might still be growing on the body of Earth. Joining these branches together, Asintmah built the first loom. And upon it she wove the fibers of the fireweed, the willow herb that Earth so favoured, weaving them into The Great Blanket of Earth.

Once the weaving was completed, Asintmah began her long walk to spread the sacred blanket across the vast body of Earth. Securing one corner to Sharktooth Mountain, she tied another to The Pillar of Rock, the third to Levelhead Mountain and the fourth to Mount Atiksa. Then sitting down beside the edge of the blanket, Asintmah began to weave threads of music, singing of all the beauties of Earth, singing songs of how Earth would soon give birth to new lives, beings as perfect as Herself.

Asintmah's songs soon changed to those that would soothe the pangs of labour, that would ease the birth for She who lay under the fireweed cover, as Earth's contractions made the Great Blanket heave and fall—in Her efforts to give Her children life.

Suddenly all was quiet. Earth lay still and calm once again. It was in this way that Asintmah knew that the children born of Earth's womb had been delivered. Reaching carefully beneath the blanket, Asintmah felt the moving life that lay between Earth's thighs. Bringing it out into the light, Asintmah saw a small grey body with four tiny feet and a long string for a tail. It was Mouse.

Excited by this little creature, Asintmah again slipped her arm beneath the blanket and found another life, this one all covered with soft fur, its ears tall with pride. It was Rabbit. So pleased was Asintmah with these two new beings that she continued to search about, her arm reaching ever further under the great blanket that still covered Earth. In this way she soon brought out Cougar and Caribou, Wapiti and Moose, and all the other beings that now walk about on Earth.

So it was that with the help of the holy Asintmah, the woman who existed before all others, Maiden Earth became Mother Earth. And although this all happened a very long time ago, Athapascan people remember that even now they must care for their aging mother, the one who gave them life, and revere the memory of the woman Asintmah who was with Her in the beginning.

AWEHAI

Iroquois

This explanation of how the earth was formed is from the Iroquois people of northeastern United States. The Iroquois Nation was composed of five tribal groups which had formed the *Hodenosaunee,* The League of Five Nations. A similar account is known among the Huron people who also spoke an Iroquois language, but did not belong to the Hodenosaunee. Some versions of the story of Awehai (Atansic) state that the earth was built on the back of the Great Turtle, an image that brings to mind the Chinese account of Nu Kwa using the legs of the turtle as the four columns that hold up the universe. Records of early Iroquois laws and customs not only reveal a system of matrilineal descent but a great deal of political and economic power held by the Iroquois women.

In the days before the Onandaga, the Oneida and the Seneca, the Cayuga and the Mohawk, were separate peoples, in the days even before people came to live upon the earth—there were other beings, in other worlds.

One of these was the woman Awehai. Another was Awehai's husband. The third was a man that Awehai's husband thought she loved, more than she loved him. Thinking this drove the husband into such a jealous frenzy that he uprooted the tree that was at the very center of the world. And into the great chasm left by the uprooted tree, the husband threw the innocent woman to her death.

Falling, falling, through the great dark hole, Awehai grasped at the life around her. Her fingers curled about seeds of vegetables and flowers. As she continued to fall through the great space, she gathered beavers, otters and toads into her arms, clutching them to her breasts. Further and further she fell, as if there would never be an end—until the vast waters of another world spread out below her.

As her body grew closer to the water, creatures with broad feathered wings flew to the place where she would land, making a soft feathery cushion. Gathered under and around her, they carried Awehai until she was safely atop the Great Turtle. The otters, beavers and toads that she had carried with her, scurried about, gathering the dirt that had been shaken from the roots of the great uprooted tree. Pressing this dirt together, they formed it into an island—the one that we now know as Earth.

EARTH AS AN ISLAND — CREATED BY WOMAN —

Once Earth was made, Awehai scattered the seeds from the plants, those she had gathered as she fell. Soon the Earth was covered with green sprouts of nourishing abundance. When Awehai saw this New World, she brought forth children to live upon it. So it happened that the Iroquois people came into being, children of the woman Awehai who had made the new land in the great waters, the woman whose heart had refused to surrender, the woman whose arms had reached out for life.

SOMAGALAGS
BRITISH COLUMBIA (BELA COOLA)

The stories of Somagalags are from the Bella Coola people who live along the coastal areas of British Columbia. Though the latter part of the story presented here appears to be based upon social concerns, the brief references to the birth of the three mountains suggest that Somagalags may once have been the name associated with Earth as Mother.

Down from the heavens that stretch over the lands of the North Pacific waters, in the land of the river known as the Skeena, came Mother Somagalags.

There by the waters where she descended, she found a man and taking him to her, she soon grew great with child. Greater yet, she grew, until she gave birth to Kuga Mountain. Again she took the man and again she laboured. This time she bore Zaychisi, not quite as high as Kuga. Yet a third time she took the man and thus brought forth the Mountain Segos, even smaller than the others.

When the mountains were fully grown, Somagalags left the Skeena River and made her way to the smoothest of beaches. Once there she went from beach to woods, from woods to beach, again and again, until she had carried out all the dry fallen cedars that she needed to make a home. Cleaning off the branches, smoothing off the bark, she built herself a fine cedar cabin in which to live.

There upon the drifting sands that lay by the great ocean waters, in the cabin of cedar, Somagalags once again gave birth.

This time she bore four young wolves, cubs that howled for food and warmth. Placing the infant cubs in the warmest corner, she walked to the water's edge, filling her basket with the tasty clams that had been sleeping in the ocean waters. When she returned to the cabin with her basket of clams, she was surprised to hear the laughter of human children coming from inside. But when she entered through the doorway, all she saw were four cubs, deep in newborn sleep. So Somagalags made the fire, and over it she cooked the clams to feed her hungry wolves, trying to forget the puzzle of the voices.

The ocean waters glistened red in the light of the sun that was bringing an end to the day, as Somagalags once again made her way across the sands from shore to cabin. She held her digging stick in one hand, her clam filled basket in the other. Wearily, she recalled how long it had been since the birth of the cubs, how many times she had fetched the clams, how many times she had made the fire, how many times she had fed her young. But upon reaching the great cedar tree that stood near the cabin, the sound of voices and laughter brought a halt to her thoughts.

In silence, she drew close to the window. Peering inside, she was astonished to see four nearly grown young men—in place of her four wolf cubs. Anger rose in her heart. Fatigue filled her body. She thought of the entire day, the many long days that she had spent standing in the waters in hopes of finding a new bed of clams, the many times she had carried the basket full and heavy with the clams that she had found, the many times she had gathered the fire wood and carried it home so that she might feed and warm the four young cubs.

Furious, digging stick in hand, she climbed through the window. With it she chastised the four young men for tricking her into believing that they were only cubs, that they could not gather their own food, that they could not fetch their own wood, that they could not make their own evening fire. Though quick to protest and offer excuse, the young men finally admitted that they had wronged their mother. Each agreed that if she would teach them how to care for themselves, they would pay her back for all that she had done for them.

So it happened that Somagalags took them to the beach to teach them the secrets of how to find the clams. She took them into the woods where she pointed out the straightest cedars and told them how they could be felled, could be used to build new shelters that would keep them from the cold sea winds. She showed them which trees could be used to carve the sacred totem, so that they and their children would never forget that they were from the Clan of Somagalags. She taught them how to carve the totem form of Somagalags, First Mother of the Clan, She who gave birth to Kuga, Zaychisi and Segos mountains, She who still watches over Her children who live upon the land of the North Pacific waters.

QUESKAPENEK
BRITISH COLUMBIA (SALISH)

The Okanagan Valley in southern British Columbia is even today known for its fertile soil and the excellent food that it produces. This explanation of the abundant growth of food in the land that borders the Okanagan River is told by the Salish tribe of that area. The account describes Queskapenek as a mortal woman but the results of Queskapenek's efforts may well reveal this account as a derivation of an earlier image of Earth as Mother.

Along the blue waters of the Okanagan River, to the south of Chu Chua and Pukaeshun Mountain, the Okanagan people of the Salish tribes remember the Mother Queskapenek. They remember her as the Chieftainess, the First Woman, the one who gave them the abundant Okanagan lands.

Many, many years ago, Queskapenek was a young woman who spent long and pleasurable hours by the waters of the Okanagan. It was there that she gave birth to children. It was there that her children gave birth to their children, as the autumn skin of Queskapenek grew rich with wisdom lines. Her face, then carved with the intricacies of the art of the finest sculptor, told of she who had seen much, she who knew the many secrets of life.

There came a time when Queskapenek knew that she had little time left to spend with the family that she had created, with the tribe that now knew the Okanagan Valley as their home. She worried about what might happen to her children, wanting to be able to provide for them, wanting to be able to mother them, even after her departure from earth.

It was with this concern deep in her mind that Queskapenek put her basket on her arm and walked into the woods. There she sought out the tastiest of roots and plants that she could find, placing each in her basket until it was full. In much the same way, she walked along in the grassy meadows, gathering the seeds of fruits and vegetables, the tastiest that she could find. Each time the basket was full, Queskapenek took the riches in her basket to the place where the soil was most nurturing to growth, where the clear mountain waters made the earth most fertile—and in this land she planted all that she had gathered.

It was in this way that the lands of the Okanagan Valley soon became known for their abundance of fine foods, for this was the legacy left by the Mother Quescapenek. It is for this reason that Salish people remember the ancient Queskapenek, the mother who still provides for them, still cares for them, even though naught but her spirit is to be seen in the Okanagan Valley.

SPIDER GRANDMOTHER
Kiowa

In the account of Spider Woman included in this section, the image of Spider was perceived as Primeval Creator. But there are numerous accounts from the Pueblo peoples of a somewhat less omnipotent image of Spider, as Spider Grandmother. Although some scholars of Native American religion claim that connections between Spider Woman and Spider Grandmother are purely coincidental, the events associated with Spider Grandmother suggest a more careful examination of the links between the two images. The following account is from the Kiowa people. The Kiowa are not Pueblo, but perhaps through contact with the Pueblo people they include some of the accounts of Spider Grandmother in Kiowa legend and belief.

The council of the animals met in the eternal darkness with hopes of finding a solution to the constant night—and to the difficulties of seeing the very ground on which they walked. Many tried to solve the problem. Rabbit dreamed up a plan—that didn't work. Fox devised another—that ended in failure. Eagle tried to find light—only to throw his wings up in discouragement. Woodpecker thought he could do better—only to find that the new world still remained in darkness.

After each had bragged in loud voices, and after each had failed, there was silence. Then from the darkness came a voice, a little voice that sounded very old. It was Spider Grandmother, suggesting that she might be able to remedy the problem. The others responded with laughter and challenging jeers. Surely this old grandmother could not do what Fox and Eagle could not do. But the wisdom of patience made her deaf to their answers. In hope of helping her people out of the blinding darkness, Spider Grandmother set off towards the East, set off towards the land of the Sun People.

The walk was long and arduous. Over vast dry deserts, over perilous mountain trails, across wide rivers and around wide lakes, Spider Grandmother continued to walk—the thread of her webbing spinning out behind her. In the darkness, she came upon a bed of soft wet clay and from it she fashioned a bowl. Once again, she began to walk, now carrying the new bowl in her hands. Many nights of darkness passed. Many days of darkness passed. And then a glow of orange appeared before her in the distance, telling her that she had reached the land of the Sun People.

Fatigued from the long walk, she rested, not far from the blazing fire that wondrously lit the night—hoping that she would not be noticed. As the evening went by, closer and closer she drew to the great fire that lit the land of the Sun People. And then, so quickly that no one saw, she pinched off a small piece of the bright orange flame, popped it into her bowl, and walked quietly away.

Following the strand of web that she had spun behind her, Spider Grandmother began the long walk home. She carried the bowl with great care, so that the piece of fire would not fall out. But much to her surprise, the fire grew brighter and larger as she walked, until its brightness and its heat became so unbearably intense that she flung the blazing fire ball into the air. Tiny and old as she was, she flung the fire so high up into the heavens that it

*After each had bragged
in loud voices*

stayed there and became the sun. So it was that Spider Grandmother brought light for her people, ending the darkness that had
been in the New World.

Yet even at the moment that she tossed the sun into the sky,
Spider Grandmother thought to keep a small piece. This she
placed in the bowl and brought back to her people, giving them
this second gift of fire for the cooking of the food, for the baking
of the clay and for the light of the evening campfire. It is no
wonder that when people, even today, sit about the council fire,
they tell these and other wondrous stories of the ancient Spider
Grandmother.

SUN SISTER
Eskimo

The following account of how the sun and the moon came to be in the sky
is generally simply designated as Eskimo. But it is important to realize
that so called Eskimo people are a group that is spread from Siberia,
through Alaska and Northern Canada, and on Greenland. Within this
group are separate peoples such as the Tahagmiut, Chugach, Netsilik,
Aleut, Iglulik, Nunamuit, and many others. It is also worth noting that
the word Eskimo was applied to these people by a Jesuit. So called
Eskimo groups refer to themselves as *Inuit*, the plural of *inuk*, which
simply means human, as Inuit means The People. Though the legend of
Sun Sister is known among many Inuit groups, there are several variations of it.

In the singing house, the voices of young women, the voices of
young men, sing and laugh together as the snow falls outside. By
the soft light of the whale oil, they watch one another as a great
wind blows across the whiteness. The wild wind grows wilder,
angrily whipping the snow up into its own path until, even fiercer
than before, it forces its way into the singing house—blowing out
the lamps.

Dark as when one's eyes are closed, the singing house was
silent. And then from the silence, a muffled sound came forth, a

frightened crying. Who could it be? And where, in the invisible room? Only two people knew. Sister, and he who attacked her in the darkness, afraid to show his face. What kind of man could this be? Sister rubbed her palms in the soot on the floor and when the lamps were once more lit, Sister knew—from the handprint of soot on his back.

'My brother, my own brother', Sister thought, as disbelief turned into shock. The pain of betrayal joined the pain of violation. From the corner of her eye, Sister saw the whale light flicker on a knife. In hatred, in outrage, in shame, she seized the knife and thrust its blade deep into the chest of her brother!

With her heart pounding heavily, pounding loud inside her own chest, Sister pulled a log from the pile. Lighting one end of the log in the fire, Sister ran towards their home, her log torch lighting the way, cold tears chilling her cheeks. But Brother too took a log and tipped the end with fire. Determined that Sister would not tell what had happened in the singing house, he followed her, making a path of bloodstained footsteps in the snow. Though he tried to run, his steps became ever slower, the ache in his chest ever greater. Finally, when his legs could no longer hold him, he fell upon his torch, lay there upon the blazing heat of the small fire, upon the icy cold of the snow, lay dying on the great flat whiteness.

Glancing behind her, hoping to see the distance between them grow greater, Sister saw the light go down. She saw it dim. Though the handprint of soot and the blood on the knife were clearer to her than the torch that went down, Sister turned to help Brother.

Almost before she had a chance to move towards him, she felt her cold and tired body being lifted from the ground. Higher and higher she rose, until she knew that she was in the highest heavens. Still she held her blazing torch, still she held the log tipped with fire, for now as she took her place in heaven, She became the sun. And to this day, Her torch glowing brightly, we know Her as Sun Sister.

Brother too was lifted into the heavens. But Brother had fallen on his torch and his light was dim. Thus his half extinguished light became the moon, placed in heaven to remind all men of the terrible wrong that he had done, so that none would follow his ways.

So it came to be that in the singing house, young voices can still be heard, telling the story of Sun Sister and Moon Brother—and how they came to be in the heavens.

WARRIOR
POHAHA
PUEBLO

Although this account of Pohaha is based upon an actual woman, the association of the story with the Mask of Valour has helped it to remain as a legend among the Cottonwood Clan of the Pueblo people. Beyond existing as a record of a woman's courage in combat, Pohaha's insistence upon being recognized as a woman as she entered battle, offers a mythic symbolism that speaks of more than the specific events described.

Among the people of the Cottonwood Clan who lived in the great houses set into the massive pink rock cliffs, young Pohaha laughed and played, fished in the streams, climbed the mountains, hunted small animals for dinner—but seldom stayed home to help her mother grind the corn.

The uncles would often tease the young Pohaha, telling her that what she did was the way of boys. But Pohaha went about her day, explaining that if she did what she did, then this must be the way of girls—since this is what she knew herself to be. Even after nineteen summers of life, Pohaha continued to roam the woods, bow and arrow in her hand, refusing to marry, refusing to be kept at home to grind the corn to feed the children they wanted her to have.

When an enemy raid fell upon the people of the Cottonwood Clan, her teasing uncles challenged that such an able hunter should perhaps ride forth and help to drive out the enemy. Much to her uncles' surprise, Pohaha answered their challenge by reaching for her bow, reaching for her arrows, reaching for the war rattle that hung upon the wall—and joining the young men who rode to battle. Her courage and determination shining so brightly, Pohaha soon found herself leading all the others. Though some mocked from behind, even they followed Pohaha to the camp of the enemy.

Along the open stretches of rock and river, Pohaha led, while singing chants of victory to give the others courage. Approaching the enemy campsite, seeing those who had so mercilessly attacked their village, she pressed her horse to move faster. But just before she loosed her first arrow, she raised her deerskin skirt waisthigh. Four times she lifted her skirt, so that neither comrade nor enemy would have a doubt that this brave leader was a woman. Then into the intruder's camp, she led the youths of her village. With war cry and arrow, with command and strategy, it was not long before those who had attacked their homes—and camped only to repeat the slaughter—fled before the angry archer.

Riding home, certain that the attackers would not soon return, Pohaha now sang songs of peace, as those who had fought behind her, now followed with joyous pride replacing their earlier doubts in the one who led them.

When the members of the Cottonwood Clan saw that the protectors of the village had returned victorious, they chanted in relief and celebration. They danced the dance of weapons laid to rest. They feasted upon the food of safe living. And then the great moment arrived, the moment for the presentation of the Mask of Valour, the sacred face that would be given to the one most courageous in protecting the people of the village. Four long teeth jutted from its wide mouth. One side was the blue of deep waters; the other was the golden yellow of sunshine. It was the mask of magical properties, the mask of bravery and daring—and it was about to be presented.

There was never a question of who the new owner of the mask would be. The elders of the village called the brave Pohaha forth and in the light of the evening fire, they placed the sacred mask of courage in Pohaha's hands. Even the uncles agreed that Pohaha must be Potai, Chief Defender of the Clan.

From that time on, for all the summers of her life, for all the winters of her life, Pohaha kept the Mask of Valour of the Cottonwood Clan of the great Pueblo people. In a year of great age, Pohaha returned the mask to her village, saying, "This mask contains my spirit. May it protect you always and be with you forever." And then, deep in sleep that very night, Pohaha went to the land of the ancestors, leaving the mask and the memory of her woman courage as legacy to her people.

PASOWEE, THE BUFFALO WOMAN

Kiowa

The story of the woman Pasowee is from the Kiowa people, an Athapascan tribe related to the Athapascans of Alaska and Canada. The Kiowa are believed to have lived in the Wyoming area before their later settlements in Kansas and Oklahoma. Although it is not mentioned in this account, the story of Pasowee may be connected to one of the sacred societies of the Kiowa, the Buffalo Women. This sacred society is especially associated with ritual dance and healing.

Stolen from her family in the middle of the night's darkness, Pasowee lived for many years in the stranger's campsite. So torn was she with longing for those she had once known that one day she ran into the woods, escaping, only to find herself lost in a place that she did not know at all.

There, lying before her at the end of the day's flight, was the hide of a long dead buffalo, a shelter for the night. Creeping in under the heaviness of the fur, Pasowee slept, as strange dreams flowed as rippling water through her mind. The buffalo had come to life. It spoke to Pasowee in a tongue that she understood. It told her of cures that could be found within its body and how they should be used to heal the ill. It told her that its skin could be used for shelter, just as it had kept her warm throughout the night. It whispered the wisdom of the ages into her sleeping ears. And then, just before the dawn, it told her of the campsite filled with the people from whom she had been taken so many years before, and which brooks and streams to follow to reach them again.

When the morning light lifted her eyelids, she did not forget the night of dreams. Sitting for a moment upon a nearby hill, she watched two wolves kill another buffalo, just as the spirit of the long dead buffalo had prophesied. Gnawing upon the buffalo they had killed, the two wolves then appeased their empty stomachs just as the spirit of the long dead buffalo had foretold in her dreams. Now trusting the spirit of the buffalo, Pasowee waited until the wolves had had their fill and then cut off enough meat for herself. When the meat was dry enough to eat along the way, she started upon her journey.

Following the fast running waters described by the buffalo, Pasowee rejoined her people. With joy, they welcomed the woman they had not seen since her childhood and asked her to tell of her time since she had first been taken. In silent answer, Pasowee showed a piece of buffalo hide that she had carried with her. Then she dried it over stones that were still hot from the fire. Everyone watched as Pasowee then stitched a circle of the buffalo hide to a circle of deer hide, carefully tying the hoof and tail of the buffalo to this leather pouch. Into this pouch she put the medicine that had been made known to her in the buffalo dream.

The miracle of the buffalo medicine brought joy and good health to the Kiowa people. But there was still more wisdom that the spirit of the buffalo had given to Pasowee to pass on to her people. So it was that she led the young women and the young men of the camp into the forest where the great trees lived. Circling about a grove four times, they entered the grove as Pasowee chose a tree, a cottonwood, upon whose lowest branch she hung a cloth. There in the grove the young people stayed until the sun disappeared. There they stayed all through the night of stars that glistened between the leaves of the highest branches.

When the light of the morning came, Pasowee sent the young men to find a buffalo. Then surrounded by the women, she stood before the tree which held the cloth, an axe held tightly in her hands. Three times she swung the axe towards the tree and on the fourth swing she began to cut. When the great tree toppled to the ground, Pasowee showed the women how to paint a carbon black upon its trunk, a clay red upon its branches. Then stripping the red branches from the black, the women made the first *deodogiada*, the first central post of a tipi.

Pasowee then chose the site upon which the tipi was to stand and taught the women how to tie the ropes, so that by pulling upon them the circle of women made the deodogiada stand as tall and as straight as it had done in the forest. Around the central post, the women then placed smaller posts, twenty-two in number. And close to the base of the deodogiada, they placed the small red branches, whistles, feathers and pebbles, and a bowl of cedar shavings—as Pasowee instructed them to do.

The smell of the burning cedar welcomed the young men as they returned with the buffalo. Ten suns passed as the skin was dried and joined and fastened into place. So it happened that from the spirit of the buffalo, Pasowee taught the Kiowa people how to build their homes. It is for this reason that Pasowee is long remembered as Buffalo Woman, Medicine Woman, she whom the spirit of the buffalo chose as teacher of the Kiowa.

WILD PONY
Apache

This legend of primeval times, as explained by the Jicarilla Apache people, is especially interesting in that it includes a description of the origins of a ritual for young Jicarilla girls. This account of the First Woman, Wild Pony, offers some insight into the value placed upon dreams as a manner of gaining knowledge, a value also evident in the Kiowa account of Pasowee. The Jicarilla Apache, though related to the Athapascan peoples of Canada, are now settled primarily in the northeastern area of New Mexico. The name Wild Pony and the part of this account that concerns the use of horses can date no further back than about 1600 A.D., the period that horses brought by the Spanish first became available to Native Americans.

In the days when days began, an old woman and an old man appeared upon the plains. The woman called the man Smoke. The man called the woman Wild Pony. As they walked upon the new Earth, a magic being, a hatsin, came to join them. This hatsin greeted them with welcoming words and then explained their future to them.

'You shall be the parents of a great and noble tribe. It is for you to learn to live upon this land, for one day the Jicarilla Apache people will remember you as their first ancestors.' Wild Pony and Smoke were astonished by this prophesy. Still they heard the hatsin's words about the greenblue rocks in the distance and the shining silver metal that was to be found in them. They turned to look at the rocks, following the direction of the hatsin's pointing finger. By the time their eyes returned to where they stood, the hatsin had disappeared.

'The silver in the rocks is all very interesting,' Wild Pony said, ''but how shall we become ancestors of a great tribe when we cannot even find enough food for the day?' They searched about the rocks and looked across the plains but there was no food to be found. As they found themselves growing closer to despair, the magic hatsin returned as suddenly as it had left.

'You must go to the South. There you will learn of the corn and the grain. There you will learn how to plant seeds so that Earth will feed you and your people forever.' It was for this reason that Wild Pony and Smoke went to the South. There they came to understand the corn and the grain that would feed the tribe they would bring into being.

113

When their stomachs were full, the hatsin appeared for a third time. This time it came to speak to Wild Pony alone. The woman and the magic being walked out upon the plains. As they walked they saw wild horses galloping across the plains, moving faster than any person could walk or run. 'Now I shall tell you of the horses', the hatsin said. 'They have strong backs and can travel great distances. But remember, these horses shall help you only as long as you treat them as your friends.'

After these words had been spoken, Wild Pony expected the hatsin to disappear as it had done before. But the hatsin stayed, continuing to walk by her side. Further and further they walked, until they came upon a stretch of soft red ground. And it was there that the hatsin told Wild Pony about the clay. It kneeled upon the ground, scooping a handful of the soft wet earth into its hand. It was this clay that it rubbed upon Wild Pony's hands, saying, 'This clay is yours to use. With it you can make bowls to hold the corn and grains. And when you find water, you can carry the water in the clay.'

Encouraged by the hatsin, Wild Pony sat by the stretch of soft red ground and formed some of it into a bowl. It was the first bowl ever made on earth. She looked up to show the bowl to the hatsin, but once again it had disappeared. Sitting alone on the ground, Wild Pony decided to make another bowl, and another, thinking how pleased Smoke would be when she brought them back.

Tired from the events of the long day, four clay bowls by her side, the sky red with the sun's descent, Wild Pony fell asleep. The sleep was deep and as heavy as the red hills of rock that lay close to where she slept. And in this deepness, in this heaviness, Wild Pony's mind slipped into dreams. She felt the red clay in her hands. She pressed and pushed. She rolled it and smoothed it. Soon she held a large round red bowl in her hands. She took the bowl to a stream of clear water that raced over small rocks and there she filled the dream bowl with water. But suddenly the bowl began to grow soft in her hands. The water trickled out over the collapsing sides, until she held only the soft red clay that had been a bowl for but a moment.

Wild Pony stared at the clay, deep disappointment filling her heart. It was in this sleep, in this dream that Wild Pony had by the clay bed, that the hatsin appeared for the fourth time. It told the dreaming Wild Pony how to make a bowl so hard that it could hold water and never again return to soft clay. 'First, you must dry the bowl in the sun. When it is dry and hard, wrap it in the bark of the pine tree. Seal the bark with the resin of the pine. When this is done, place the bowl in a fire that smoulders for three days.' With these instructions, the hatsin taught Wild Pony how to make bowls that would hold all the water that she needed.

Years blew across the wild grasses. Horses found by Wild Pony and Smoke became their friends and carried them to far places. Corn and grain kept them from hunger. Silver was hammered into rings for arms and necks. Wild Pony and Smoke were happy upon the Earth. Children came to Wild Pony and children came to her children.

It was many years later that Wild Pony decided to teach her daughter's daughter how to form the clay, how to make the fire and keep it smouldering for days. I shall not live forever, thought Wild Pony. I shall teach the child of the clay and the pine bark so that she may have bowls even after I am gone. Wild Pony rolled the clay and pressed it into shape, explaining to her grandaughter of eight years how a bowl was made. But when the girl tried to form a bowl, the clay cracked and slipped apart. The girl could not turn the clay into a bowl.

As Wild Pony fell asleep that night, she felt the sadness of realizing that the knowledge of the bowls would be forgotten. Her heart was again filled with disappointment, as it had been when she was young and the bowl had grown soft in her hands. And as she remembered that dream, the hatsin again appeared to her, though it had not visited her since that time.

This time it reminded Wild Pony of how it had rubbed the clay upon her hands and told her that it was hers to use. 'This you must do for the young one, as I did it for you. When you have passed along this gift, she too will be able to make bowls.' Wild Pony smiled and nodded in her sleep, remembering the day of that precious gift. Again the hatsin remained. For even as Wild Pony's dreaming mind was on that day so many years ago, the hatsin said, 'I have one more gift of knowledge for you. It is perhaps the greatest gift of all and when I have told you about it, you will know all there is to know.' It was in this dream that the hatsin told Wild Pony how to make the sacred pipe of peace and the wisdom of using it. Once the words had been said, the hatsin vanished, never to appear again.

When the morning sun brought the light, Wild Pony took her grandaughter to the place of the red clay. There she took a handful of the clay and rubbed it into the small hands of her daughter's daughter. As she did this, she said the words that have been repeated to Jicarilla Apache girls ever since that day, 'Now the clay is yours to use.' But when they sat down together alongside the red clay, they did not make a bowl. Instead they made a peace pipe. Together the grandmother and the daughter's daughter made the very first peace pipe on Earth.

When the time came to take the sacred pipe from the smouldering fire, they allowed it to cool in the air. It was this pipe that they filled with the tobacco leaves that they had gathered in the hills. And sitting side by side, Wild Pony lit the pipe, drew upon it four times and then passed it to her grandaughter. The grandaughter too drew upon the pipe four times, making four puffs of smoke in the air. Grandfather Smoke watched the women and tried to imitate what he saw. Rolling a leaf of a yucca plant, he filled it with tobacco. But after four puffs on the yucca pipe, the pipe turned to ashes. Smoke took a branch of sumac wood, and from this he carved yet another pipe. The sumac was not much better than the yucca and Smoke was soon surrounded by more smoke than he intended.

Feeling sorry for her grandfather, the grandaughter asked Wild Pony if she might give the clay pipe to Smoke. And so the custom came into being that each girl of eight years has her hands rubbed with clay and makes a sacred peace pipe, each reciting the story of Wild Pony, the First Mother, as she presents the sacred peace pipe to her people.

the golden mirror of ise

_ _ JAPANESE

rom the blazing fires of volcanic Fuji and the brilliant golden light of Amaterasu to the misty nearly forgotten images of the female spirits of the sea, Goddess imagery in Japan is as varied as the many peoples who came together to form this island culture on the western edges of the great Pacific.

Despite a lack of material on Upper Paleolithic habitation in Japan, the evidence of Upper Paleolithic cultures in Siberia, China and Indonesia suggest that Japan may have been inhabited since Upper Paleolithic periods. We do know that the Jomon culture of later Neolithic periods left numerous small statues of women that are similar to the Neolithic Goddess figures of other areas, as well as stone circles that resemble those of the Near East and Europe.

To understand the sources and the eventual synthesis of Goddess reverence in Japan, one must consider the evidence of migrations into Japan of: Ural-Altaic peoples from eastern Siberia, Sino-Monogolian peoples from China and Korea, and Polynesian peoples from the South Pacific. Yet even as Japanese records reveal continuous confrontations between these various cultural streams, they also reveal an astonishing willingness to synthesize diverse beliefs into a composite perception of life and existence.

It is generally accepted that the Neolithic Jomon culture was developed by the ancestors of the Ainu peoples who once inhabited nearly all of the islands of Japan. The greatly diminished

117

population of Ainu is today centred primarily on the northern island of Hokkaido. The Ainu appear to have migrated from eastern Siberia and to have spread from the island of Sakhalin into the islands of Japan, through the Ryukyu islands immediately to the south of Japan, and into parts of Melanesia. Ainu people have even been associated with a group of indigenous Australians known today as the Gippsland people.

The Ainu have been most closely linked to the Tungus people of Siberia, an Ural-Altaic group whose reverence for the polar bear as deity and/or ancestral totem may offer some insight into Ainu beliefs. Similar beliefs concerning the Samoyed dog occur among other Ural-Altaic peoples of Siberia. Affinities between Ural-Altaic languages reveal the widespread habitation of the Ural-Altaic speaking peoples, including those of northern Sweden, Finland, the Samoyedic groups of the arctic tundra, the Tungusic groups of eastern Siberia, and inhabitants of Manchuria, Mongolia, Turkey and Hungary.

Much more study on the various groups of Ural-Altaic speaking peoples is needed to clarify the similarities and the differences, but from the existing Ainu of Hokkaido we have learned of their reverence for mountains, especially volcanoes, and their association of Mount Fujiyama with the Goddess Fuji. Ainu beliefs about the North Star may have resulted from observations on the nomadic travels of many Ural-Altaic peoples, the seemingly stable North Star perhaps important in establishing direction and position on the tundra lands of Siberia.

Although most material suggests that the general movement of Polynesian peoples was continually eastwards, there is evidence that reveals that many Polynesian peoples also migrated to Japan and became part of the general population. Information on the Goddess as the volcanic Mahuea of New Zealand and on the volanic Pele of Hawaii raises the possibility that the concept of the sanctity of Fuji arrived with the Polynesians. Yet Ainu reverence for Fuji may actually be the source of this spiritual concept, later spread by Ainu peoples who migrated at least as far as Melanesia and were absorbed into the Polynesian population (see Polynesian section—Vol. I).

The later influx into Japan of peoples from Korea and China may have brought Confucianist attitudes towards ancestor worship, along with an emphasis on a male-oriented rule of states that were forming at about 500 A.D. Similarities between Chinese ideas and those of Japan surface in the accounts of Amaterasu, as well as in the legends of sea serpents and sea princesses. There is no question that the Chinese Goddess Kuan Yin (see Chinese section—Vol. I) was the origin of the Japanese Goddess Kwannon. Still revered in a temple in the Asakusa district of Tokyo (Yedo), Kwannon's association with the sea is evident in the portrayals of Her riding upon a dolphin or fish.

In studying the Goddess imagery of Japan, it is extremely important to realize that none of the written records of Japan are earlier than the eighth century A.D. It is perhaps even more important to know that nearly all of the early material was recorded by scribes who had been commissioned by the Imperial Dynasty or other important ruling families. It is also helpful to note that at the time of the initial recording Japan did not possess a method of writing. Thus the records of Japan were recorded in Chinese characters, at times even in the Chinese language. What we today refer to as *Shinto*, a major religio/political system in contemporary Japan, was actually the *Kami No Michi* of Japan, written in Chinese as *Shen Tao* (Shinto), literally The Way of the Spirits.

The most important texts of ancient Japan are the *Kojiki* and the *Nihongi*. These books were initially commissioned by the *TEXTS* Emperor Temmu, ruler of the state of Yamato on the island of Honshu. Temmu's stated intention was to collect the ancient beliefs of the land, and to do so he selected the writer Yasumaro to record the words of Hieda No Are, a member of the royal guild of reciters. Yasumaro completed the Kojiki in 712 A.D. He then presented the Emperor with the more varied Nihongi, a work that includes slightly different versions of the more linear account in the Kojiki. Most studies of the ancient beliefs of Japan are based upon these two major works. There is some additional material from that period and slightly afterwards: the *Kogushui*, the *Manyoshu*, the *Engi Shiki* and the *norito* (the ritual prayers). The Kogushi and the Engi Shiki were also commissioned by ruling families, those who felt slighted by Kojiki and Nihongi biases towards the Imperial Dynasty.

Though political biases are obvious, biases concerning female imagery are seldom discussed by scholars of Japanese literature. It is true that the major deity of the Kojiki and the Nihongi is the Sun Goddess Amaterasu. Yet the emphasis on the secondary status of the female in the accounts of Izanami, and the lineage of Amaterasu that leads to the claim that the rulers of the

Imperial Shinto Dynasty descended from Amaterasu's grandson Ninigi, whom Amaterasu is said to have appointed to be in charge of Japan, not only reveal state biases but perhaps masculist ones as well.

Even in comparisons of the Kojiki and the Nihongi, certain conflicting accounts are apparent. The Kojiki, and some versions in the Nihongi, describe the birth of Amaterasu from the eye of the male Izanagi, the mate of Izanami. Yet one version in the Nihongi clearly states that Izanami gave birth to the sun as one of Her first children. Since this occurs in only one version, it would be difficult to claim that this was the original account of Izanami—as mother to Amaterasu—yet in nearly all Kojiki and Nihongi versions, Amaterasu does refer to Izanami as Her mother. The idea of the sun being born from the eye of a primeval deity may have been derived from a Chinese account of P'an Ku, literally Ancient Serpent. In the Chinese account, the sun is born from the eye of P'an Ku. The possibility of the image of Izanami once having been regarded as a serpent is further suggested by Kojiki and Nihongi passages about Izanami first giving birth to Yebisu (Hiruko), a water serpent.

The possibility of early ideas of a divine serpent of the sea may help to explain the rather puzzling repetition of the number eight in many of the images and symbols of Japanese beliefs. Both the Kojiki and the Nihongi state that at the original Creation by Izanami and Izanagi, eight islands were made—despite the fact that Japan has four major islands and an almost infinite number of smaller islands. The sacred mirror that is the symbol of the Sun Goddess Amaterasu is described as the eight handed mirror. Eight pairs of deities are said to have preceded the existence of Izanami and Izanagi. The Japanese idiom meaning great or massive, as used in the ancient records, is 'eight fathoms deep'. In the Kojiki version of the slaying of the serpent (the account so similar to the one of Yakami included in this section and the Chinese account of Li Chi) the serpent is described as having eight heads and eight tails, and it was said that eight daughters of one family had been sacrificed to it. In the account of Li Chi, the sacrifices were made in the eighth month of each year. (Each of these legends is told to explain the conquest of the serpent and thus who brought an end to this practice.) As a purely speculative guess, may I suggest the possibility that the number eight may be related to very early ideas of a sea creature, such as the octopus, holding up the islands.

Similar ideas are found in Chinese accounts of the earth resting upon the back of a great turtle, an idea that is also known among the Iroquois (see Awehai—Native American section). Aztec accounts include images of a massive alligator holding up the earth. It may be relevant that in one Nihongi account a divine princess who lives in the sea takes her true form—as a crocodile. Legends still linger in Japan, of a great fish *namazu* who lies beneath the islands, its movements and wriggling said to be responsible for the many earthquakes in the area. In the effort to see past the conscious and intentional recording of Goddess imagery in eighth century Japan, the speculation of an ancient Sea Goddess linked to the image of Izanami, and the repeated use of the number eight, may provide a direction in understanding the many Japanese accounts of female spirits of the sea.

Echoes of ancient *miko* priestesses in the Japanese texts suggest that female clergy once held a much greater role in the religious affairs and rituals of the numerous shrines, than was known in later periods. *Noros*, shamanesses who acted as prophets, much like the Chinese women known as *wu*, may have been the origin of the more structured role of miko. Relatively recent evidence of sexual rituals at Shinto shrines may reveal vestiges of a form of worship that was similar to that of the Goddess as the Tantric Shakti in India and the worship of Inanna, Ishtar, and Ashtart in Sumer, Babylon, and Canaan (see Indian, Sumerian and Semitic sections).

One aspect of Japanese Goddess imagery that is rather puzzling in its strong resemblance to images of the Scandinavian Goddess Frigga is that of the celestial weaving house of Amaterasu. It would be difficult to think of two more strikingly contrasting peoples than the Japanese and the Scandinavians. Yet both Amaterasu and Frigga (see Scandinavian section) are described as living in celestial palaces surrounded by semi-divine women of the weaving room in the palace. It is tempting to consider the Ural-Altaic connections between Japan and northern Sweden, but realizing that most of these Ural-Altaic peoples relied upon furs and skins rather than the weaving of textiles, this uncanny resemblance may be purely coincidental, perhaps each drawn from early communal weaving houses as they developed within their own cultural millieu.

Along with each specific image of Goddess reverence, it is important to understand that inherent in nearly all legend and ritual of Japan is a perception and experiencing of the natural environment: mountains, rivers, sea, rocks, trees, flowers, birds, animals, fish—that may best be compared to the Tao of China or Native American concepts of Mother Earth. The one word most important in understanding this perception of the world is *kami*. Defined as spirit or spiritual essence, it is the acknowledgement of the kami in each manifestation of natural life that endows the perceiver with an understanding of the spiritual dynamics of the world. This concept, often associated with the later Zen Buddhism of Japan, probably originated with the indigenous Ainu. The Japanese word kami is derived from the Ainu word *kamui*. The Ainu people of Hokkaido still consider the process of climbing mountains as spiritual pilgrimage.

The following accounts of Izanami, Amaterasu and Ukemochi offer some idea of Goddess imagery as it was known in Japan during and after the eighth century A.D. Yet glimpses into earlier beliefs may emerge from these mirrors of womanhood, even as one stands on the coastline of these great mountains that jut out from the sea and is warmed by the golden glow of the reflection of the morning sun, as She rises from the vast Pacific waters to look first upon the islands of Japan.

FUJI
(A I N u)

The Ainu, the indigenous inhabitants of the islands of Japan, paid homage to the Goddess of Fire as Fuji (Fuchi, Huzi). The site most sacred to those who revered Her was the volcanic Fujiyama located on the main island of Honshu. The Ainu population diminished as migrations of peoples from Korea, as well as from the Pacific Islands, formed the population we today refer to as Japanese, most of the Ainu retreating to the island of Hokkaido. The image of Fuji is extremely similar to images of Mahuea of New Zealand and Pele of Hawaii. The concept of Goddess as a volcano may have formed from observations of the spreading of volcanic lava in ocean waters, such lava creating new islands or adding new areas to existent land. The Ainu association of the bear with the North Star offers a puzzling similarity to the Greek account of Kallisto as the bear constellation that includes the North Star.

Guardian of the Fire
upon the blazing mountain
that stands not far from ancient Yedo,
Her sacred throne floats in the flames
so that all may know of Her sovereign power,
of Her sacred place upon the Eternal Mountain,
towering rock that touches earth as it touches heaven,
as Fuji looks upon Her own beauty
in the mirror surface of the lakes
that lay about Her feet.

Some say that She descended from the heavens
as the woman Turesh who lived upon Mount Fuji,
first woman of the world
who brought the knowledge of existence
to those on earth,
for though it is the mighty Goddess Fuji
who governs from the mountain of flame,
it is Her daughter who is the spirit of the hearth,
the one who taught of warmth from the cold,
the one who taught of the fire beneath the pot.

Ancestress of the once mighty Ainu people,
was it She who lived as Mother Bear,
great white furry being
who lived upon the guiding light that never moved
from the ancient Ainu home in heaven,
polar star where souls may rest
before returning once again to earth?
Each year, at the time of the Iyomande,
the messenger cub was sent to heaven
by those who lived in the caves
upon the islands that floated in the waters,
to remind the Mother of the constant star
that they would one day return home.

IZANAMI

Both the *Kojiki* and *Nihongi* accounts of Creation described Izanami as the divine woman in the eighth pair of deities that arrived at the beginning of time. Little is said of the other seven, but Izanami is credited with most of the activities associated with the formation of land and life. What is especially interesting in these eighth century A.D. records, is the specific emphasis on the female acceptance of secondary status. This emphasis raises the question of the possibility that this aspect of the account of Izanami was added to justify a role reversal from the customs of earlier periods. The eventual placement of Izanami in a castle in the land of the dead may be connected to this effort to justify role reversal, or perhaps was intended to explain the double role of Izanami as Creator, as well as Goddess of the Dead. The eighth century descriptions of Izanami's first child as an ugly and unacceptable water serpent may indicate an earlier image of Izanami as a deity of the sea, perhaps comparable to the fish tailed Chinese Goddess Nu Kwa, or to the Goddess of the Sea and of the Land of the Dead known among the Inuit (Eskimo) under the name of Sedna. Remnants of images of a Sea Goddess occur in the accounts of Urashima and of Fireshade, as told in the *Nihongi*. Several scholars have suggested that the small island of Awaji was the sacred centre of reverence for Izanami, associating this island that lies between Honshi and Shikoku as the Onogoro of the Creation accounts.

Holy Izanami, She Who Invites,
once stood upon the Floating Bridge of Heaven,
once stood on the Ama No Uki Hashi.
In those ancient days when Izanami was young,
She decided to take brother Izanagi as Her mate,
thus the sister and the brother
circled about the Pillar of Heaven,
She from the left,
he from the right,
and upon meeting as agreed,
She spoke of Her desire for him,
suggesting that they mate.
From this mating came the child,
the Water Serpent Yebisu,
the one She sent off in the Boat of Heaven.

But those who wrote for Emperor Temmu of Yamato
regarded this offspring as a tragedy,
claiming that a breach of courtly etiquette
had caused the birth of such an unseemly child,
thus explaining that it was the male who must speak first—
and that the woman should answer only in compliance.
So it was said that the two had once more circled
around the Pillar of Heaven,
the brother then speaking first of his desire,
Izanami echoing his words.

From the mating of the two
came forth the islands of Japan—
as the two moved together like the wagtail,
like the bird of perfect song
that Ainu people had said made the islands
by the wagging of its tail in the waters,
even as others spoke of the tail of the great fish
that stirred up the waters
until the lands came forth.
The island of Onogoro was the first,
and from this home on the waters,
eight great islands came forth from Izanami.

125

From Izanami came the sun and the moon,
the sea and the rivers,
the mountains and the valleys,
the trees and the herbs,
thirty two beings She brought into existence,
thirty two beings filled with sacred kami spirit.
But upon the birth of the thirty third,
the male that was the kami of fire,
the one known by the name of Kagu Tsuchi,
the womb of Izanami was so badly burned
that She was forced to leave
all that She had created
and to retire to the Land of Yomi,
The Land of the Dead.

It was in the land of Yomi
that Izanami built Her castle,
thus living peacefully among the dead,
but there came a day
when Izanagi thought to visit Izanami,
and ignoring Her request that She not be seen in death,
Izanagi entered the Land of Yomi.
The reunion was far from joyful
for when Izanagi saw Izanami in a state of death
he fled in repulsion and fear.
Enraged by Izanagi's actions,
Izanami sent the Shikome after the fleeing man,
these angry female spirits of Yomi
causing Izanagi to run even faster,
until the terror stricken man
placed a great boulder between the Yomi
and the land above,
and from behind the massive rock
spoke words of divorce
to the divine woman who had died
bearing his son—
as She had borne all existence.

AMATERASU OMIKAMI

The *Kojiki* relates that the Sun Goddess Amaterasu was born from the left eye of the male Izanagi, *after* the death of Izanami. Yet a *Nihongi* version of the Creation mentions that Izanami gave birth to the sun and the moon *before* giving birth to the water serpent. The *Kojiki* also states that brother Susanowo was born from Izanagi, but includes passages in which both Amaterasu and Susanowo speak of Izanami as their mother. These conflicting accounts reveal the existence of at least two separate bodies of beliefs, and the attempt to create a composite statement of origins. In examining the process of the amalgamation of religious beliefs, we are fortunate in having access to information about the intentional synthesis of Buddhist and Shinto imagery in eighth century A.D. Japan. Initially based upon the writings of Kobo Daishi in 774 A.D., Pure Land Buddhism developed the idea that Amaterasu had returned as the Amidha Buddha, a concept that bears comparison to the Buddhist idea that the Chinese Goddess Kuan Yin was a reincarnation of the male boddhisatva Avalokitsevara. The symbol of the mirror of Amaterasu, regarded as a sacred Shinto object even today, may be associated with the ancient Ainu idea that the volcanic Goddess Fuji enjoyed looking down upon Her image—as reflected in the lakes at the foot of the mountain. Images of the sun as female and the moon as male are echoed in the accounts of the Khasis of Assam and the Inuit Sun Sister (see Indian and Native American sections). Several lines of the Icelandic Volupso reveal that the sun was once regarded as female among Scandinavians as well. Shinto is still a major religion in Japan, an interesting synthesis of a deep reverence of nature alongside what may be viewed as the political structure based upon beliefs in a divine heritage from Amaterasu, as confirmation of the royal family—not unlike beliefs in divine right as long expressed in Christian nations of Europe

On the banks of the Ise Wan, near the town of Uji Yamada in the district of Mie, stands the Ise Shrine of Amaterasu Omikami, holiest Shinto shrine in all Japan, humble wooden temple that houses the Most Sacred Mirror, eternally reflecting the shining glory of the gracious sun, She who chooses to shine upon Japan before all others, She who is the Divine Ancestress of those who rule Japan.

Heaven Shining She is called, Great Woman Who Possesses *NAMes* Noon, She who reigns over The Plain of High Heaven, Her sacred five strand necklace made of the magatama beads that call upon the spirits adorning Her golden throat, as She watches over all on earth, guiding the building of the canals of irrigation, guiding the *DUTIes* fields of growing rice, guiding the silken threads left by

Ukemochi, guiding the great Weaving Hall of Heaven, the Imino Hataya, where women live and spin in Her celestial palace.

Her brother Susanowo was assigned the dominion of the sea, and displeased that his sister held greater power, he formed a scheme to take that power as his own. With cunning, he announced that he planned to visit their mother Izanami, She who lived in the Land of the Dead. Thus he gained the right to approach the domain of Amaterasu, pretending to tell Her of his plans, but he arrived with such loud and crashing noises that Amaterasu suspected that he intended to challenge Her higher rulership. Swiftly, Amaterasu prepared Her defense, taking up three swords and Her quiver of one thousand arrows that She placed upon Her back; She held Her bow in one hand and five hundred arrows in the other. Arming Herself in this way, She planted Her great legs upon the ground, so firmly that She could not be dislodged.

But upon his arrival, Susanowo denied his intention to cause harm, denied any intention of challenging the power of Amaterasu. And as a gesture of good will, he suggested that they mate, stating that to have children together might mend their loyalties and trust in each other. So it was that Amaterasu mated with Susanowo, and became the mother of the three daughter goddesses, Oki Tsu Shima, Tagi Tsu and Ta Giri Hime.

Yet it was not long after this claim of honorable intention that Susanowo blocked the canals of irrigation, the canals so dear to Amaterasu. He piled them with mounds of dirt so that the waters could no longer flow to the thirsty waiting plants. Still not satisfied with this attack upon what was dear to Amaterasu, he then entered the places in which the rice plants grew and stomped upon each and every plant until the rice paddies lay in muddy chaos. As if he had not already caused enough destruction, and fully proven Amaterasu's original suspicions, Susanowo then thought to smear the celestial weaving house in the palace of the Goddess with the excrement of animals and humans. Finding that his patient sister had been willing to overlook these hostile deeds, excusing Susanowo's acts of destruction by saying that he had swallowed too much saki wine, which often was his habit— Susanowo then murdered a piebald colt and heaved its body into the celestial weaving house. It was then that Amaterasu filled with rage, for as the weight of the horse struck the looms and tables of the hall, they fell upon the women who wove the tapestries in the sacred weaving house, sending several to the Land of the Dead.

murder is too much!

128

The Goddess of the Plain of High Heaven, She Who Is Heaven Shining, filled with anger, but refusing to fight on such a demeaning level, She decided to announce Her rage by the absence of Her warmth and light that brought the goodness of life. Thus She retired to the Cave of Heaven, the Ama No Iwayato, from which Her light would not shine, and pulled the great door tight behind Her—so that the world was in darkness.

THE WORLD IN DARKNESS

No longer was there day and night. No longer did the golden light help the rice to grow. Life was impossible. The deities of heaven assembled on the banks of the celestial river to discuss what might be done to restore the treasured presence of Amaterasu Omikami. They decreed that Susanowo would be punished and fined, and then banished him from the heavens. But how to tempt Amaterasu from the cave? How to let Her know that Her brother had been sent away?

It was for these reasons that the plan was conceived. The playful Goddess Ama No Uzume would dance by the entrance of the cave, making motions and faces that would bring such a laughter from those who watched Her that the curiosity of Amaterasu would be aroused enough to open the door and peer out.

LAUGHTER

Thus the wild dance of Ama No Uzume took place before the Rock Cave of Heaven and when the golden Goddess was tempted to discover what caused such joy and laughter, She found Herself facing the mirror of eight hands that had been hung upon the sacred Sakaki tree of Mount Kagu. So intense was Her brilliant image, so beautiful the reflection upon the polished bronze surface, that She stepped further out to take a closer look, while those who watched quickly closed the door to the cave that had been Her home of anger.

Some say this story was told each year as the days that had darkened earlier each night reversed into the mirror image of each day's light lasting moments longer, the winter solstice remembered by the Sakaki tree laden with jewels and the mirror that would shine with the light of the returning sun. But most remember the mighty Amaterasu as She who shines on the Land of the Rising Sun, Divine Ancestress from whom all rulers were born, She whose mirror now rests in sacred wrappings in the holy place of Ise, She who won not by confrontation but retreat, She who still shines from the Highest Plain of Heaven.

UKEMOCHI

The association of the Goddess Ukemochi with all food, whether found in the sea, planted in the fields or hunted in the mountains, as well as with the silk used for clothmaking, suggests that this deity may once have been revered as the Goddess of a particular community or area. This explanation of Her death and the transfer of Her attributes to a deity appointed by the Shinto Amaterasu may again reveal the efforts of the writer of the *Kojiki* and the *Nihongi* to formulate a centralized theology. The language and concepts in the material concerning Ukemochi suggest that Her image may have been derived from early Korean beliefs. The account also includes yet another explanaton of the understandable idea that the sun and the moon avoid each other as a result of personal antagonism. This idea, which is present in the accounts of the Khasis of Assam and the Inuit of Alaska and northern Canada, even appears in the Mayan account in which the moon is regarded as the Goddess Ix Chel (see Native Americans of Mexico—Vol. I).

From the Goddess Ukemochi came the abundance of the rice fields, the fish of the rivers and the sea, and the animals of the mountains. Long had She been revered as the Goddess who provided all until there came a day when the moon god Tsuki Yomi, brother of Amaterasu, was sent to Ukemochi to serve within Her heavenly palace, to help Her feed the people of Japan.

Arriving at Her home in the heavens, Tsuki Yomi was offered the rice, the fish and the meat that poured forth from Ukemochi. But Tsuki Yomi refused the food that appeared upon the table as a great banquet to welcome his arrival and chose to view Ukemochi's gracious hospitality as insult to his pride, claiming that She had vomited these foods from Her own body.

Already angered at the humility of his assignment, further angered at what he regarded as insulting, Tsuki Yomi drew his sword and murdered the Goddess who had provided for Her people. Yet even as She lay in death, Ukemochi left a legacy of much that was of value, for from Her stomach the rice still came, and from the black silk of Her eyebrows came the threads of silken cloth, and from Her divine head came the horses and oxen, while the wheat and the beans, that were the staple foods of those who tilled the land, continued to come forth from Her womb.

When Amaterasu heard of the murder, She filled with rage and indignation that Tsuki Yomi should have committed such a crime. It was at this time that She appointed Ogetsu Hime to tend the work that Ukemochi had once done but in anger at Her brother, She banished him from the heavens. Filled with shame, he dimmed with the dishonour of his act, shrunk with the knowledge of the evil that his pride had instigated, and from that time on Tsuki Yomi was careful not to show his face in heaven when he knew that his sister was awake.

Some say that when Ukemochi died, it was the Goddess Tamiyo who was appointed to to do the work of Ukemochi, but that Amaterasu put the silkworms into Her own mouth, so that the strands of radiant colours poured out from the mouth of the brilliant Amaterasu.

YAKAMI

The Buddhist tale of the heroine Yakami, still known along the southern coastline of the island of Kyushu, bears some resemblance to a Kojiki account of an eight headed, eight tailed serpent that was slain by Susanowo —a serpent to whom young girls were sacrificed. The resemblance of the two accounts is all the more puzzling in that Yakami is the name of a divine princess mentioned in other Kojiki accounts associated with the island of Kyushu. It is possible that the young woman Yakami was substituted for Susanowo in this legend, but also possible that the original story was altered upon being recorded in the *Kojiki*. The possibility that the image of the young heroine, as the slayer of the serpent to whom young girls were sacrificed, is the original account is further suggested by the ancient Chinese legend of the young woman Li Chi. The valour of Li Chi is still celebrated in ballads of the Fukien province of China, an area whose coastline lies across the East China Sea from Taiwan and the Ryukyu Islands that are stepping stones to Japan. It is quite possible that the Li Chi legend was absorbed into Japanese culture, just as Buddhism and so many other aspects of Chinese culture have been. The Shinto Kojiki account that credits Susanowo with the slaying of the serpent states that he then married the young woman whose life was saved, thus revealing the importance of this legend in Shinto records. The Li Chi account, somewhat like the Chinese legend of Gum Lin, describes how the serpent was lured to its death by tempting rice and malt cakes, Li Chi afterwards remarking to the remains of the previous sacrifices that the sorrow was that they were punished for their gentleness and timidity.

On the southernmost tip of Japan, where the waters of the Pacific flow gently in and out of the inlets along the coastline of Kyushu, there lived the brave Yakami. Golden in the daily sun, almost a being of the sea, she spent her childhood years diving in the waters filled with oyster beds, her young legs firm with muscle, her heart as calm and fearless on the floor of the deep ocean as upon the mat in her own cabin.

Happy young voices could be heard along the rocks of the shore when a perfect pearl was found or when baskets of fish were so full that parents would be pleased. But at times there was the sadness of the loss of a dear friend to the great shark or an illness that could not be cured, and all the sunshine and the sea would not be enough to drive away the quiet grief. Yet for all the events of her young life, never had Yakami been more full of sorrow than when the news came that her parents had been sent to the south, exiled to a prison on a far off island for speaking out against those in power.

There was little work done that day. Young women who usually spent the days diving down to the sea floor now sat around Yakami, their eyes filled with compassion for their comrade—she who had helped them carry their baskets on days when she found little of her own, she who had offered some of what she had on days when others had found none. But royal rulers were not the dangers of the sea, and despite the fearless and courageous lives they led, all felt weak and powerless to lift the heaviness from Yakami's heart.

Her grief too great to search for oysters, Yakami wandered by the wharves, wove her way in and out among the fishing boats, watched the masts lean and sway on the rocking waters of the cove, watched the repairing of the rope nets, staring at the fishermen who climbed from the wharf to deck—from deck to wharf. Surely these boats could travel further than she could swim. Looking out at the open waters, she wondered just where, just how far away her parents might be. 'Do you go to the islands of the south?', she asked an old fisherman, as he sorted his fish on salty wet boards. He nodded, as he threw two smaller fish into a basket.

'I would like to go with you', Yakami ventured. 'I can help with the sorting and I know how to tie the knots when the nets are damaged.' The elderly man smiled in assent, helping Yakami feel some of the heaviness lift from her heart as she knew what she must do. 'My parents have been put into prison', she explained. 'Perhaps on Tenega, peraps on Yaku. They may be even further south. But I must begin to search.' Although no word had passed from the old man's lips until that moment, his eyes then began to dart from side to side, anxious to see that no one was in sight. And then he whispered to Yakami, 'I cannot. My family might suffer. No one will take you on such an errand.'

By the time that Yakami asked the others, all seemed to know the purpose of her trip. Young or old, rough or gentle, all refused and moved away from where she stood, as if afraid of an illness. How strange, she thought. Daily these people risk their lives among the coral and the shark. Daily they risk their lives against the chance of typhoon winds and the tsunami waves that could come upon them like moving mountains. Yet all were afraid of the rulers and those who did their bidding. It seemed that the perils of humans held more terror than all the perils of nature. But more determined than ever, Yakami waited until the dark blanket of night kept the secret, as she untied the ropes of a small unguarded boat. In silence, she slipped the oars through the waters until the mainland was out of sight, raising two small sails in the grey of a dawn of endless waters.

Twice, the sun rose to her left. Twice it arched over her. And twice it slipped into the waters until the time that Yakami saw the island. The moon had reached the top of the heavens by the time she tied the boat to a rock at the island's edge. But when daylight came again and she made her way among the people of the island, all she learned was that prison was not a subject for conversation. Knowledge of her mother and her father was as distant as on the day they were first taken. With half the sun in the sky and the other half floating on the waters, Yakami noticed a holy place set upon the top of a hill, the craggy grey rocks along the side of the hill making an inviting stairway to the summit. Though exhausted from all that she had done, Yakami felt that if she could climb to the shrine, all would be well. As if the very wind carried her on its currents, Yakami floated past the yellow and orange flowers that sprung from the rocks, so that she soon found herself on the top of a cliff that hung out over the ocean below. And there, not far from the small shrine of cypress wood, she lay beneath a wind-blown tree, smelling the familiar salt of the waters, listening to the familiar roar of its ever falling waves as the surf licked against the wall of rock below, and closed her eyes in sleep.

When her eyes opened to strange sounds, the stars were gathered about a top heaven moon. The sleep had been long and heavy, but now her eyes opened wide to see two figures standing at the very edge of the ocean cliff. The taller one recited the norito prayers, while the smaller figure's sobs were caught in the wind. The hems of the white cloth robes they wore blew behind them like sails on a fine day. And then, as if in a bad dream, Yakami saw the taller one reach out, as if to push the smaller one from the cliff. With almost no thought in mind, Yakami leaped to where they stood, grasping the arm of the little one, surprised to see the face of a girl even younger than herself.

The other, a priest grey with many years, gave no apologies but instead explained that the girl had been chosen as the sacrifice to the dragon of the sea, the evil god who lived in these waters and stirred up tai fung winds that played havoc with the boats of these waters if he were not appeased by the yearly sacrifice of a young girl. Yakami, thinking that with the loss of her parents she had little for which to live, insisted that she take the place of the sobbing one, and taking the white robes from the girl, she put them on her own body. Still the fires of hope had not gone completely from her, for as she stood upon the edge, waiting to meet her death, she slipped her diving dagger between her teeth, as she had done so many times before.

As the priest and the young girl watched from the cliff, Yakami's body slid silently into the icy ocean waters. Even as the priest said the prayers of death, Yakami's strong legs swam between the creatures of the sea, pushing deeper and deeper until she saw the skates and rays that hovered on the ocean floor. It was not long before she found the glowing entrance to the rocky cavern so deep beneath the sea. And there she saw the pearly scales, the eyes

Still the fires of hope had not gone out

as red as rubies, the body as great as a fallen tree—the evil dragon of the sea. But though the great thing moved towards her, Yakami quickly circled about its head, and from above she plunged the dagger so that green blood flowed from its eyes. Blinded by its own blood, the dragon stirred the waters into such a rage that Yakami fought the tow of a whirlpool. Then raising her arm with all the force that she could summon, she drove the dagger deeper into the dragon's chest. Suddenly all was calm, as the life fluid of the dragon seeped into the sea.

Astonishment was clear upon the faces of the priest and the young girl who still prayed for the dead Yakami, as they saw her surface upon the water. It was not long before the entire island heard the joyous news and of the courage of the fearless young Yakami. Amidst the cheers of celebration, they again heard the story of why she had come. The word of what had happened sailed off to all the other islands, until it reached the officials of the prison where Yakami's parents had been kept. In gratitude for what she had done, orders were given for the parents release so that they joined Yakami in joyous reunion.

Though Yakami left the island, never was her memory forgotten, as each year at the time of the ancient sacrifice all families gave thanks to Yakami that their daughters would be safe. Never forgotten at the hilltop shrine, her name was called upon as The Brave One, The Good One, as voices floated over the waters singing the story of her courage.

in the land of elves and giants

— — SCANDINAVIA

From the misty fjords of Norway, from the steamy frost of volcanic Iceland, from the dense forests of Finland, from the lakes and rivers of Sweden, from the peninsula of ancient Jutland, come accounts of ancient Goddess reverence that linger in the nature spirits and the magic chants of Scandinavia.

In any exploration of Goddess imagery in Scandinavia, there are two important yet seldom mentioned factors that should be considered. The first of these is that the population of most of central and northern Sweden and Norway, and all of Finland, was initially composed of people known as Finns, a Mongolian, Ural-Altaic speaking people. Related to the Arctic Siberians, the Finns were quite physically different than the tall, light haired, blue eyed Teutonic/Germanic groups we generally think of as Scandinavian today. As northern Germanic tribes such as the Norse, the Danes, and the Swedes, pressed further from central Europe into the north, the Finns retreated even further north, many remaining in the area known as Finnmark or Lapland. Each group left reminders of their encounters with the others in ancient lore and legend. It has been suggested that accounts of small dark elves and dwarves, the beings of Svart Alfaheim (Dark Elf Land), may have emerged from northern Germanic perceptions of Finnish peoples. Since Finland is regarded as a Scandinavian country today, Finnish Goddess images are included in this section, but the reader should be aware of the existence of these two diverse cultures that were the foundations of pre-Christian Scandinavian beliefs. It is for this reason that I have referred to the accounts of northern Germanic peoples as Nordic, rather than Scandinavian, reserving the designation of Scandinavian to encompass both Nordic and Finnish cultures.

The second factor that is often ignored in studies of early Scandinavian beliefs concerns the specific passages within early Nordic records which clearly state that the deities of the Nordic peoples had come from ancient Turkey (Anatolia). According to the thirteenth century A.D. *Prose Edda* of Iceland, the Assembly of Deities known to the Nordic peoples as the *Aesir* came from Troy on the northwestern coast of Turkey. This idea may have developed during the period of 800—1000 A.D. when Norse Vikings were known to have travelled as far as Russia, Turkey and even to Jerusalem. But it is possible that a Nordic connection with Turkey was much earlier, possibly related to the Indo-European speaking groups that entered Anatolia in the second millenium B.C. The province that included the area of Troy at about 1500 B.C. was known as Assuwa. This was the province that became known to the Romans as Asia, the name Asia later used to refer to all of Turkey. (When the use of the name Asia was extended to the Asian continent as we know it today, Turkey then became known as Asia Minor.) The Nordic references to Troy are especially interesting in that they refer to the early Nordic deities as—'The Asians'. This possible link between the people we later know as Nordic and the people of the ancient province of Assuwa may explain the name of the area in which the Nordic deities were said to dwell—*Asgard*, the Land of As or Asa. The Norse storm god Thor, often referred to in the Nordic literature as Asa Thor, was said to have been one of the first deities 'born' in Troy. The name and image of Thor may be related to the Anatolian storm god known in the fourteenth century B.C. as Taru, Tarhund or Tarhuis.

This possible relationship may also help to throw some light on the name of the Queen Goddess of the Aesir—Frigga. Though some scholars link the name of Frigga with the Sanskrit *prija*, meaning love, the name Frigga (and the variations of Freyja and Frija) may have been based upon concepts of the Goddess as known among one of the Indo-European speaking peoples of ancient Turkey, the Phrygians. Just as Aphrodite on Cyprus was spoken of on the Greek mainland as Cypria, and Artemis of Mt.

Cynthus as Cynthia, the Phrygian Goddess most widely known as Kybele (Cybele) and as the Mother of All Deities, may have been remembered by Nordic peoples as Phrygia—Frigga. (Tacitus wrote that the Germanic Aestii tribe revered the Goddess as The Mother of All Deities.) It is truly unfortunate that we have so little material concerning Nordic beliefs until some two thousand years after the Phrygians inhabited Anatolia.

The material that provides us with most of the information about Goddess reverence among the Nordic people is drawn from: the Icelandic poetry of about 900 to 1100 A.D., referred to as the *Elder Edda* or *Poetic Edda*; a compilation of ancient Norse beliefs and traditions brought together by Snorri Sturluson of Iceland in the thirteenth century A.D., referred to as the *Younger Edda* or *Prose Edda*; some records by Saxo Grammaticus of Denmark, a contemporary of Sturluson; and the *Germania* of the first century A.D. Roman writer, Tacitus. One of the most interesting and informative Eddic poems is the epic known as the *Voluspa*. literally *Wise Woman's Prophecy*, sometimes referred to as *The Sibyl's Vision*. This epic takes the form of the words of a *volva*, the Icelandic term for prophetess or sibyl. It is in the Voluspa that the volva not only reveals her knowledge of the past—from the very beginning of time—but foresees the future and the time of Ragnarok, Doomsday. The Norse account known as *Eirik's Saga*, dated to about the twelfth century A.D., provides a detailed account of the physical appearance and actions of such a prophetess, and her use of magic chants that invoked the spirits that provided her with prophetic knowledge. (This incident, which takes place on Greenland, and may reveal Finno-Lapp influences, was clearly regarded as pagan by the new Christians who had quite mixed feelings about gaining information about the future in this way.)

From the Eddic materials we learn that the sun, Sol, was regarded as female, while the moon, Mani, was thought of as male. Although this gender identification of sun and moon differs from Greek, Roman and other Indo-European beliefs, it does agree with the Indo-European Hittites of fourteenth century B.C. Anatolia (see Anatolian section—Vol. I). The Eddas also reveal that the Nordic people believed that there had once been a war between the Aesir and another group of deities known as the *Vanir*. The Vanir were described as living in *Vanheim*, the Land of Van. It has been suggested that the Vanir may have been the deities revered by the people who lived in the area of Vannoy in northern Norway (Lapland). An even more speculative suggestion is that Vanheim may be associated with the Lake Van area of eastern Turkey. When the war was over, some of the deities of the Vanir were taken into the Aesir. One of these Vannic deites was the Goddess Freyja. Despite this account of the late adoption of Freyja into the Aesir, She was apparently an extremely popular image of the Goddess among the Nordic people. Sturluson commented that at the time he was writing, two centuries after Christianity had been made the official religion of Iceland, 'only the Goddess Freyja is still alive'.

Aside from the Goddess images included in this section, other names and images of divine or magical women appear briefly in the Nordic records. Gollveig, which may mean Golden Witch, is mentioned in the Voluspa as the major victim of the 'first war on earth'. The volva explained that Gollveig had been burned in the Hall of Hor three times over, smitten with spears, yet still lived and would live eternally. The volva also mentioned Heitha or Heartha as a 'far seeing witch', 'wise in magic'. Most interesting are the few Eddic lines referring to a divine cow who existed before all else. Her name Audhumla, may mean Creator of Earth. Four rivers came forth from Her udder. Described as The Cow of the Abyss, living in the land of flame and frost, She disappears from Nordic record after She creates the first human. One can only wonder about possible connections between Audhumla and the bovine images of the Greek Goddess as Hera, and the sacred cow as Hathor of Egypt (see Egyptian section). The name of the Goddess Ostara appears in southern Germanic record, associated with spring festivals. The reference is late and may be derived from the Semitic Ishtar or Ashtart.

There are many Eddic references to *Jarnved,* Ironwood, as the homeland of Giant Women. One of the most intriguing and puzzling statements about the Giant Women is the line in the Prose Edda, "That age was called the Golden Age before it was spoiled by the arrival of the women who came from Giantland." The Voluspa mentions three Giant maidens who arrived shortly after the world was created, at the time when no lack of gold was known. The concept of giants among a people as tall and large as the Norse is certainly puzzling. Any attempt to gain some understanding of this may well begin with ancient Greek accounts of Giants who lived in Thrace, accounts thought to have been associated with the Celtic tribes to the north of Greece.

Sources of early Finnish beliefs are even more sparse than those of the Nordic people. The primary sources are the collections of chants known as *Magic Songs,* and the epic poem *Kalevala.* Although we are fortunate in having the information preserved in the Kalevala, it is unfortunate that this compilation of Finnish lore by Elias Lonnrot was made as recently as the nineteenth century A.D. Fragments of names and ritual have also been found in the sacred chants of Finnish groups that settled in Estonia where the Earth Goddess was known as Maa Ema, and among the Votyaks of Siberia where She was known as Muzjem Mumi. The Goddess names that were preserved in Finland were Ilmatar, Mielikki, Maan Emoinen and Rauni. The name Rauni was associated with the ronn or rowan tree, the mountain ash. It is difficult to say whether the Finnish peoples adopted the sanctity of the rowan from the Nordic peoples or vice versa. Throughout many parts of Scandinavia, the rowan became the centre of rituals on Rowan Witch Day, May 1st. The tiny orange berries of the rowan were used to ease childbirth, which probably led to its alternate name of quickbaum (life tree). The rowan was long considered to be a protection against evil in Scandinavia, twigs and branches kept as amulets, the berries also said to restore youth.

Finnish spiritual beliefs reveal similarities to other Finno-Ugric/Ural-Altaic speaking peoples of the Arctic regions. The early Finns were related to Samoyedic and Siberian groups, as well as to Eskimo groups of North America and Greenland. The twelfth century A.D. Vinland Sagas describe a people on what may have been Newfoundland as much the same people as the Lapp or Eskimo groups of Greenland. Although the possibility is seldom if ever discussed, it does seem likely that some Native American peoples may have entered North America from Greenland. The concept of Earth as Mother, as well as the reverence for the bear as ancestor, spiritual ideas that occur in both Finnish and Native American cultures, may be more than coincidental.

Evidence of the Chancelade people of Upper Paleolithic periods of France, whose remains exhibit Eskimoid or Mongolian features, suggests that Proto-Finnish peoples may once have lived as far south as the caves of France. Eventually retreating to the most northerly regions of both the eastern and western hemispheres, many Finns were assimilated into Nordic groups and settled into agrarian societies, while others continued to follow a nomadic way of life, building only temporary shelters, moving as the reindeer moved.

It may well have been some of the early Finns who were described by Tacitus as the Fenni tribe. Tacitus placed them to the northeast of the Germanic tribes, explaining that among the Fenni the women did as much hunting as the men. There is still too little known about these Arctic peoples who may well have given us snow shoes, skis, sleds and kayaks. Perhaps their ability to do what astonishes us most, survive in the most frigid zones on earth, is what has protected them from our prying questions. (Most scholars prefer to do their research in sunny Greece or Italy.) Yet stories of the ancient Creatress Ilmatar, Mistress of the Forest Mielikki, and the ancient Sacred Chants that call upon the spirits of nature, flow south with the sparkle of snows melting in clear blue northern rivers.

It is evident that Goddess imagery in Scandinavia is a complex study of both Nordic and Finnish beliefs, and the synthesis of these two diverse groups of people. Images of women as Divine Mother, as Queen of the Witches, as Queen of the Elves, and as the one endowed with knowledge of the future, linger in Scandinavian perceptions of nature, as surely as the foggy mist so often veils both forest and fjord, transforming what is solid and tangible into that which is hidden, ethereal and *myst*erious.

ILMATAR

Ilmatar, literally Sky Mother, is most often referred to as Water Mother
in the *Kalevala*. Her image bears comparison to Inuit accounts of the
Goddess Sedna, Nuliajuk or Nerrivik. Since the written records of Finnish beliefs are from such a recent period, it is difficult to ascertain the
age of this image or how much influence Nordic groups may have had
upon it. The Kalevala presents Ilmatar as a passive being who creates the
earth almost by accident, yet at the same time describes Her as Creator
and as possessor of immense powers. The account of the teal's eggs, and
the later Creation by Ilmatar, suggest that Lonnrot may have combined
two quite separate creation legends in his compilation of the Kalevala.

Descending upon the billowing waters
of the never ending ocean,
Ilmatar was rocked in the waves of the wild sea,
blown along in the foamy tempest
of winds from the East.
Carried for centuries upon the swelling waves,
She floated to the East,
She floated to the West,
She floated to the South,
She floated to the North.
Feeling only cold and dreary,
Ilmatar began to regret
that She had left Her home of gentle breezes.

In the deepest moment of Her sadness,
a lovely teal came flying over,
seeking land on which to rest
seaching for a nesting place—
and finding only moving waters.
It was then that gracious Ilmatar
lifted Her great knee from the sea
creating the first hill of land established.
It was on that knee the teal soon built her nest.
Knee as green as spring's blossoming,
held the teal's nest up high,
held the six eggs of gold,
held the seventh one of iron.

But how long could the Water Mother
hold the stillness of Her knee?
Thus Ilmatar moved to find comfort,
causing the eggs to fall into the waters,
causing them to shatter into fragments.
From the lower shells the earth took form,
from the upper shells came the arch of heaven,
from the yolk came the lustrous sun,
from the white part came the moon,
and from all that was speckled in the eggs—
the stars came forth.
Still Ilmatar floated on the waters,
now peaceful and serene.
For ten more years She floated,
until the day when She raised Her head
from beneath the waters—
and thus began Creation.

Pointing with Her fingers,
She formed the fjords along the ocean.
Her toes created the underwater caves
where fish might lay their eggs in safety.
With the deepest part of Her body,
She formed all that was on the ocean floor.
Her feet created beaches.
Her head made the long curving bays.
Even the craggy rocks that stood in open water
were formed by the ancient Water Mother—
She who made all earth.

Oldest of all women,
loveliest of all women,
first of all mothers,
then formed the pillars
that held the sky in place
and upon the rocky cliffs
She engraved the forms of figures.
Still Ilmatar remained in the ocean waters,
owner of powers too numerous to count,
possessor of magic too deep to comprehend—
and perhaps She lives there still.

FREYJA

According to Snorri Sturluson, author of the thirteenth century _Prose Edda_, of all the ancient Scandinavian deities only one was still 'alive' at the time he was writing—the Goddess Freyja. The name Freyja, cognate with the Sanskrit word _prija_ which is translated as love or friendship, was used in the Eddic accounts to mean Lady—as the counterpart to Lord. Freyja, often referred to as Freyja Vanadis, was known as the Queen or Mother Goddess of the group of deities known as the Vanir. The legends of Freyja's relationships with the elves of Svart Alfaheim may be purely mythical or perhaps revealing of some connection with the Finnish peoples. Sturluson gives alternative names of Freyja as Mardoll, Horn, Gefjon, and Syr, stating that these were the names She was known by among other peoples. The golden boar on which Freyja and Her twin brother Freyr rode through the forests was identified by Tacitus as a major emblem of the Mother of All Deities, as known among some of the Germanic tribes. The account of the Goddess as Gefjon (Gefion, Gefn), which occurs in the beginning of the Prose Edda, bears some resemblance to the image of the Goddess as Nerthus in Her cow drawn wagon, perhaps suggesting Gefjon's island of Sjaelland (Zealand) as the one on which the image of Nerthus was kept.

Proudly did She ride about, Freyja, Queen Mother of the Vanir, Her chariot drawn by cats as dark and sleek as the night, until just at the moment one might catch a closer glimpse, She would be off through the forest, mounted upon the back of Golinborrsti, golden boar charging between the trees. But if one chanced upon Freyja in the woods, She would gather up Her falcon wings and soar past the tops of the highest pines, the tips of Her vast wing span brushing against the clouds.

In the arrival of the spring greening, one might see Her eyes peering out from the very centres of the wildflowers of the field, Her silky hair glimmering between the branches of the trees, as the sun angled in the sky. And when night's darkness veiled the meadow, one might spy the wondrous Freyja as She stayed to watch the faerie folk, the dark and tiny elves who danced upon the golden ribbons that fell from the moon, perhaps even fortunate enough to see Freyja tossing fragrant flowers to applaud the graceful dancers or to watch Her gather honey to feed the little ones.

Many sides had Mother Freyja, as familiar with the battlefield as with the field of wildflowers. How often did She ride

CAT

BOAR

FALCON

across the battleground, choosing from among the slain those She wished to keep with Her forever, those who would then dwell in Her heavenly castle of Folkvanger. It was they who saw the war helmet on Freyja's head. It was they who saw the sword and spear in Her hand, while others spoke of mounted Valkyrie maidens taking the slain to Odin at Valhalla.

Some said that She was one with Gefjon, for it was She who did the giving, and in this form of ancient Woman Giant She drove Her wagon through the land, speaking to the oxen four that pulled the yoke, as if they were Her sons. As Gefjon, She ploughed so deep into the earth that She pulled it with Her to the sea, thus creating the great island of Zealand and the Kattegat Sea as a moat of protection. Though some say that the hole that was left behind became Lake Malaren, others say that Zealand clearly came from the place where Lake Vanern now stands. Yet all agree that it was Gefjon who formed this island in the sea and remember Her by the Gefjon Fountain that graces the city of Copenhagen.

It was Freyja who taught the magic songs of the mystic Seydur, taught them to the women whom She chose to look into the time of what was yet to be. Sitting high upon a seat before the people of each village, the chosen women would chant of what was to come, foretelling the lives of newborn babes, imparting knowledge of the summer's crops. The holy Volva, blessed women prophets, sang to Freyja in ecstatic trance, exchanging answers for questions, providing the Nordic people with a knowledge of the future.

And when people were in need, Hindluh the Sorceress was there by Freyja's side. Some tell the story of the time when Ottar called upon Freyja in his argument with Angantyr, claiming that it was his land that Angantyr used as a home. Thus Freyja devised a scheme, arranging that each would speak in the assembly and that the one who could recite the longest list of ancestral names —that one would have the land.

As the good but simpleminded Ottar lamented about the few names that he knew, Freyja transformed Ottar into a bear and upon his back She rode into the deepest woods, to the cottage of Hindluh. There, life by life, Ottar heard of all who had owned the land, all who had used the name that was now his. Though Hindluh took him back through time, Ottar fretted more than ever. Freyja felt ever more certain that She could not trust the memory of this man. It was for this reason that She bade Hindluh to brew a potion for Ottar, so that upon drinking it, he would not forget all that he had heard. When the day came that Ottar's case was heard in the assembly, and each name tumbled from his mouth with ease, Ottar dropped upon his knees in gratitude to the compassionate Freyja.

There came a day when, deep in the northern forest, Freyja wandered into Svart Alfaheim, the Land of the Dark Elves. Close by the great oaks She saw a cave, and the four little men who lived there. Hard at work by a glowing forge, their tiny hands held the pieces of glistening gold that were soon to be parts of the most perfectly formed necklace ever seen by mortal or deity, the necklace we now know as the magic Brisingamen, made of the brilliant jewels known as The Brisings.

Watching in silence until the work was done, Freyja grew in determination that the necklace would belong to Her. She brought forth handfuls of silver, as if from the air, but the elves refused Her offer. She brought forth handfuls of gold, more than anyone had ever seen, but again the little men refused to sell the necklace. 'What do you ask?' She declared in growing impatience, and was not a little surprised when they asked for a night of love—for each. Four days and four nights Freyja spent in Svart Alfaheim, so pleased with the four little men that She nearly forgot the necklace. But on the fifth morning, true to their word, the four led Her out into the morning sunshine and there in the greenest of meadows they placed the precious Brisingamen on the Queen Mother of the Vanir. As the clasp was fastened about the neck of the Goddess, the rainbow appeared in the sky. From the necklace came blazing fire. From the necklace came brilliant light. It brought the glow of the dawn and the dancing lights of the setting sun upon the waters. It glistened with a light that created the morning star. And most precious of all its magical presents, it brought the heat of the forge on which it had been made and the knowledge of forming gold as if it was as soft and pliable as clay. Leaving the land of Svart Alfaheim, the treasure of the Brisingamen about Her neck—Freyja brought these gifts to the people of Scandanavia.

NERTHUS AND URTH

Ancient Goddess

The rituals for the Goddess as Nerthus are known from the *Germania* of the Roman writer Tacitus. He explained that Nerthus was revered by the north Germanic tribes known as the Reudigni, Aviones, Angles, Varini, Edoses, Suarines and Nuithones. These first century A.D. references to Nerthus have been compared to the thirteenth century A.D. passages about Urth, the eldest of the three Norns. Thus, I have combined the available information about both Nerthus and Urth in the following piece, but it should be understood that these two images appear in texts separated by some twelve centuries. The Norns are most often associated with the Greek Moirae, the Roman Fates, who in turn have been linked to the Anatolian sister deities who spun destiny. Hallfred Ottarson, writing in Iceland at about 1000 A.D., told of shunning the rites for the Norns for the new Christianity.

Mother of the Northern Earth,
called upon as Holy Nerthus,
dwelled upon an island in the Northern Sea,
Her image deep within a sacred grove
hidden beneath protective veil.
Yet each year She came forth,
as those who joined in joyous festival
greeted and welcomed Her appearance,
as Nerthus rode by in a wagon of finest timber,
drawn through the streets by sacred cows.
All weapons were put aside,
all iron objects locked away,
in hopes that Nerthus would bring prosperity and peace.
Though none were there to know,
they say Her image was then bathed
in the waters of a secluded lake upon the island—
and that those who bathed Her
then met their death beneath those waters.

Freyja, Queen Mother of the Vanir

Those who tell of ancient Urth
do not forget Her sacred Well,
the spring pond of magic waters
that bubbled above the white clay beds.
It was by these waters
that Urth lived with Her sisters,
for as Urth had all knowledge of the past,
so Sister Skuld foretold the future,
as Verthandi understood the vastness of now.
Three Norns they were,
living beside a root of Yggdrasil,
the root of the World Tree
that was closest to the home of the Aesir,
the dwelling place of all goddesses and gods,
the root that was kept alive
by the magic waters of the Well of Urth.

So powerful were the Three,
it was they who appeared at each birth,
allotting the fate, decreeing the future,
for each new born babe,
spinning the threads of destiny,
weaving the golden fibers of what would be,
even as they carved the laws of humanity
upon the root of Yggdrasil,
making laws so wise and righteous
that even the deities of the Aesir
held their daily court of justice
at the dwelling place of the Norns—
The Three Sisters who knew all there was to know.

IDUNA

Iduna's primary role is that of the possessor of the golden apples of immortality. Her image is one of eternal youth and springtime. The golden apples that kept the deities of the Aesir eternally young may be linked to beliefs about the orange berries of the rowan tree, the rowan berries thought to restore youth as well as to ease the pains of childbirth. The Finnish Earth or Forest Mother known as Rauni was regarded as the essence of the rowan tree, perhaps suggesting that the Nordic image of Iduna may be much the same as that of the Finnish Rauni. This account of the Nordic Iduna is drawn from the *Prose Edda* and from the tenth century poem *Haustlong* of Thiodolf of Hvin, a Skaldic poet of southern Norway.

Into the land of Asgard walked the ever young Iduna, born of the spring air, birthed from the flowers of the field, Goddess of the fruit of the orchard. With Her came Her golden treasure chest, Her gracious gift to the deities of Asgard, the glowing box containing that which so many mortals yearn to gain but is reserved only for the holy ones of the Aesir—the golden fruit of immortality.

In Her voice they heard the music of ever running brook and stream, the lovely quiet that follows the roar of thunder, that stays the din of late winter storm. As She walked among the deities of Asgard, presenting each with a golden apple, each deity became as youthful as Iduna—even as the treasure chest remained as full as when She first arrived. Delighted with Her presence, a great feast was spread in Asgard, with more than mead enough for all, each drinking horn filled to overflowing. And at this joyous celebration, Iduna took each deity to Her fruitful, loving body, so that none knew a lack of the abundant love of Iduna. Throughout this wondrous evening, Iduna's mate, he who had arrived in Asgard with Her, Bragi of the delicate features and gentle disposition, sang sweet verses that harmonized with the golden strings of his harp—verses of the miracle of the eternal youthfulness that Iduna had given to those of Asgard.

But springtime cannot last forever, and when Thiassi of snowy Thrymheim heard of the eternal springtime of life that had been given to those of Asgard, his resentment and envious desire grew. So it happened, that with the help of evil Loki, Thiassi swooped with snowy eagle wing upon the unsuspecting Iduna and took Her as a captive to the land where all is cold and dead with winter. The deities of Asgard once again grew old—as all that grows in summer dries and dies with autumn wind to lie silent and dead beneath the winter snow—as prisoner Iduna shivered in the Thrymheim cold.

Sadness fell upon the holy Aesir as they watched themselves grow older with each day, their faces gaunter, their hair greyer—each day that Iduna did not appear. In the sorrow of looking upon Iduna's empty seat, the deities of Asgard cried to Frigga, asked the Queen of the Aesir who knew all— what had happened to Iduna, and how they might restore Her presence at the table. How they missed Iduna's tasty golden fruit, the warmth and gentleness of Her springtime being, the juices of eternal life. How they missed the sound of harp strings and the lilting voice that Bragi, in his grieving for Iduna, could no longer offer to the Aesir.

Frigga looked deep into Her knowing mind and saw the sad Iduna held prisoner in Thrymheim, now guarding the apples of eternal life from Thiassi, even as She fought to repel his efforts to mate with Her springtime being. Thus Frigga ordered Loki, he who had put Iduna in this peril, to now rescue Her from Her winter plight. Loki then dressed in Freyja's falcon coat, perhaps a reminder of a time when it was Freyja who brought Iduna home to Asgard. Flying north to Thrymheim, Loki arrived to find Iduna all alone; Thiassi was flying over the ocean waters searching for fish. Quickly transforming the ever young Iduna into a seed of springtime, Loki took Her up in Freyja's falcon beak—and in this way they flew across the heavens to Asgard.

But Thiassi, with the eagle sharpness of his eyes, spied Iduna leaving. With his wide eagle wings, Thiassi flew to intercept the falcon, drawing close above the mountains close to Asgard—in clearest view of those who wished Iduna to return. In their anger at the bold Thiassi, the deities of Asgard made a great fire on the mountain top. Unable to stop his flight before his wings touched the leaping flames, Thiassi met his death in the blazing fire. So it was that the great eagle of Thrymheim died, as precious seed Iduna returned to the deities of Asgard—once again giving them youth and immortality.

MIELIKKI

(handwritten: Goddess of Forest)

The evidence of Mielikki as Goddess of the Forest occurs in the *Magic Songs* of the Finns, and in the *Kalevala*. The image of Mielikki bears a surprising resemblance to the Greek Goddess Artemis, as the protector of animals of the woods and as the Goddess of the Hunt. The references to Mielikki nurturing the young bear may be associated with the ancient Finnish custom of placing a bear skull in the forest as sacred totem. This reverence of the bear appears all across Ural-Altaic speaking regions of the Arctic and raises questions about the bear rituals for Artemis, and the relationship between Artemis and the Bear Goddess Kallisto (see Greek section).

(handwritten: Like Artemis)

Mistress of the Forest,
fair and bountiful Lady,
nurtured the bear cub
with the honey of the bees,
yet it is Mielikki who allows the woods
to grow grey and shabby
when the snows of winter melt away,
even as the skull of ancestral bear
sits high upon a branch in the forest,
facing the rising sun,
in the hollow where light pierces
through the roof of heaven touching leaves.

Delighted by the magic sound of flute,
Mielikki then dons Her golden bracelets,
slips golden rings into Her ears,
threads golden beads around Her throat
and takes Her seat
in the mansion of golden windows
where She watches over the creatures of the woods,
providing game only to the worthy,
directing the maiden spirits,
the fleet metsanhaltija of the forest,
to open the mansion doors—
only to those
who know that Mielikki dwells within.

FRIGGA
Queen Mother

The attributes of the Goddess Frigga are so similar to those of Freyja that the two names are often thought to refer to the same Goddess image. The major differences between the two are Frigga's much closer relationships with Her husband Odin and with Her son Balder. Since both Frigga and Freyja are associated with the magic Brisingamen necklace, the account of Odin's attempts to steal it may help to point out some of the differences. The idea of a sacred necklace was also associated with the Greek Goddess Harmonia, Aphrodite's daughter. It is interesting that the amber used in Mycenaen Greek jewellry (at about 1500 B.C.) is believed to have been imported from Jutland, ancient Denmark. Tacitus wrote of the Germanic Aestii tribe, both as worshippers of the Mother of All Deities and as the only ones who gathered amber for the Romans. The account of the death of Frigga's son Balder has been compared repeatedly to the accounts of Attis, Adonis, Osiris, Tammuz and Damuzi, the dying son/lovers of the Goddess in the Near East. Although Frigga is continually referred to as the wife of Odin, She is described as living in a separate palace, Fensalir, surrounded by other goddesses or divine women. Sturluson lists one of these women as Gefjon, the Goddess image earlier described by him as the creator of the island Sjaelland, and the name he gives as a variant of Freyja.

High upon Her throne in the Palace of Celestial Marshes, in the women's hall of mist and sea, in the fabled Castle Fensalir, sat the Goddess Frigga, Queen Mother of the Aesir. It was She who spun the golden threads of fate, weaving universal design of past, of present, and of future.

With Her were the holy women who dwelled with Her at Fensalir. Gracious Fulla was friend and confidante, advisor whose ears were always open to mortals as they prayed on Midgard, especially to women who asked for ease in childbirth, or asked Fulla to prevail upon Frigga to weave fine destinies for little ones whose lives were waiting to be spun. And there was wise Gna who rode upon the swift steed Hofvarpnir, to learn all that had occurred so that She might convey these messages to Frigga, causing many to say that Frigga said little—but knew all.

In the Hall of Fensalir lived Eira of the magic herbs, skilled physician always willing to aid those who suffered from disease or wound, and Hlin who protected those in danger, while Syn acted as the counsel for defense of any innocent who was wrongly accused. Sjofn turned the minds of mortals to thoughts of love, while Lofn helped those whose love was forbidden. Var watched over vows and contracts, wreaking vengeance on those who did not keep their word, while Gefjon cared for all women who chose to live their lives without a husband.

In the midst of all these holy women, Frigga sat upon Her throne, clad in long white robes that darkened with the coming of each night, the feathery plumes of the sacred heron rising from Her royal crown, so that many said that Frigga flew as the heron flies, ascending straight up into the heavens, but others said that it was the wings of the falcon that She wore. The golden girdle of heaven's arch circled about Her holy waist, as the belt of stars circle in the sky, yet some say that this jewel encrusted girdle was the magic necklace, the brilliant Brisingamen.

Memories of Mother Frigga of more ancient days drew visions of delicate young Balder, who died leaving his holy Mother to mourn, though Frigga had begged all living things on earth to spare the life of Her gentle son when She heard that Hella, Divine Queen of Nifhelheim, wished to take him for Her own. But the evil giant Loki, he who thwarts all that is good, hearing that Frigga had not spoken to the tiny mistletoe that grew at the foot of the great oak, used the hand of Balder's blind brother to shoot a dart of mistletoe into Balder's chest. Thus was Balder sent to Nifhelheim in deathly sleep.

Learning of the tragedy, Frigga sent Hermodar to the Underworld of Hella, the dark and gloomy Nifhelheim, to arouse compassion for the grieving Frigga. Though Hella thought to keep the gentle lad for Herself, She promised the return of Balder—if all living things on earth would weep as Frigga wept. Once again, Frigga travelled far and wide, speaking to each thing that lived on earth. From each She received a promise that they would mourn for Balder, and would weep as Frigga wept. But evil Loki, this time posing as the Giant Woman Thiokk, refused, and once inside his cave he only laughed at the trick he had played on Frigga. Thus Balder remained with Hella, and shall until the day of Ragnarok will come—they day of doom and final battle that will bring to an end to Midgard as we know it.

Frigga not only mourned for Her son but was often saddened by Her marriage, for husband Odin thought so much of himself that he had little time left for thoughts of Frigga. Thus Frigga chose the company of the elves or the brothers of Odin, Vili and Ve, to join Her in Her bed at Fensalir. So unloving was Her husband Odin that he took the golden necklace that had been Her most prized treasure. When Frigga saw it on a village gate above Her, adorning a statue that Odin had made in his own image, She filled with righteous anger and demanded its return.

Odin with arrogant refusal, recited magic runes over the statue, thus empowering it with speech so that it could name the name of any who might try to remove the precious necklace. Perhaps Odin would have kept it always, had gracious Fulla not cared so deeply for Mother Frigga. So it was that Fulla made arrangements with a friendly elf, and with him laid the plan to place a magic spell of sleep upon the guards of Odin who watched the gate. With this done, the elf climbed upon the arch and pushed the statue to the ground. In this way the shattered statue told no tales, while Fulla retrieved the necklace for Queen Frigga. Thus the ancient Brisingamen, that which Freyja had once earned , was reclaimed as the possession of the Goddess.

SKADI

Goddess of Winter/Snow Queen

The image of Skadi is as the Goddess of Winter. Although descriptions of Skadi mention Her robes of white fur and Her icy crystal arrows, the name Skadi (cognate with the Greek *scotos*, the Gothic *skadus*, and the Norse *skadi*) literally means the Dark One. As hunter with the bow and arrow, the image of Skadi may be compared to the Finnish Mielikki. Her name and image have been compared to Scathach of Scythia who appears in Celtic accounts as 'wise in weaponry'. The accounts of Skadi were later incorporated into Hans Christian Andersen's story of The Snow Queen.

Though some said that Skadi was dark and full of harm, the ancient Mother of the North taught Her people how to make the skis and skates and sleds to slide across the miles of whiteness of Norwegian winters. Great woman of Thrymheim, it was Skadi who stirred up the snowflakes of heaven so that they swarmed like bees around Her white fur robes and boots. Even upon the broadest

snow shoes that She invented for Her people, Skadi remained
fleet and agile, as She used Her bow and arrow in the snowy
woods.

They say She came to Asgard upon hearing of the fiery death
of Thiassi, eagle father of wintry Thrymheim, his feathered wings
burned to ashes when he had tried to keep Iduna from the deities
of Asgard. Standing before the deities of the Aesir in Her snow
white fur and crystal armour, Her arrows sparkling with the frost,
Skadi demanded a life for a life. Thus the deities of Asgard, seeing Her determined anger, offered Her a husband in Thiassi's
stead.

Though in Her mind delicate young Balder was the object of
Her fancy, those of Asgard insisted that Her choice be blind and
wrapped a linen cloth about Her eyes so that She could see no
higher than the ankles of all the men who stood about Her in a circle, waiting for Skadi to make Her choice. So it was that Skadi
had to pick, almost as if with eyes shut tight, as so many women
are wont to choose their mates, thinking that the feet most
perfect, most delicately formed, were those of Frigga's sweetest
son, the gentle Balder. But when the blinder was removed, it was
Njord of the foggy seacoast, he who had come from the Vanir,
that She had taken as Her husband.

All went rather well as long as they remained in Asgard. But
when the time arrived that they should choose a marriage home,
Njord insisted that Skadi join him in his home along the mild misty beach where the sounds of gulls pierced the air, while She insisted that he return with Her to the snow covered mountains of
Thrymheim, where the call of wolves was music more familiar to
Her ears. Trying to devise a plan that would be suitable to both,
the year was evenly divided, so that half the time was spent in
Njord's Noatun home, dwelling then in snowy Thrymheim for the
remainder of each year.

What seemed such a fair and reasonable solution ensured
that one of them always would be saddened, whichever place was
taken as their home. Though She had won him fairly, Skadi finally announced to Njord that they must part. Some who tell this tale
say that She left with love and friendship. But others claim that
She flew into a rage and breaking up the timber of their marriage
bed, She strapped the boards upon Her feet and thus invented
skis. Walking flat upon them until She reached the hills of sliding
snow, She then skied across the mountains and the valleys—back
to Her Thrymheim home.

Once again in the land of constant snow, Skadi found Uller, he who liked the winter. Some say Uller's mother Rind was the Mother of the northern forests who some call upon as Rauni. Those of northern Norway, who say that Skadi and Uller were their parents, tell of calling upon Skadi in blinding blizzards, asking Her to help them in their plight. And some say they see Her hunting in the moonlit snow, Her arrows glistening with ice, or see Her riding in Her sleigh of icy crystal, its ski runners almost floating over the packed whiteness, as great white furry dogs pull Her to Her palace built of bricks of ice.

Those who later came to Norway with stories of a holy child born to a virgin in Jerusalem, spoke of Skadi as the evil Snow Queen who tempted innocent children from their homes, keeping them as captives who had lost their souls. But there are those who say that one day Skadi left the land of Thrymheim and skied across the waters of the great Norwegian Sea, landing on the shores of the island to the west—where She was called upon as Scota—Great Mother of the Scots.

HELLA
Goddess of the Underworld

Hella, the Goddess who ruled Nifhelheim, the land of the dead, appears in the Eddas only in this connection. It is quite likely that Nifhelheim was associated in early Norse minds with the island of Iceland, the volcanic Mt. Hekla and the nearby town of Hella probably named in this way. Hella was described as treacherous and frightening, yet quite human in Her desire to have the beautiful Balder join Her in Nifhelheim. Germanic material on the Goddess as Holla and Holda may indicate that the most ancient nature of Hella had been much more complex. The connection between these two Goddess images, Hella and Holla, is made clear by the German word for Hell, *Holle*. The German Goddess Holla was later regarded as Queen of the Elves or Queen of the Witches. The name Holla, which may have been a title, is extremely interesting in that it is not only cognate with the term hell, but also with holy, heal, hallow, hello, whole, all, halo and holly. The name as Holda is probably related to the various names given to elves, witches, Valkyries and Giant Women—as Hild, Hulda, or Hilda. It is somewhat ironic that Holla, initially the Goddess of the hearth fire of each home, was later associated with the burning fires of Hell. The imagery associated with Hella and Holla is reminiscent of the Goddess Hecate as known in Anatolia (see Anatolian section—Vol. I), though Her name may be linked to the Greek title of Hellotia. Holla too was woven into later Germanic fairy tale, as the witch Frau Holle described by the Grimm brothers.

Riding on the dark and moonless night,
Her hounds barking at Her horse's heels,
Mighty Holla, Queen of the Elves,
Mistress of Witches,
made Her way through the Black Forest,
blessing what was righteous,
laying spells on those who had done wrong,
causing the hellebore to grow
for the essential herb of Her cauldron,
called upon by the mysteries of the alfablot rite,
so that dead souls could rise
on the sacred hallowed day of late autumn,
the highest day of Holla.

Those who spoke of Holla as the mighty Hella
said She was the daughter
of the Giant Woman Angroboda
and that Her body was alive on one side,
blue and corpselike on the other,
for it was Hella who ruled the land of Nifhelheim,
living in the great hall of Eljudnir,
served by Ganglati and Ganglot.
It was in this land of Nifhelheim
where fields of shrouded dead
lay beside the root of Yggdrasil,
ash tree at the center of the world,
while serpent Nidhogge gnawed upon the root.

To enter the domain of Hella,
one rode through northern glens,
each gloomier and darker than the one before
until the waters of the Gjoll
brought an end to the path.
Over the water stretched the bridge of gleaming gold
the bridge that hung upon a single hair,
guarded by the maiden Modgud
of the white and bloodless skin
who took her toll of blood
from all who passed her way.

Nine regions made up Nifhelheim,
surrounded by walls taller than any other,
as the rust red bird crowed as sentinel
before The Gates of Hel.
Therein rested the departed of the earth,
in fields of bliss for the righteous,
in caves of icy streams of venom
for those who had lived lives of evil.
And for the worst, their bones were washed
in the cauldron of Hvergelmir
and fed to ever hungry Nidhogge,
while their flesh and blood dripped from ferocious jaws
of hounds that bayed and howled for more.

Though Norse memories of Hella
were filled with fear and terror,
still the Goddess Holla shook Her feather bed
causing the snowflakes to fall in the northern woods
as Her image could be seen in the halo of the moon,
and Her presence could be felt
in each sacred grove or hollow
where the hidden people danced about
bringing joy to She who sat upon the throne,
to Holla who protected all souls
and all spirits of the forest lands,
perhaps those who had once roamed Finnish Forests
as the mystical Haltija.

the primeval prophetess

The names, images and symbolism associated with Goddess reverence in ancient Greece are so much more familiar to most of us than those associated with the Goddess images from the many other cultures of the world, that this has truly been the most difficult chapter to present.

On the one hand, many of the names and legends are so well known that, in a sense, they need not have been included in these two volumes at all, since my primary intention in this study has been to reclaim what has long been relegated to obscurity. On the other hand, the source materials concerning Goddess images in ancient Greece are so numerous, both in the area of Classical literature and accounts of archaeological evidence, that lengthy volumes, not only on individual Goddess figures but on their specific temples, have been written in recent times, e.g. *The Argive Heraeum* by W. Waldstein and *Eleusis and the Eleusinian Mysteries* by G. Mylonas. Comprehensive studies on ancient Greek religion, such as the works of L.R. Farnell, M. Nilsson, H.J. Rose, A.W. Persson and J.E. Harrison are widely read, while the writings of Bulfinch and Hamilton are even more so.

Yet to research and write two volumes on our worldwide Goddess and heroine heritage, but exclude the wealth of material about the Goddess images of ancient Greece, seemed unthinkable. The solution I arrived at in dealing with this problem, one that I hope readers will regard as reasonable, was to cite the familiar aspects of the most widely known Goddess figures of Greece but to also include lesser known details of shrine sites, rituals, and symbols, that are generally not included in popular studies of Greek religion. Thus drawing directly from the extensive works of Homer, Hesiod, Herodotus, Aeschylus, Euripedes, Pausanius, Plutarch, Strabo, Diodorus Siculus and several other ancient Greek writers, I chose statements that I felt would be of particular interest to the readers of this study. It is true that these classical sources are less easily available and therefore less widely read than the books mentioned above, but for any reader interested in further study of any or all of the Goddess images of Greece, it is these primary sources that must be studied, along with the accounts of the archaeological excavations of Greece, such as the work of H. Schleimann, S. Casson, S. Marinatos, B. Petracos, A. Evans and L. Drees.

Even as I tried to keep this chapter from requiring many more pages than any other in these two volumes, it did eventually emerge as one of the longest sections included in this study. Added to this problem of preferring an egalitarian spacial allottment, I had to deal with my personal feelings about retaining the account of Athena in the form in which I first wrote it. That is, the entire two volumes had originally been written in what some have referred to as 'staggered prose', the form in which many of the shorter accounts still appear. When I made the decision to transpose the longer accounts into the more usual prose form, I hesitated to change the account of Athena. I do hope that the reader will forgive my self indulgence in this decision, or will, upon reading the final paragraph, at least understand my reasons.

In considering Goddess reverence in ancient Greece, it is important to be aware of the numerous influences upon early Greece: Anatolian, Cretan, Cyprian, Canaanite (Phoenician), Egyptian and Thracian. Archaeological excavations have revealed the existence of Neolithic Greek cultures such as the Sesklo and the Dimini, as well as the Cycladic of the Aegean Islands, each of these producing numerous Goddess statues, and each believed to have been influenced, if not originated, by cultures from Anatolia.

The earliest written records from Greece, and minimal they are, are the partially deciphered Linear B tablets of the Mycenaeans of the fifteenth century B.C. It was not until some seven hundred years later that the works of Homer and Hesiod appeared, and with these two writers came the beginnings of the continuously literate Greece that has provided us with the written records of

Greek ideas about the world, including their religious beliefs and customs. The important books of Herodotus did not appear until about 425 B.C., and most of what we refer to as the Greek Classics are from the time of Herodotus onwards, the valuable books of Pausanius written as late as the second century A.D. Thus our knowledge of ancient Greece is a patchwork quilt drawn from the literature of some nine hundred years, while what we know of the periods before the eighth century B.C. relies on archaeological finds and the sources that Hesiod, Homer, and other writers drew upon.

It is clear that as the historically known groups, such as the Achaeans and the Dorians, gained power in specific areas of Greece, religious beliefs and practices that were known to the earlier inhabitants were affected accordingly, e.g. the superimposition of an Apollo temple on the shrine of the Goddess Gaia at Delphi, and the increasing importance of Zeus at Olympia where, archaeologists explain, a temple to Hera long preceded even the smallest altar to Zeus.

By studying the evidence produced by archaeological excavations, alongside the words of the writers of ancient Greece, we can see that over a long period of time, divine attributes were often absorbed under various names, some elaborated upon, some pared down. Family trees were constructed to explain the relationships of one deity to another, for Greece was filled with a multitude of names and images of the divine, many drawn from the cultures that were the Greek's neighbors in trade and war. Thus the Goddess Dione of the dove oracle at Dodona in northern Greece (described in detail by Herodotus, Bk. II) was said to be the mother of Aphrodite who, according to Herodotus in Book I, was brought to the Greek island of Cythera by Phoenicians from the dove oracle at Ascalon. The pomegranate as the symbol of death and rebirth not only occurs in the rituals for Demeter and Kore but also in those of the Goddess Kybele in Anatolia, while it is found in the hand of a statue of Hera at Argos, and in one of Aphrodite at Sikyon. Shrines to different deities often stood side by side in most Greek towns and cities, while the rituals and symbolism at temples, said to be in honour of one particular deity, were often quite different from those for the same deity in a different area, e.g. Demeter the Healer at Patrai, Demeter of the Underworld at Hermione, and Demeter the Law Giver at Drymaia.

Greece was a nation of religious eclecticism, drawing from east and west, north and south. Despite the many efforts to form a centralized theology, Greek writers reveal that this was never truly accomplished. Yet classical Greek culture, occurring well over two thousand years after writing was known and used in Mesopotamia and Egypt, is not only presented to us as the foundation of western culture, but as if it arose out of a cultural vacuum. Reading of the Goddess images of Greece, in the context of these two volumes, we find many of the images beautiful and inspiring, yet we can also see that they are but a part of the treasures in our wealth of ancient mirrors of womanhood.

NIKTA

NIGHT

Nikta (Nichta), literally Night, is known from passages in Hesiod's *Theogyny*. Her association with the Hesperides and the Gorgons, both described as living far to the southwest of Greece, may indicate that the image of Nikta was drawn from ancient beliefs of northern Africa. Perhaps associated with Nut or Nekhebt of Egypt, or Neith of Libya, Nikta does not appear to have had any shrines or temples during the time of Classical Greece, though Her image was an important one in the Orphic Mysteries.

Possessing powers greater than all other deities,
Nikta came forth from primordial chaos,
black as the midnight heavens,
and then gave birth to day,
and then gave birth to all of airy space.

gave birth to . . .

From Nikta came forth the Sister Gorgons,
Sthenno, Euryale and Medusa.
From Nikta came forth the Sister Hesperides,
Aigle, Erytheia and Arethusa,
those who guard the golden apple trees
that grow in an orchard of the westernmost lands,
yet are owned by Mother Gaia,
who gave them as a wedding gift to Hera.
From Nikta came forth the Sister Fates,
Klotho, Lachesis and Atropos
those who allot life's destiny
and punish those who go against life's laws.

Her black wings sheltering Her nest,
Nikta brought forth the Egg in the Wind,
the egg from which Erotic love, Eros,
came into the world at the beginning of time—
so that the race of mortals might begin.

GAIA
Mother Earth

Descriptions of Gaia as Creator appear in Hesiod's *Theogyny*. Though revered throughout the land of Greece, the best known shrine of Gaia lay beneath the later temple at Delphi. The image of Gaia, literally Earth, was closely associated with the sacred serpent variously known as Delphyna, Python, and Typhon. This serpent symbol also appears in accounts of Hera and Athena, both of whom absorbed many of the attributes of Gaia. The presence of Mycenaean artifacts at the shrine of Delphi suggests that the image of Gaia may have been linked to Goddess reverence on Crete.

Primeval Prophetess, most ancient Earth, came before all else and brought the world into being. They lit fires to Her on the mountain tops. They entered the depths of Her oracular caverns set deep into the mountains, to hear Her tell of what was yet to come. Alone, She created the heaven, and naming him Uranus She took him as a lover—thus giving birth to the deities of heaven. Alone, She created the sea, and naming him Pontus She took him as a lover—thus creating the deities of the sea.

Her shrines were known across the lands of ancient Greece, at Tetrapolis and Claros, at Patara and Patrai, at Aegira and Argos, at Erythrae and Kyme, at Athens and Tegea, at Salamis and Phyle, and at Gaios where the most ancient wooden images stood in Her sanctuary. There they celebrated the ancient rites, at these holy places where they called upon Her name, on sacramental ground enlightened by the words of Her priestesses, sacred Sibyls, wise Pythias, devout Mellisae.

But intruders came from the northern lands, claiming Her sacred shrines for their own, daring to diminish Her ancient majesty, yet unable to deny Her primacy—so that when speaking of their own god Zeus, they said that She must have been his grandmother, so long had She been known. Even Achaean adoring Homer, centuries after the intrusion, could not forget Her as he sang, "I shall sing of Gaia, Universal Mother, firmly founded, Oldest of all the Holy Ones".

At the site of Olympia, She was called upon as Gaia Olympia, oldest deity of that divine mountain, site where they later said Zeus reigned, as they changed the mountain's name to the masculine Olympus. Yet long before Zeus was born, Gaia had been known in the deep cleft that faced the southeast, the one where a laurel stood sentry at the entrance, where Her knowing priestesses sat dispensing Her wisdom, reciting Gaia's law on each decision.

Tales of Gaia's serpent child Typhon lingered, each telling of the battles that Typhon faced from the assaults of Zeus. First in the Corycian cave in far off Cilicia, the Anatolian home where Typhon had been born. Then at Mount Casius in the land of Syria, and later yet upon the fiery Aetna on the isle of Sicily. Do these long held memories of Zeus attacking Typhon tell of the many shrines that those who worshipped Zeus had stolen from Grandmother Gaia—and claimed to be their own?

Where shall we know Gaia best? Surely at the foot of Mount Parnassus, the site of ancient Pytho, sacred Delphi, that place of holy oracles of divine word given by prophetic tongues. These were the words that were heard throughout the world, Gaia's mystic cavern held in highest repute by both the poor and the powerful, as holy Pythian priestess spoke of what Gaia had placed inside her mind. Though men of Zeus had taken Olympia, Dorian priests claimed Pytho for Apollo. And though they still spoke of it as Delphi, Womb, Apollo spoke in louder voice—so that the gentle voice of Earth no longer could be heard.

But deep beneath the sanctified land, Gaia left silent proof of Her ancient ownership—Gaia sitting upon Her throne, the divine lioness that spoke of Ashtart and even of Sekhmet of the Nile, and much that told of dwellers from the isle of Crete, perhaps those who once knew Knossos and left its memory in the name of Parnassus. Yet even as the treasures of the Mother of Crete lay at the deepest level of Delphi, Dorian Greeks claimed that Apollo had taken the form of a dolphin and stopped a boat of merchants who had sailed from Cretan Knossos. These were the men, they say, that he appointed to control the Delphian rites, to teach the Pythian priestess to call upon Apollo—and ignore the word of Gaia.

Some say that Delphi's priestesses were as young as the leaves of springtime, innocent of the great knowledge they conveyed. But other memories speak of long white hair and faces creased with lines of wisdom that only many years of life can bring. Each crowned with laurel wreath, sitting upon the ancient tripod, they threw the barley, hemp and laurel, into the fire on which the sacred cauldron burned—though some say the fumes of Delphi were natural vapours pouring from a fissure in the deep rock secretness of the subterranean chamber that was Earth's Holy of Holies.

Those who came with questions, confused in heart and mind, purified themselves in the water of Her flowing Castalian Spring, as it cut deep into the pink earth. There they called upon the names of the divine woman spirits of the Corycian cave, perhaps in honour of those who had once attended Typhon's birth. Deep in cavern shrine, the Pythia quaffed the waters of the bubbling Cassotis that ran into the holy chamber—and once in touch with Earth, the Pythia began to speak of what she heard, answering questions in riddles of allsense, ordaining the law as she told of the future.

Some say that Dionysus, the one Egyptians speak of as Osiris, was buried deep beneath the stone in the heart of Gaia's Delphi cavern—and that this sacred rock was the navel of the centre of the earth, the core of Gaia's being—holy omphales of Pytho, knitted bout with woven fillet. Yet they also said that it was the grave of slaughtered Python, murdered Typhon, Gaia's virgin born serpent child who was once known as Delphyna. But all of these tales are memories of bygone days, as long ago as when women built the first small shrine at Delphi.

Homer sang that young Apollo, finding the site of Pytho to his liking, decided to take it for his own. But upon seeing Gaia's priestess Delphyna blocking his path to the holy chasm, Apollo used his torches and his arrows and dropped Pythoness Delphyna in untimely fiery death—thus declaring the ancient shrine as his own. Yet centuries later, Aeschylus wrote that the holy shrine had not been stolen by Apollo, but was given as a gift, placing these words in the mouth of a player upon Hellenic stage.

> First in my prayer, before all other deities,
> I call upon Gaia, Primeval Prophetess,
> Next Themis on her mother's oracular seat
> sat, so men say. Third by unforced consent,
> another Titan, another daughter of Gaia,
> Phoebe, gave it as a present to Apollo,
> and giving it, gave her name as well.

Euripedes tells yet another version, writing that a serpent, a child born alone of Gaia, guarded the cave of Gaia's oracle. Apollo then struck the serpent dead, and Gaia in Her wrath at the brutish thing that Apollo had done, sent nightmares to the men of Apollo, laying bare the past, the present and the future, so that they would know what penance they would someday pay. And who can help but wonder at the memory that Apollo once tried to rape the maiden Daphne so that the young woman was grateful to be transformed into a laurel, for Pausanius wrote that Daphne was the name of the most ancient Pythian priestess that Gaia chose to prophesy at Her Delphi shrine. Though we know little of the young Creusa, what shall be made of the tale that she was raped in a cave near Delphi—by that same Apollo—who is said to be the fountainhead of Hellenic logic and rational thought? Were these memories of the time when Gaia lost the shrine, the time that Boio spoke of when she said that Delphi had been claimed by sons of the remotest North?

Still more we know from what they tell of Apollo's attempt to heal his guilt, for they say that after he murdered Python he went to Tempe Valley to purify himself by working as a shepherd. Yet each eight years thereafter, at the time of the Septerion, a hut was built upon the halos circle, not far from the Delphian stone of the Sibyl Herophile, the site where that ancient prophetess from Anatolia once spoke the sacred prophecies. Described as the dragon's lair, each eighth year women marched with young lads to this hut, the boys overturning the tables within, setting fire to the tiny shrine. And as the fire blazed in grievous memory of what had happened so long ago, they called upon one lad as young Apollo, and afterwards pretended that he must leave for Tempe to atone for the evil he had done.

Even at the time when Pythian priestesses had learned to call upon Apollo, and the shrine grew from a tiny sanctuary to a temple rich with treasures of silver and gold, the sibyls held vague memories of ancient days. For when a plague struck four centuries before the days of Roman Caesar, the Delphic priestess decreed that the worship of the Mother of All Deities must be brought from Pessinus in Anatolia, that the rites for Mother Kybele must be brought to Athens. Two hundred more years had gone by when the Sibyl then called for the holy black stone of Kybele, insisting that it must be installed in Rome, and that all religious procession and custom for Kybele must take place in the heart of Rome.

Sacked for its treasures by the Celts, claimed by the Roman empire, looted by Christian Constantine who took the treasures to Byzantium, Delphi remained as holy oracle. But Emperor Theodosius closed the holy site as a danger to Christianity, and Arcadius, succeeding to the throne of early Christendom, took an axe to the ancient bricks and stones—until the ancient temple lay in silent ruin.

Diodorus said that the written records of Delphic prophecies and the Delphic laws known as Sibylline were written in the hexameters of familiar Delphic rhythm, and that these Sibylline records were the source of Homer's stories, the font from which his tales came forth. Rumour upon rumour grew about the final resting place of the Oracles Sibylline, nine books in all they said—once kept in stringent secrecy in Rome. Destroyed by Stilicho? Burned at Alexandria? Yet can we help but wonder if they do not still exist, perhaps hidden away in library sacrosanct, available only to those who qualify by intent—and gender—for Roman ordination? For just one century ago, the Cardinal named Mai revealed the presence of ancient Sibylline verses that he had drawn from the dust of Vatican shelves. Thus the voice and wisdom of ancient Gaia may still lie deep within Her own body—the knowledge of Earth kept hidden within earth—kept from the light of day by those who have forgotten the primacy of Mother Gaia.

THEMIS AND DIKE

Both Themis and Dike are defined as Justice. The survival of the name Dike emerges in the modern Greek word for judge, *dikasta*. Though Themis was regarded as the daughter of Gaia, Dike was said to be the daughter of Themis, one of the Horae, the Seasons. The image of Themis bears a strong resemblance to the very ancient Greek Goddess of Wisdom, Metis, while the Scales of Justice so often shown in the hands of Themis suggest a connection to the Egyptian Maat (see Egyptian section). Although references to Themis appear in many of the Greek Classics, Dike was a much lesser known figure, appearing primarily in the work of Aristos and Ovid.

Ancient Themis, She who held the Scales of Justice, righteousness, and moral law, was She not first known as Metis who tried to teach Achaeans the rules of fairness to all? Hesiod said that Metis was wed to their wrathful Zeus, claiming that She was the first bride of his youth. Yet when Zeus could no longer bear the wisdom and good counsel that came from Her womanly wisdom, he swallowed Her whole—explaining that he then received Her sagacious words from inside his bloated belly.

Thus they spoke of Themis, in vague memory of Metis, perhaps hoping that by inverting the pronouncement of Her name, Her womanly justice might be inverted too. Still Themis spoke of what was right, still She held Her scales up high, above prejudice, above bribery, Her word protecting the innocent, punishing the guilty. And though Achaeans once again announced Her wed to Zeus, this time as Themis, and his second bride, they soon forgot the marriage, realizing that Her indomitable strength, Her independent voice, were not the makings of an Achaean wife.

Hopes of entrapping Themis in marriage frustrated and forgotten, Greeks then spoke of Themis as the aunt of Zeus, sister to his mother Rhea, both daughters of the ancient Gaia. But Aeschylus confessed that he thought of Themis and Gaia as 'One with many names'. Themis birthed the Horae, thus creating the daughters of time, those who made the seasons come and go, those who were known as the Seasons, Eunomia, Eirene and Dike. Themis birthed the Moirae, though some said Nikta was their mother, three sister Fates who wove the future of each life, Klotho who spun the threads of life's destiny, Lachesis who allotted each year's portion, and Atropos who clipped the thread when life was done. But though they said these were the Seasons and the Fates, and that they were the daughters of Themis, were they not the many sides of Ancient Mother Justice?

Euripedes remembered that Gaia was Her mother, and that for Themis, Gaia tried to save the ancient shrine at Delphi, so that the daughter might carry on the mother's work. At Olympia too, the name of Themis was revered, long before the men of Zeus claimed that Olympia was theirs. But when the evil deed of usurpation at Olympia was done, the men of Zeus set aside a portion, an altar very small near the mouth of the sacred cavern of prophecy, not far from the tiny altar that was set aside for Mother Gaia —altars for those who could not forget the ancient days when the Mother and the Daughter had taught the ways of right. Their family share was meagre, after having owned it all, still the memory of Themis was endless large for even now we see Her as the brave Olympia, Liberty, Justice, Goddess of the scales of righteous judgement, ancient Themis, more ancient Metis, perhaps most ancient Maat.

Diodorus told us that it was Themis who first taught of the

peace that comes with divine and moral law among a people, and that it was Themis who first revealed that argument and doubt could be settled by Her ancient priestesses, those who could hear and understand the words of Themis, those who served at Her ancient shrines, those who spoke Her words and decrees aloud—so that in this way the written laws were formed, the ordinances we know as Themisteuin.

Though Themis was honoured at Troezen and Tanagra, at Athens and Aegina, at Olympia and Thebes, Pindar claimed that Themis sat upon Mount Olympus, directly next to Zeus, holding a branch of laurel and a cup of invocation in one hand, Her scales of justice in the other. They say that it was Themis who announced when the holy ones of Olympus should join together for discussion, calling each from wherever they might be, thus sharing Her words of wisdom with those who stole Olympus. Yet they listened carefully to each word of advice that She gave, wise enough, at least, to know true Wisdom's voice.

Yet one might doubt the truth of Pindar's claim, for some say that Themis sits at greater heights, missing nothing, as Her starry Scales of Justice light Her Libran home in heaven. And many say that daughter Dike sits by the side of Themis, Virginal Justice once known as Astraia, for though Dike too once lived on earth when the world was in a Golden Age, She fled to the mountains in the time of Silver, and finally escaped to heaven when those of the Bronze Age created sword and spear. Joining Mother Themis in the heavens, Dike still glistens—as the stars of ever virgin Virgo.

DIKE = Virgo

THEMIS = LIBRA

DEMETER AND KORE

The image of Demeter, which is best known from the accounts of the important temple at Eleusis, was also revered in many other temples and shrines throughout Greece. Though it is clear from statues and references that Demeter had a daughter, Kore, who each year descended into the Land of the Dead, the name Persephone as Queen of the Dead may have been a quite separate image in earlier periods. Persephone's Latin name of Proserpina, First Serpent, may indicate that this earlier image was linked to images of the serpent child of the Goddess, perhaps even associated with the Egyptian Ua Zit (see Egyptian section). Several of Demeter's shrines were also built on Mycenaean foundations, further suggesting a possible connection with the beliefs and rituals of Crete. Both Hesiod and Diodorus directly link Demeter with Crete, while Diodorus also mentions that Isis of Egypt was much the same deity as Demeter, provider both of law and agriculture. Upon reading the material for this account, the desire to unravel the meaning of the Mysteries was intense, but the more I read, and learned upon my visit to the site of Eleusis, the greater was my understanding that even if understood—they should not be described in so public a manner.

Abducted from the garden of earth and thrown into a chariot, the Maiden was carried off through the dark crevices of earth's chasm, to the depths of the Land of the Dead, leaving Mother Demeter to sorrow at Her death. Holy Maiden, Sacred Kore, She had only meant to find a perfect flower and instead, this blossom of young womanhood was forced to become the wife of Aidoneus Hades, Queen Persephone of the Land of the Dead, as Mother Demeter searched for Her by torchlight, wandering about the earth in Her grief.

In the month of Boedromion, when the crops of Demeter were harvested all through the land, and the autumn chills and winds began, it was the time of the Sacred Mysteries, the Thesmophoria of Syracuse, the nine days of the Greater Mysteries of Eleusis, the time to remember the abduction of the daughter, the time to remember the sorrow of the mother who searched for nine days, the time to retell all that occurred in that most ancient of times.

Near Eleusis, the initiates bathed together in the sea at Phaleron, cleansing the piglets that absorbed all sins, before they started, upon the Sacred Way from Eleusis to Athens, from Athens to Eleusis. Returning with the sacred images of Demeter and the Maiden, they passed the holy fig tree that was given by the Mother, they paid homage to each shrine along the way, and bathed the images in the sea as they had bathed themselves. Some say that when the sky protected them with its dark cover, they lit their torches and wandered over the sand and the rocks of the beach, as if in search of the missing Maiden—as Demeter had once searched along the shore.

The Mysteries of Demeter were known throughout the land. Some tell of winding passageways that the waters had cut deep

M.T.
DIKTA
eppergence

into the rocks, and women making their way through these damp caves filled with unknown terrors—to recall the darkness that the Maiden must have seen, to recall the fright that the Maiden must have felt. Some speak of the opening at the other end of the darkness, the green and gold of the fields, where wreaths of flowers and myrtle leaves were placed upon each woman as she once again emerged into the wondrous sunshine, to dance and sing on the Rarian Field, the first field in Greece ever to be ploughed and sown, near the Well of Kallichoros where women first danced for Mother Demeter to bring the harvest.

So the memory was kept alive, the memory of the time that Death took the young Maiden to a land beneath the earth, and the Mother grieved and searched for nine days long. But when Demeter heard from Hecate and Helios that the Maiden had been abducted by Aidoneus Hades, only to serve as his wife and queen, to become the feared Persephone, Demeter's rage became manifest. Holding back the rain, parching the summer's crops, Demeter caused the land to lay in unproductive drought. So frightened were the deities of Olympus that Aidoneus Hades was finally prevailed upon to let the Maiden go, to return Her to Her Mother, so that the threshing floor might once again be covered. Thus the Maiden returned to be reunited with Her Mother, and those who loved Demeter joined Her in joyous song and dance to celebrate the coming home. Yet even this joy was dampened by the knowledge that the Maiden had partaken of the pomegranate seeds, some say four, some say six, and for the seeds that were eaten, the Maiden was to return each year to the Land of the Dead—one month for each seed.

So it came to be that the women carried sacred molloi cakes, the honey and sesame that was shaped and baked in the image of that sacred part of the body from which each and every human life emerges, that which is possessed only by women. Carrying the sacred molloi that symbolized the arrival upon earth, each year it was remembered that the Maiden must part from Her Mother, yet each year She would return—in the midst of laughing, dancing, singing, celebration.

Yet deep in the Eleusis shrine of the Telesterion, from which only the sounds of laughter could be heard, were enacted the Greatest Mysteries, that none have revealed until this day. The Mysteries. The Mysteries. Shall we ever know? Did they tell of Demeter as Thesmophorus, the Giver of the Law, and explain that it was She who first established the law of the land? Did they speak of the gift that She gave, the knowledge of the seeds and the growing of the wheat, so that the fruits of Demeter's harvest might feed the people of the world? Some hint at cups of barley water, mushrooms, and poppies, and accounts of Triptolemus. Some speak of resurrection, new incarnations, and the rising of the Phoenix from its ashes. Did they enact the abduction of the Maiden, or tell of how She sat upon the throne as Queen of the Dead, as mighty Persephone?

Some say that the Mystery was that the story had been turned around and that it was Adonis who had been kept by Queen Persephone for four months of each year. For even as Aphrodite begged for the return of Her son/lover, Persephone claimed that he belonged to Her, and thus was his time divided throughout each and every year.

The Mysteries. The Mysteries. Who was it that ever said that women cannot keep a secret? Yet Diodorus claimed that in times more ancient still, for those at Cretan Knossos the sacred rites were open to the eyes and ears of all who wished to know. And was it not Cicero who said that the Mysteries of Eleusis mellowed people's hearts, transformed barbarian natures into beings truly human. And even before Cicero it was said that the Mysteries for Demeter softened the dread of death. For although each year the Maiden descended to the Land of the Dead, in payment for the pomegranate seeds, always She returned, to be greeted by Her Mother Demeter, She who moved heaven and earth until She succeeded in bringing Her daughter back into the sunshine of alive.

At Patrai, they came as pilgrims to be healed by Demeter of the Mirror on the Lake. And at the Mysaion near Pellene, Demeter was honoured in the sacred grove of abundance, among the fruit laden trees and clear spring waters. Though the days of the Pellene festival were numbered as seven, on the third day all male beings were excluded from the sanctuary, as women performed the rites for Demeter throughout the night, just as they did at the shrine of Demeter in Pyraia, just as Roman women did for the Goddess Bona Dea, those whom Plutarch said 'played amongst themselves' throughout the night. Near the Corinthian grave of the Sea Women who died in battle against Perseus and his men, stood the shrine of Demeter of the Pelasgians, the first of the peoples to inhabit Greece. It was there that they dropped burning torches into the pit, hoping to light the way for the Maiden beneath the earth. At Lerna on the sea near Argos, Lernians claimed that theirs was the site at which Persephone had been taken to the Land of the Dead, yet others said that the Maiden was abducted near the River Erineos that runs by Eleusis. Megarians pointed out the Calling Rock where Demeter had called out to the Maiden, and each year the women of Megara called to the Maiden, as Demeter had done. And though they speak of the Mother as Demeter Europa at Lebadeia, and Demeter Chthonia at Hermione, and Demeter Thesmophoria at Drymaia where they said the Mother first gave the law, at the town of Potniai they simply called the Mother and the Daughter—Potniai, The Goddesses—knowing that there was never one without the other.

Was the secret known to early Christian emperors who so despised the Mysteries that Byzantine Theodosius banned them from the land, forbade the baking and the carrying of the sacred molloi cakes, silenced the singing, halted the dancing, doused the torches of the searchers—and brought about the end of the reverence for the Mother and the Daughter? What was it, Theodosius, that made you close the temple at Eleusis until the day that its lands were taken as a Christian graveyard—and the knowledge of the rebirth of the Daughter was all but forgotten?

HERA

By the time of Hesiod and Homer, the Goddess as Hera was linked to Achaean Zeus. Yet references to Metis and Themis, as earlier wives of Zeus, perhaps reveal the continual transitions in Hellenic beliefs as Achaeans gained a firmer foothold over the indigenous peoples of Greece. As with Gaia and Demeter, the symbols of Hera are linked to Crete, but also to the western coast of Anatolia and the Ionian island of Samos, where many Cretans had settled.

Shrines of the Holy Mother Hera once bejewelled the lands of the blue Aegean Sea, for though She was born on Samos near the coast of Anatolia, Mycenaeans made a home for Her at Argos, at

Tiryns, and Mycenae, yet long was She remembered on the isle of Samos, and known as the great one on the isle of Lemnos where She birthed Her son Hephaistos. Yet they say that She had been known as Mother upon the land of Crete and that at the Cretan temple of Phaistos, Her son was called upon as Velchanos, he who lived to die each year.

Some say that She was one with Gaia, though Gaia's daughter Rhea was said to be Her mother, yet She was heir to Gaia's sacred tree of golden apples that was guarded by the serpent Ladon, serpent child of Typhon who was born from ancient Gaia —though others whispered that Hera was its mother. Holy Hera, Cow Eyed Hera, was She not once known as Io, for though Achaeans said that Io was Her priestess, serving at Her great Argolian shrine, Io was the Holy Heifer of the heavens who reigned o'er all of Egypt. Thus came the tale that it was Hera's fault that Io was turned into a heifer, yet Io's wanderings reveal Her sanctity as the lands of Ionia took Her name, Ionia where the isle of Samos rose from the waters. Still they say that Io reached the land of Egypt where She took the name of Mother Isis, even as they spoke of Hera as bovine, naming the sacred hill that lay close by Her Argos temple as Euboia, rich in cows.

Thus were the holy heifers moulded from the clay, and left as evidence of votive reverence deep beneath the earth of Argos, of Tiryns, of Mycenae, homes where Mycenaeans had first settled. And at Mycenae lay the bovine head of hammered silver and golden horns, the rosette of the Holy Mother shining upon its forehead, just as the bovine head of darkest marble, crowned by golden horns was once held sacred at Cretan Knossos. Though some would see these heads as bulls, those who first found them in the ancient ruins wrote of them as images of the Holy Heifer of Egypt, horned as Nut, as Hathor, as Isis long had been—horned as the cows that still roam upon Aegean lands.

Yet more than Mother's milk was Hera, for carefully hammered plates of gold formed the double axe between Her sacred horns, and upon the Samian isle armed women ran in contest for the sacred shield of Hera. At Greek Sicyon, Hera wore the helmet and the spear. Was it for these reasons that they said that warlike Ares was Her son, and that warlike Eris was Her daughter, declaring a twinship between the two? How can we forget that it was Eris who possessed the golden apple, that which must have come from Hera's tree, the apple that rolled the Greeks into the Trojan

War? And what is to be made of the tales of Ares' temple in Papremis, that shrine of Ares on Egyptian Delta lands, for Egyptian priests of Ares each year enacted Ares' first attack upon the temple, citing memories of times long ago. And was it not these priests who said that the temple had first belonged to Ares' mother, and when he, unfamiliar to those who served at Her temple altars, had been refused entrance to Her door, forced his way into the holy place with violent assault—so that it now was known as his?

Various are the stories of Hera's early childhood, for some say that She was raised by Titan Tethys in times ancient even then, when Olympian deities fought the Titans for supremacy, yet others claim that She was nursed by the three women, Euboia, Prosymma and Akraia, at the site where the great Argive temple then was raised. It was Callithoe, so they say, who first served as priestess at this fabled Heraion of Argolis, and they add that at that time all Argive time was reckoned by the names of Hera's priestesses, as each in turn spent their years as guardian of the temple rites. Leading festival processions, holding sacred branches as they walked, these priestesses of Hera paid honour to the ancient Mother, as Founder of Civilization, Goddess of Battle, She who taught Her people to sow and reap the crops. And to the image of Hera that dwelled within the sacred Argive walls, Argive women purified in the nearby Eleutherion stream, those who had wreathed their heads with Hera's wild marjoram rigani — brought the sacred plant as offering of deepest reverence and honour. It was then that they saw the image of the Mother, a sceptre in one hand, a pomegranate in the other, so that they understood that Hera ruled in death—as She did in life. For was She not both Mother and Virginal Maiden, bathing in the clear waters of the Spring of Kanathos each year, forever renewing Her youth, infinite in Her cycles?

Those who thoughtlessly repeat that Heracles, emblem of the Dorian invasions, was the Glory of Hera, surely do not know of what they speak, for Heracles was he who quelled Hera, and the tales of the labours and life of Heracles make this all too clear. Was it not Hera's golden apples that Heracles stole after striking Hera's serpent Ladon dead, just as Zeus had murdered Typhon, just as Apollo murdered Python? And did Heracles not destroy the children of Typhon too, the serpent that some said had been born to Hera? And were these evil deeds not done at Lerna where

Typhon's Hydra was laid to rest, and at Nemea where Typhon's lion was laid to rest, towns that lay so nearby Hera's home at Argos. And was it not Hera who warned the Amazon women at Themiscyra, when Heracles came to take their Queen Hippolyta? And did Heracles not steal the cattle from Hera's sacred isle of Erytheia, and when Hera tried to fend him off, did he not shoot an arrow deep into Her breast? There are those who say this deed was done after Heracles told Molorchus to pray to him—in Hera's stead. Was it not for all these reasons that foresighted Hera had tried to prevent Heracles from ever being born, and when he had been birthed against Her will, that She sent two serpents to strike him dead? Yet even then Zeus had slyly tricked Her by bringing the infant Heracles to Her breast, placing him there while She lay deep in sleep, so that unwittingly Her milk had gifted Heracles with some of Her immortal essence. Thus they spoke of Her outrage when She awoke and found the infant Heracles at Her breast, and how She had thrown him aside so angrily, so fiercely, that Her milk spurted across the heavens—and became the Milky Way. It was said in ancient times that Heracles first took his name when he was told that from Hera he would have undying fame, and would no more be known as Alkaeus, but remembered ever after as Heracles, Hercules. But fame is gained in many ways, and as the Queller of the faith of ancient Hera, so did the prophecy for Dorian Alkaeus come true.

There are many ways to make a Goddess seem less than She might be. For even before the time of Alkaeus, Achaeans spoke of Hera as the wife of Zeus. Yet there were few who did not understand what marriage meant to an Achaean who set out to conquer many lands that had long known the worship of the Mother. To those who questioned the appearance of a father god, rather than a delicate young consort, Achaeans promised the fidelity of their father god of thunderbolts to the long beloved Mother, in each place that She dwelled. Thus was Zeus pledged in marriage, or assigned seducing role, to many woman names of power, and in this way the conquering Achaeans gathered up the names of Alkmene, Aegina and Anaxithea, of Callisto, Calyce and Hesione, of Danae, Demeter and Dione, of Metis, Maia and Mera, of Leda, Lato and Semele, of Eurynome, Eurymedusa and Europa, of Themis, Taygete and Persephone, of Io—and even his own mother Rhea. For these are but some of the women with whom Achaeans said that Zeus had had his way, as they thought it doubly useful to paint an image of ancient Hera as fraught with petty jealousy. For had Her name not been chosen as the most important wife of Zeus, only to ring in hollow echo of diminished ancient memory of She who had been sovereign, almighty Mother in Aegean lands?

Was it chance that appointed Hera as the best known wife of Zeus, or was it that when Achaeans claimed Olympia as the home of Zeus, they came upon the sacred temple of Hera, ancient before Zeus had even a tiny altar in the town? Thus was Hera wed to Zeus, though some say that he spent three hundred years courting Her upon the isle of Samos, where She had long been known as Parthenos. Yet they spoke of a child being born to Hera beneath the willow on the bank of the Imbraxos River that runs through the island of Samos, and some say that She was one with the Holy Mother of the nearby Ephesian temple. Still Achaeans said that She came to live upon Olympus, Her throne then set beside the one of Zeus.

Even then, those who remembered earlier days when Hera had been Queen alone, told of the time that She grew so great with rage that She bound Zeus to his couch with thongs of leather, threatening to push him from Olympian throne. But Acheaen weaponry aborted the rebellion and once Zeus had been untied, he threw Hera's loyal son Hephaistos, perhaps Her consort of more ancient days, down from the heights of Olympus for aiding and abetting Her. Thus was Hephaistos lamed, as the faith of Hera had been lamed. Still Zeus' vengeance was not yet satiated, for he then tied Hera's wrists to heaven, and hung the heavy anvils of metalsmith Hephaistos as weights about Her ankles, so that thoughts of further revolution were crushed beneath the weight of torture—as Achaeans then said that Hera was the Goddess of Marriage—for was She not the wife of the mighty Zeus?

APHRODITE

According to Herodotus, the worship of Aphrodite was introduced to Greece by the Phoenicians of Canaan. In turn, when the Greeks colonized areas of Canaan, they referred to the shrines of Ashtart as those of

Aphrodite Urania, literally, Aphrodite, Queen of Heaven (see Semitic section—Vol. 1). Initially revered as a more multifaceted deity concerned with oracular prophesy and with battle, the Hellenic Greeks came to regard Aphrodite primarily as the essence of erotic love. This attitude may have developed in response to the sexual rituals, so closely associated with the Goddess as Ashtart and Ishtar in Canaan and Babylon, continuing in the Greek temples of Aphrodite, especially at Corinth. The Romans knew Aphrodite as Venus, the star that had been sacred to Aphrodite, Ashtart, Ishtar and Inanna.

White bird of the heavens, dove wings gliding over the sea, Aphrodite Ourania, Queen of Heaven, came from ancient Phoenician Ascalon in the land of Canaan to the nearby isle of Cyprus. Landing at Kition, landing at Amathus, landing at Paphos, those who saw Her shake the water from Her wings upon the rocks of Petra Tou Romiou thought that She had been born of the sea, the whiteness of Her feathers blending with the whiteness of the aphros foam.

They say Phoenicians carried Her to the Cyprian isle, even to the Holy Island of Cythera that Homer spoke of as divine. Still some say that Her home is on the Holy Hill of Corinth in the land of Greece. Once called upon as Ashtart, Queen of Heaven known throughout Canaan, Her April festivals continued along the coast of Cyprus. Her sacred essence was in the milkwhite marble stone, Galatea stone that Pygmalion adored, stone anointed with the oil of olives by pilgrims who travelled from far across the sea, to receive a phallus and a lump of salt on the first day of the month of Nisan. In this way they paid their respect at the holy shrine of Paphos where Aphrodite Ourania, Queen of Heaven, had chosen to make Her new home.

With Her came the memories of Adonis, he who had been Her son/lover Tammuz in Canaan, the sweet young shepherd of the myrtle tree whose gentleness and beauty were lost in untimely death, his blood escaping from the wild boar wound, colouring the poppies of the Cyprian Troodos Mountains, so that women in their sorrow at Aphrodite's loss, wove poppies and myrtle leaves in wreathes about their heads. Lamenting with Aphrodite, the women carried the pomegranates of Persephone, Queen of the Land of the Dead, and planted basket gardens of seeds that would die as Adonis died, before full maturity could come. Such were the sacred rituals for Aphrodite, enacted only by the women, for

Lucian complained that these were the mysteries from which all men were excluded. And in his anger, Lucian claimed that they were lascivious orgy, mere corruption of the mind.

Holy women, sacred women, served Aphrodite in Her temples, taking lovers from among those who came to pay respect and honour to Aphrodite Who Gives Life, to Aphrodite who blessed Her devotees with eternal youthful vigour, to Aphrodite who took Her bodily pleasures from both deities and mortals. Many were the men She had possessed—gentle Adonis, rocklike Hermes, warlike Ares, royal Anchises, watery Poseidon, delicate Dionysus, metalsmith Haephaistos, and oar pulling Butes. Thus the women who served at Her temples, both princesses and peasants, followed the ways of Aphrodite, burning myrrh and frankincense in sacred invocation, while bedding any they desired within Her holy shrines. Those who worshipped Aphrodite kept the love of women in their hearts, as poet Sappho of the isle of Lesbos, who called out to Cypria, Queen of Paphos, Golden Crowned Aphrodite, wrote of the blessing of 'sleeping on a tender girlfriend's breast' and of 'girls who lay upon soft mats with all that they most wished for beside them'. To those who entered the holy places of Aphrodite, love was love. Thus at Her Oschophorian rites, young boys dressed as girls. And at the Argive feasts for Aphrodite, men put on the robes of women, while women donned the clothes of men.

Yet some remembered Aphrodite as the Mother, First Mother of the Race, She from whose body the first Thebans had sprung. Essence of Love, essence of Motherhood, Oldest of the Fates inscribed upon Her shrine at Athens, Aphrodite was known as Goddess of the Spear at Paphos, She Who Battles in Mylasa, and as Armed Aphrodite on Cythera and at Akrocorinth. Thus when Her broken image was raised from the sea at Milos, perhaps it spoke not of perfect female body, but of arms that had been wrenched away.

At Sikyon, even then the ancient site of Mekone, Aphrodite held the sacred mekon poppy in one hand, the pomegranate in the other. It was here they say that Demeter first discovered the poppy. And at Hermione, where the shrine of Demeter Chthonia stood, a shrine for Aphrodite was the site where all virgins came to sacrifice to the Queen of Paphos, before accepting the love of a man.

Though some would say that Aphrodite thought only of physical pleasures, Aeschylus heard Aphrodite say:

> I am the Goddess Cypria, mighty among people.
> They honour me by many names.
> From the tides of Pontus to the Pillars of Atlas
> These lands are mine to rule.
> To those who acknowledge my power,
> I give honours and rewards.
> But those who dare to defy me,
> I shall swing them by their heels.
> For how can I be joyous in my heart,
> If I am not honoured by my people?

Though many centuries have passed, and churches have been built upon the ancient sites, echoes of Panagia Aphroditessa linger in the Shrines of Maria, as the ancient corner stone of Paphian church is anointed with the oil of olives, and a candle lit before the ancient stone—in honour of Holy Aphroditessa—as the Maid of Bethlehem.

HESTIA

Primarily associated with the fire of the hearth, and the eternal city flame that was carried by torch to colonies to indicate their acquisition, the image of Hestia appears to have arrived in Greece at an extremely early period. Though Her name was known on Mycenaean Crete, Her presence among the Scythians may reveal a northeastern origin. Hestia was described as sister to Demeter and Hera in Hesiod's Theogyny, but She had few shrines in Greece. Yet Romans, who spoke of Her as Vesta, regarded Her as an extremely important deity. In Plutarch's account of the early Roman leader Numa Pompilius, the temple of Vesta and the roles of the vestal priestesses are described in some detail. The reverence for Vesta may have survived in Celtic Britain and Ireland in the worship of the Goddess as Bridget.

Banding together by the light of lava
bursting from volcanic heights,
Scyths once gave Her name as Tabiti Vesta,
though Greeks came to know Her as Hestia,
whose name was used to seal each oath,
as spiritual communion rose from Her flame,
kept bright by the women of the mountains.

Some left the land where fires burned brightly
upon Caucasian mountains,
and roamed along the Black Sea's northern coast,
passing through Thrace and Thessaly,
entering the lands of Greece,
carrying Her eternal flame,
everburning heart of tribal light,
blazing core of council meetings
which one may borrow to start the hearth,
or carry to ever distant lands,
planting as a memory of home
that which can be taken
and at the same time left behind—
Mother Flame whose children grow
and yet She never dies,
while sacrifice and incantation
pay honour to Her name.

Hestia of the Hearth,
given a family seat upon Olympus,
was spoken of as one most ancient,
yet almost forgotten by Hellenes
who preferred to think of mountain fires
as the property of Zeus.
Yet Hestia's flame burned brighter
in the air of ancient Rome
where gracious marble temple
circled about Her constant light,
and Vestal priestesses of pure and perfect being,
those who were called upon to judge,
for their voices could speak nothing but the truth,
lovingly tended Her ancient light,
now glowing upon the Palatine Hill of Rome,
and offered cakes of Mola meal

to the many women who came to pray
and to celebrate the June Vestalia,
at this most sacred of temples,
where Hestia was called upon as Vesta.

ARTEMIS

Though the names of Themis and Artemis bear a puzzling similarity, the
descriptions of these two images of Goddess are quite different in both
imagery and symbol. As if to further confuse a comprehension of the
nature of Artemis, we find Artemis of Anatolian Ephesus as a sedate
Mother Goddess, though clearly associated with Amazons, while Artemis
in Greece was regarded as the fleet young huntress and protector of the
animals of the woods. The worship of Artemis is often linked with Crete
(as Dyktynna and Brito Martis), and may be compared to images of Libyan Neith, but the Artemis symbols of bear and stag, and Her association
with Bendis of Thrace, may reveal a northern European origin. Her role,
both as hunter and as protector of the animals, may well be compared to
Mielikki and Skadi (see Scandinavian section). Romans regarded Her as
the one they called upon as Diana, this name perhaps linked to the Greek
Dione of the Dodona Oracle, and to the Greek word *diania*, meaning intelligence.

Numerous were the stories of the women of the mountains of
western Anatolia, and Amazon troops coming to the aid of Troy
near the waters of the Sangarius, and how these women had once
come from far off Libya to found the Anatolian towns of Priene
and Prusa, Smyrna and Sardis, Pergamon and Kyme, Myrina and
Mitylene, Astyra and famed Xanthos, and the most honoured site
of Ephesus where the Mother of the Amazons was called upon as
Proto Thronia, First Upon the Throne—and as the mighty Artemis. So sacred was the Mother known at Ephesus that it caused-
Pausanius to say, "All cities worship Artemis of Ephesus, and in-
dividuals hold Her in honour above all other deities. This is due to
the renown of the Amazons, those who first consecrated the land
of Ephesus, those who dedicated the first image of the Goddess,
long before Ionian Greeks arrived."

Though Amazon murals adorned the Anatolian temple sites of Artemis at sacred Magnesia upon the waters of the Meander, and at long remembered Halikarnassos where priestess Artemisia called upon Her name and built great walls of stone that were carved in honour of the valour of the Amazons, Artemis also travelled far from Anatolia. They spoke of Her as fleet Dyktynna of the Cretan isle, and Crete's sweet maiden Goddess Britomartis. Yet did not Strabo speak of Her as Artemis Bendis who carried spear and torch, as She rode Her swift steed throughout the lands of Thrace. Others told the story of the maiden Iphigenia, at Chersonese on Lake Maeotis, at the northern edges of the great Black Sea, and how Iphigenia brought the ancient sacred statue of Artemis to the town of Brauron in the heart of Greece. Yet Hesiod claims that Iphigenia was transformed into the threefold Hekate, the mighty Artemis as known among the Taurians.

Perhaps confused by Her allness, as She who was at one with the animals, the bear, the stag, the wolf, the lioness, while at the same time The Mighty Huntress, the Birth Easing Nurse, Protector of Girls, Fleet Maiden Daughter of the Woods, giving life, taking life—Hellenic Greeks, masters of dualities, perceiving in opposites, divided Artemis in two. Thus naming the rocky isle of Delos as the birthsite of holy Artemis, they declared Her Artemis name of Lato to be Her own mother, while Her Artemis name of Eilythia was said to be the midwife—at the birth of the Artemis who had existed always. For on the ancient isle of Delos were the offerings of silver labia and silver vulva—that had so long before been dedicated to Mother Ashtart by Phoenicians.

Though Greeks spoke of Artemis as the Daughter of Lato, who some describe as Dark Robed Night, the daughter was known as Artemis Eilythia still, as many remembered that the Mother and the Daughter were but one and the same, and that giving life and living life are inextricably entwined, and that the multitude of epithets of the Goddess were merely the many names and titles of the Holy One. Thus they spoke of Artemis as Pheraia, Aphaia Aegina, Kurotrophos, Opis, Agrotera, Brito Martis, Dyktynna, Bendis, Aritimi, Limnaious, Lady of the Lake and Lioness. Even as She was being born on Delian Mount Cynthus, they pointed to the moon and said Her name was Cynthia. Pausanius gave Her name as Artemis Astratia, explaining that each month holy rites were held for Her at the time of the new moon, even as such rites were held for Her at Anatolian Halikarnassos.

But at Greek Pyrrichos, the temple of Artemis was built to honour Amazons who had fallen there, while inscriptions in the temple spoke of Artemis Ashtart.

Was there a province in all of Hellenic Greece that did not see by the light of the flames of the great bonfires built in Her honour, and by the light of torch processions that celebrated Artemis all through the land. Young girls dressed as bears at Brauron, at the temple of the Taurian Artemis image that had been brought from the Black Sea, while at Patrai the priestess of Artemis rode in a wagon drawn by deer, to celebrate Her festival in wide and glorious procession.

In Sparta, at the festival of Tithenedia, the goat was sacrificed to keep young women 'safe from marriage', as the young lads held tight to an image of Artemis, the willow branch upon bare skin reminder of the rage that Artemis might feel towards any who defied Her laws.

Memories of Kallisto lingered, though some said that this was but another name of Artemis. Yet long was the story told that Zeus had taken the form of Artemis, and in this form had tricked the nymph Kallisto into love. It was for this reason that Kallisto was turned into a bear and placed in the northernmost heavens, perhaps remembered by the girls who dressed as bears at the festival of Artemis in Brauron. Yet the island that held the great temple of Artemis, so close to the volcanic mountain, the island Greeks later spoke of as the lovely Thera—was once known as the Isla of Kallista.

Many were the legends of Artemisian nymphs, the women who ran with Artemis in the woods and forest, spoken of as nymphs for they were as fleet and nimble as the deer that were sacred to the swift Artemis. Yet when their strong legs and the perfect aim of their arrows could not match the ones from whom they might have need to flee, they called upon Artemis for protection, even as the Pleiades of heaven felt safety by the side of Artemis.

Daphne, running from Apollo, in fear of being captured and abused, cried out to Artemis for help and found herself transformed into a laurel, able to whisper her gratitude to Artemis only in the rustling of her leaves. Arethusa, a woman of the woods, fled from Alpheus, who thought to violate Arethusa in the forest, and merciful Artemis changed her into the clearest of spring waters so that she might flow along in safety, yet still roam through her beloved woods. Atalanta, swiftest runner of all Boetia, nursed in infancy by a bear, kept her vows of independence by the fleetness of her legs, thus spurning all who mentioned marriage by challenging suitors with races that she always won. But when tempted by the gold of an apple, laid as lure upon her racing path, she entered into tragic marriage, sorrow and misfortune. Yet even after her mistake, Atalanta was rescued by watchful Artemis who transformed her into a mighty lioness so that she might still run side by side with Artemis.

Some say that the hunter Orion dared to violate a woman of Artemis and that for this he was severely punished by the perfectly aimed arrows of the Mighty Huntress. Hunter Aktaon paid the penalty for arrogantly spying upon the unclothed Artemis as She bathed in the stream of a cloistered morning forest. So enraged was Artemis at this impudence that the Goddess made of him a stag, so that the very dogs with whom he hunted, tore him limb from limb.

Artemis Parthenos they called Her, parthenos so long defined as virgin, only revealing the strange nature of patriarchal mind. For parthenius was the child of a parthenos, and parthenos was simply one apart, one free to follow the wind, one free to follow the beds of streams and rivers, one free to enjoy the company of the women of the woods. So was the world a better place when both men and women knew that the spirit of Artemis was close by, forever ready to help, forever ready to punish any that broke the laws of parthenos. For still She came to the side of the mother and eased the pains of childbirth, as She came to the side of the lioness that was bringing forth her cubs. And as provider of the juniper and hellebore that could be used for healing, Artemis taught of the medicines of the woods.

Romans called upon Her as Diana, Huntress Moon who sent Her perfect arrow beams down from the night time skies, She who rode in great procession upon the isle of Sicily, Her chariot drawn by lions. For as they say the lion is the sun, so must the lioness, mightiest hunter of the jungle, be the moon. Far did She travel, on earth as in heaven, for Trojan Brutus told the story of how his ship landed upon a silent island in Mediterranean waters and there, kneeling before an altar of Diana, She told the Trojans of the island in the waters far to the west. In gratitude for these words of Diana, when these Trojans landed upon the isle of Albion that later took the name of Britain, altars were built for the

so must the lioness be the moon

ancient Diana whose women may still be seen dancing upon the
heath, with only the stars lighting their celebration of the monthly
return of each new moon—the eternal return of Artemis Diana.

ATHENA

How much clearer
the riddle of your Athena being grows,
when first I think of Metis,
'wiser than any deity or mortal',
Metis, full with child,
prophesied as danger to Achaean Zeus,
who in his cowardly fear
swallowed the wisest one—whole,
and later on the shores of Tritonis,
from his then pregnant head,
split apart by the axe of Hephaistos,
brought you forth full grown,
Goddess image made in male fantasy mold,
gestating in his arrogant warrior mind,
umbilically attached
to placental thunderbolts of wrath—
yet not untouched by the genes
of She who filled his cowardly belly.

No Olympian I,
for what faith could I follow
that tried to deceive me
into thinking that life comes forth from man,
when no male being ever known
has carried a child to birth
and from his body pressed life forth.
I might be fool enough to think the earth was flat,
or that the sun moved round it,
but what child does not notice
the swelling of the belly of the woman
that precedes the emergence of new life?

Yet, dear Athene, how to find the threads
of your true Goddess being,
searching for loose strands
that were later woven
into Achaean invader design?
I search on Crete, in Libyan Africa,
at Troy and Canaanite Ugarit.
I dig about in the oldest stones and bones of Athens,
but if I miss a thread or two
of your true essence,
or mistake a recent one for old,
I beg your forgiveness, Ancient Weaver,
for I am but a novice
at the craft you taught,
a mere mortal attempting to disentangle
the threads of your usurped divinity.

IN LIBYA

I look for threads
at your Libyan festival among the Auses people,
inhabitants of the lake known as Tritonis,
so long ago by Herodotus described,
two teams of women young and strong
in ritual combat with sticks and stones,
enacted among a people
who did not believe in marriage,
and lived with whom they pleased,
worshipping the brave Athena,
though once they called upon you
as Mother Archer Neit,
your sacred aegis
but the common dress of Libyan women,
fringed goatskin thonged with leather,
as yours is fringed with snakes.
And was it not the Machlyes,
the Auses' closest neighbors,
who remembered the time of Jason's visit,
and the tripod that he coveted,
the one that would give Libyan lands to Greece?
Was it during that same time
that Perseus murdered Queen Medusa,
Ruler of the Gorgons of Tritonis Lake,

194

a murder possible only with your help,
Perseus beheading Medusa by looking into the mirror
the mirror that you gave him,
Her image in the mirror now seen upon your breast—
so that looking at you, do I see the dim reflection
of the slaughtered Libyan Queen?
O Wise One, O Brave One,
are you Medusa, Metis, or Athene?

In Crete

I look for threads
upon the silent isle of Crete,
whose voice is hidden in undeciphered text,
for they say it is your birthplace,
and that the serpents
twisted bout the arms of priestesses
travelled with you
when Mycenaeans brought your holiness
to the land of the Hellenes.
Cretan Goddess of the double axe,
Lady of the Labyris,
known in dark oracular caves,

Athena
Labrys

were you once called upon as Hella
and remembered thus in torch races
of Mycenaean founded Corinth,
known there as Athena Hellotia,
with memories of a maiden Hellotia
who hid within your temple,
seeking sanctuary from invaders
and there was burned alive—
for who can forget that beneath the foundation
of your splendid Athenian shrine,
crown of the Acropolis,
lie the fragments of Mycenaean structure,
walls and sacred images
that we know so well from Crete.

I look for threads in Troy,
fabled city of coastal Anatolia,
for it was there, from your Trojan temple,
that your famed Palladium was stolen,
your sacred image of olive wood

In Troy

195

that bore the name of one you slew in Libya,
by the shores of Lake Tritonis
where Queen Medusa died,
but this memory was spoken of as accidental slaying
of sister playmate Pallas,
she who died when but a maiden,
she whose name you took
in agonizing memory of sister lost,
or does your title Pallas, Pallados,
speak of your pallium, your mantle,
goat skin aegis of protection?
Yet I wonder if I should match
the colours of the threads
of your Palladium in Troy
with those I found in Libya,
threads that speak of accidental death,
among the women who fought in teams among the Auses,
as revelation that she had lain with a man
and was thereby weakened for the combat.
Is it for this reason
that you take the name of Parthenos,
knowing that your strength
would fade to weakness
should you take a male to your Athenian bed?
Still more tangled threads
lie about your Trojan temple,
terrorized Cassandra, fleeing to your altar,
clinging to your sacred image
to escape Achaean Ajax,
yet raped within your sanctuary,
violated before your very eyes,
Cassandra driven over the edge of sanity's cliff.
But when Achaean Odysseus,
comrade of Ajax in Trojan battle,
stole your image from the desecrated shrine—
you saw fit to see him safely home.

I look for threads upon the isle of Cyprus,
for there at Larnaca Tou Lapithou
inscriptions bear your name,
honouring you as Anat Athena,
while Sanchonthion of ancient Berytus,

196

city now spoken of as Beirut,
speaks of you and Anat as one and the same.
Truly Anat wore the helmet and the shield,
Her strength in battle well known in Ugarit,
northern coastline city of Canaan,
home of Mycenaeans who had once lived on Crete.
But Anat was also known among the Hyksos
who called upon Her name in Egypt,
drawing Her image with helmet and with shield,
with battle axe in hand,
speaking of Anat as Mistress of the Heavens,
Domina of Deities.
But there are some that say
the Hyksos, once expelled from Egypt,
fled to the isle of Crete.
Would they not have known you there
as Cretan Goddess of the Double Axe,
Lady of the Labyris,
Warrior Goddess Anat,
Holy Neit, so long known as Mistress of the Arrow,
Lady of Sais upon the Delta—
ancient owner of your temple at Sais?

Following these threads of unpatterned,
yet intricate design,
again they lead me back to Lake Tritonis,
Libyan homeland of ancient Neit,
site, they say, where Zeus pulled you from his head.
For Diodorus tells of Amazons,
mighty bands of women,
who came from Hespera,
island in the fabled Lake Tritonis,
women led by gallant Myrina and Mitylene,
courageous generals, sisters, queens,
who brought the worship of their Goddess,
The Mother of All Deities,
to mountainous Anatolia,
settling the nearby island of Lemnos,
naming its capital for Myrina,
settling the nearby island of Lesbos,
naming its capital for Mitylene.

You wear the battle of the Amazons
upon your shield in Athens,
in memory of the women warriors' battle
in that most noted city of Attica.
Was it then that you were taken captive
and imbued with the values of Achaean men—
or do you still remember your sisters
who fell in tragic defeat,
their blood soaking deep into Athenian soil?

Lady of Wisdom, Lady of Battle,
a rich tapestry of you I could weave,
born in the home of Libyan Amazons,
daughter of digested Metis wisdom,
inheritor of Neit who ruled the Libyan heavens,
sister of the helmeted Anat—
are these all one and the same,
diverse voices echoing from you
as Mother Courage Wisdom of us all,
for when I bring my unfinished weaving north,
strangely enough, I find you at Delphi,
revered at your shrine as Athena Pronaia,
most ancient spot in all of Delphi,
where, says Aristides, it was you
who was guardian of the oracles of prophecy,
and that your serpent Erechthonius
was Gaia's Python, Gaia's Typhon,
and that you were one with Gaia,
and that at the oracle of Erythrae,
you took the seat of Themis,
offering Themis counsel to Olympians—
yet answering only to the name of Athene.

Yet still I cannot weave the pattern
before I add the colours of your inventiveness
to my armful of scattered threads,
for they tell me that it was you
who first invented the wheel for the potter,
that it was you who built the first bridle,
and first tamed wild horses
so that they would pull the wheels of wagons,
even yoking the winged horse Pegasus

that grew from the drops of Medusa's blood,
that you taught the arts of medicine and healing,
carved the first flute to ever sing sweet sounds,
and, of course, Ancient Weaver,
it was you who designed the first weaving loom,
taking great pride in the tapestries you wove.

In and out of these threads,
your serpent Erechthonius slides.
Rumour has it that the serpent was born
when you fought off rape
and the semen of Hephaistos fell upon the earth,
thus birthing Erechthonius.
Though most say that the serpent of wisdom
was the child of Gaia,
Delphyna, Python, Typhon,
yet many times I have seen the serpent
hiding behind your mighty shield,
and have heard that it lives
on the great hill of Athens,
in your temple that was built
on ancient Mycenaean shrine,
the temple known as the Erechtheum,
the one guarded by Caryatid women,
though once the serpent dwelled in your own temple,
as Homer long ago explained,
causing me to wonder if it was not the Erechtheum
that was your holiest of shrines,
long before the Parthenon was built.
They tell me that it was for your serpent of wisdom
that the errephorai women brought the cakes of honey,
the young women who tended your eternal fire,
those who wove your holy peplos shirt,
so that each month the sacred serpent was fed,
and though I know your serpent lived in Athens,
I cannot help but think of the sacred serpents of Crete,
and even ancient Ua Zit of the land of the Nile.

Close by the Erechtheum,
they built your holy Parthenon,
one time jewel of Athens upon the city summit—
Parthenon for Parthenos—

woman who will take no husband,
finding strength in womanhood alone.
Was it your continual refusal to mate with men,
whether deity or mortal,
that allowed you the strength
to defeat the Giant Enceladus,
and to grasp the reins of Diomedes' chariot
so that you could pin arrogant Ares to the ground
with your everpresent spear?
Yet driving chariots was not unwomanly
for in the marble memories of your Panathenian Festival,
Parthenon images of late summer days in Athens,
I see that it is Amphitrite
who controls the reins,
while husband Poseidon sits by Her side,
as they draw close to the greatest of celebrations,
to join the horse and chariot races,
to join the procession of the torches,
to celebrate your birthday.

Standing here at the foot of the Acropolis,
I wonder, shall I hang my tangled threads in Athens—
yet I know your shrines were spread so far and wide.
Well were you known in the Rhodian city of Lindos,
and on Mount Pontinius in Argolis your temple stood;
in Sicily they called upon you as Athena Napkaia,
while Athene Alea was your title in Arkadia.
At Archarnae and Sunium, Colonus and Phyle,
at Thebes and Alalcomenae,
in Boetia and northern Thessaly,
at Mycenae and Tiryns, Delphi and Megara,
in each were you known and held in high esteem.
Yet it is to Athens
that I bring this armful of still unpatterned fibers,
and on this hot summer day
I climb the long ascent to your great Parthenon temple,
now as confused in architect design
as this tapestry that I have tried to weave—
once usurped as Christian church,
once blown apart by ammunition
stored within its sacred walls,
now background picturesque for visitors

who climb upon the broken blocks,
shouting, laughing, smiling for cameras,
and yet as I stand here in the tiring sun,
this tangled mass of threads
filling my arms, my head, my heart,
I see you sitting upon a broken stone,
your helmeted face resting upon your hand,
and I approach, explaining,
that truly do you trouble me Athena,
for though I say that you have not been born of man,
neither are your words or actions
of woman's heart begot,
for when you say that the child
is the child of the father only,
and the mother but the vessel of containment,
I ask which part of you is from man's mind—
and which of woman born.

You answer, Ancient Weaver,
with threads of your own,
telling me the story that untangles my threads,
as you take them to weave in clearer design—
the tale of how you won this sacred site,
contesting watery Poseidon
who could only bring forth a well of salt water,
while you produced the olive tree
for food and fuel and shade,
but how hollow was the victory
for it angered the Achaean men of Athens
who outnumbered the women—by one,
and thus, forced to accept your presence
as the Holy One of Athens,
since the contest had been fairly won,
in angry revenge, they voted
that women could no longer have their vote,
and from that time, the names of children
would be taken from the father's clan,
reducing the import of motherhood
to carrying vessel and nurse.

Yes, now I remember this last story,
and sit beside you on this dry and broken rock,
that was once part of your glorious Athenian temple,
and hear you say, 'What else could I do?
Forgive me, but try not to forget
that when first you learned
such a word as *Goddess,*
not long after you first began to read,
and images in books filled your growing mind,
it was I whose image went beside that word,
Athena, proud in my helmet of Valour,
Athena, proud in my name of Wisdom—
reaching out to you from the page,
filling you with a woman strength
that no one else would give.

BIBLIOGRAPHY

BIBLIOGRAPHY

Note: The sources listed here have been divided by cultural area, while sources that include several areas are listed in the final 'general' section. This bibliography has been compiled with two aims in mind. The first is to list the principal sources, both primary and secondary, employed in researching the Goddess and heroine images included in each of the fourteen sections of Ancient Mirrors of Womanhood (Vol. I & II). The second aim, and the major one, is to supply a list of source materials for the reader interested in further research on a specific area or topic. Most of the sources listed have extensive bibliographies of their own which, in turn, can lead the reader to further information on the specific subject of their interest.

Since Ancient Mirrors of Womanhood is intended as an introductory text, aimed at encouraging further research, and reclamation of important images of womanhood as known in the past and among the many cultures and racial groups of the world, it is my hope that these volumes will stimulate such studies, and eventually bring long ignored information into the mainstream of our culture. These volumes are intended as a stepping stone, to encourage interest, to point out what has existed, and to act as a germinal source for further research. Whatever one's religious or spiritual inclinations—or lack of them—the information and evidence concerning the images of woman included in these two volumes should be known and familiar to any truly educated person.

CHINA

Barondes, R. *China, Lore Legends and Lyrics* Philosophical Library 1960

Birch, Cyril. *Chinese Myths and Fantasies* Oxford University Press 1962

Bodde, Derk. "Myths of Ancient China" in *Mythologies of the Ancient World* ed. by S.N. Kramer Doubleday 1961

Chen, Ellen. *Tao as The Great Mother and the Influence of Motherly Love in the Shaping of Chinese Philosophy* Religious Heritage Series University of Chicago Press 1972

De Bary, W.T. *Sources of Chinese Tradition* Columbia University Press 1960

Eberhard, Wolfram. *Folktales of China* Routledge & Kegan Paul 1965

Ferguson, John. "Chinese Mythology" in *The Mythology of All Races* ed. by MacCulloch, J.A. Boston 1928

Giles, H.A. *Chuang Tzu* London 1889

Karlgren, Bernhard. "Legends and Cults in Ancient China" *Bulletin of the Museum of Far Eastern Antiquities* No. 18 1946

MacKenzie, Donald. *Myths of China and Japan* Gresham London n.d.

Maspero, Henri. *The Mythology of Modern China* Asiatic Mythology London 1932

Nai, Hsia. *New Archaeological Finds in China* Peking 1972

Roberts, Moss. *Chinese Fairy Tales and Fantasies* Pantheon 1979

Tao Teh King of Lao Tzu translation Bahm, A.J. Ungar 1958

Van Gulek, R.H. *Sexual Life in Ancient China* Brill, Leiden 1964

Werner, E.T.C. *Myths and Legends of China* Harrap 1922

_____ *A Dictionary of Chinese Mythology* Julian Press 1961

CELTIC

Bromwich, Rachel. *Medieval Celtic Literature* Toronto 1974

Chadwick, Nora. *The Celts* Pelican 1970

_____ *The Druids* Cardiff 1966

Cross, T.P. & Slover, C. *Ancient Irish Tales* Dunn 1969

Dillon, Myles. *Early Irish Literature* University of Chicago 1950

Dillon, M. & Chadwick, N. *The Celtic Realms* Weidenfeld & Nicolson 1967

Dunn, J. *Tain Bo Cuailnge* London 1914

Evans, J.G. *The Book of Taliesin* Llanbedrog 1910

Ford, Patrick. *The Mabinogi and Other Medieval Welsh Tales* University of California Press 1977

Foster, J.C. *Ulster Folklore* Belfast 1951

Fox, C. & Dickins, B. *Early Cultures of North West Europe* 1950

Guest, Lady Charlotte. *The Mabinogion* Cardiff 1977

Hatt, J. *Celts and Gallo-Romans* Nagel 1970

Hubert, Henri. *The Rise of the Celts* Kegan Paul n.d.

Jones, Gwyn & Thomas. *The Mabinogion* Dent 1950

Kennedy, P. *Legendary Fictions of the Irish Celts* London 1891

MacCana, Proinsias. *Celtic Mythology* London 1970

MacCulloch, J.A. "Celtic Mythology" in *Mythology of All Races* ed. by MacCulloch, J.A. Boston 1928

Murphy, Gerard. *Saga and Myth in Ancient Ireland* Dublin 1955

O'Rahilley, C. ed. *Tain Bo Cuailnge from the Book of Leinster* Dublin 1967

O'Sullivan, S. *Folktales of Ireland* London 1966

Piggott, Stuart. *The Druids* Praeger 1968

Pinchin, Edith. *The Bridge of the Gods in Gaelic Mythology* London 1934

Rees, Alwyn & Brinley. *Celtic Heritage* Thames & Hudson 1961

Rolleston, T.W. *Myths and Legends of the Celtic Race* Harrap n.d.
Ross, Anne. *Pagan Celtic Britain* Routledge & Kegan Paul 1967
Severy, Merle. "The Celts" *National Geographic* May 1977
Spence, Lewis. *The History and Origins of Druidism* Aquarian 1949
Squire, Charles. *The Mythology of Ancient Britian and Ireland* London n.d.
Thurneyson, R. *British Druids* Halle 1921
Trevelyan, M. *Folklore and Folk Stories of Wales* London 1909
Wood-Martin, W.G. *Traces of the Elder Faiths of Ireland* London 1902

NATIVE AMERICANS—CENTRAL AND SOUTH AMERICA

Braden, C.S. *Religious Aspects of the Conquest of Mexico* Duke University Press 1930
Brenner, Anita. *Idols Behind Altars* New York 1929
Burland, C.A. *The Gods of Mexico* Putnam 1967
Caso, Alfonso. *The Aztecs, People of the Sun* University of Oklahoma Press 1958
Clark, J.C. *Codex Mendoza* 3 Vols. London 1938
Coe, Michael D. *The Maya* Thames and Hudson 1966
Covarrubias, M. *Indian Art of Mexico and Central America* Knopf 1957
Dibble, C.E. & Anderson, A.J. *Florentine Codex* University of Utah 1957, 1959
Emmart, E.W. *The Badianus Manuscript, An Aztec Herbal of 1552* Baltimore 1940
Gann, T. & Thompson, J.E. *The History of the Maya* New York 1931
Goetz, D. & Morley, S. *Popul Vuh* University of Oklahoma 1952
Horcasitas, F. & Heyden, D. *Book of the Mayan Gods and Rites by Fray Diego Duran* University of Oklahoma 1971
Joyce, Thomas A. *Mexican Archaeology* London 1914
_____ *South American Archaeology* London 1912
Keeler, Clyde. *The Secrets of the Cuna Earth Mother* n.d.
Kingsborough, E. *Antiquities of Mexico* 9 Vols. London 1830-48
MacNeish, R.S. "Early Man in the New World" *American Scientist* Vol. 64 1976
_____ *The Prehistory of the Tehuacan Valley* University of Texas 1967
Mason, J.A. *The Ancient Civilization of Peru* Penguin 1957
_____ "Mirrors of Ancient America" *University of Pennsylvania Journal* Vol. 18, No. 2 1928
Means, P.A. *Ancient Civilizations of the Andes* London 1931
Meggers, B.J. "Transpacific Origins of Mesoamerican Civilization" *American Anthropologist* Vol. 77 1975

Morley, Sylvanus. *The Ancient Maya* Oxford University Press 1946
_____ *An Introduction to the Study of Maya Hieroglyphs* Bureau of American Ethnology Bull. 57 Washington 1915
Spence, Lewis. *The Gods of Mexico* Harrap 1932
Thompson, Eric. *Maya Hieroglyphic Writing* Oklahoma 1960
_____ *The Rise and Fall of Maya Civilization* Oklahoma 1954
Vaillant, George. *The Aztecs of Mexico* Doubleday 1962
Von Hagen, Victor. *World of the Maya* Mentor 1960
Special acknowledgement to Yvonne Retter for information on Colombia.

SEMITIC

Albright, Wm. F. *Recent Discoveries in Bible Lands* Funk & Wagnalls 1936
_____ *Archaeology and the Religion of Israel* John Hopkins 1942
_____ *The Archaeology of Palestine* Penguin 1949
_____ *Yahweh and the Gods of Canaan* Athlone 1968
Anati, E. *Palestine Before the Hebrews* Jonathan Cape 1963
Baramki, D. *Phoenicia and the Phoenicians* Beirut 1961
Barnett, R.D. *Catalogue of the Nimrud Ivories* British Museum 1957
Bermant, C. & Weitzmann, M. *Ebla* Quadrangle 1979
Bertholet, A. *A History of Hebrew Civilization* Harrap 1926
Budge, E.A.W. *The Babylonian Story of the Deluge and the Epic of Gilgamesh* British Museum 1920
Cassuto, U. *Anath* Jerusalem 1951
Contenau, G. *Everyday Life in Babylon and Assyria* Arnold 1954
Cook, Stanley. *The Religion of Ancient Palestine in the Second Millenium B.C.* Constable 1908
_____ *The Religion of Ancient Palestine in the Light of Archaeology* Oxford 1930
Delaporte, L. *Mesopotamia* Routledge & Kegan Paul 1925
De Vaux, Roland. *Ancient Israel* London 1965
Dossin, G. "Un Rituel du Culte d'Istar Provenant de Mari" *Revue d'Assyriologie* Vol. 35 1938
Driver, G.R. *Canaanite Myths and Legends* Allenson 1950
Farnell, L.R. *Greece and Babylon* Clark 1911
Gordon, Cyrus. *Ugaritic Literature* Rome 1949
_____ *Ugaritic Manual* Rome 1955
Gray, John. *The Legacy of Canaan* Leiden 1957
_____ *Archaeology of the Old Testament World* Nelson 1962
_____ *The Canaanites* Thames & Hudson 1964
_____ *Near Eastern Mythology* Hamlyn 1969
Harden, D. *The Phoenicians* Thames & Hudson 1962
Heidel, A. *Babylonian Genesis* University of Chicago 1951
Hitti, P. *The History of Syria* Macmillan 1951

Hooke, S.H. *Origins of Early Semitic Ritual* Oxford 1935
_____ *Babylonian and Assyrian Religion* Hutchinson 1953
Jacobsen, Th. *Toward the Image of Tammuz* Harvard University Press 1970
Jastrow, M. *The Religion of Babylon and Assyria* Atheneum 1898
Kapelrud, A.S. *Baal in the Ras Shamra Texts* Copenhagen 1952
Landes, G. "The Material Civilization of the Ammonites" *Biblical Archaeologist* September 1961
Langdon, Stephen. "Semitic Mythology" in *Mythology of All Races* ed. by MacCulloch, J.A. Boston 1928
_____ *Tammuz and Ishtar* Oxford University Press 1914
_____ *Babylonian Liturgies and Hymns* Oxford n.d.
Layard, A.H. *Nineveh and Babylon* British Museum 1853
Luckenbill, D.D. *Ancient Records of Assyria and Babylonia* Greenwood 1927
Macalister, R.A.S. *Bible Sidelights from the Mound of Gezer* Hodder & Stoughton 1906
_____ *Gezer Excavations* London 1912
Moscati, S. *Ancient Semitic Civilizations* Elek 1957
_____ *The Semites in Ancient History* University of Wales 1959
_____ *The World of the Phoenicians* Weidenfeld & Nicolson 1968
Olmstead, A.T. *A History of Palestine and Syria* Chicago 1931
Parrot, A. *Nineveh and Babylon* London 1961
Patai, Raphael. *The Hebrew Goddess* Avon 1978
Rowe, Alan. *The Topography and History of Beth Shan* University of Pennsylvania 1930
Saggs, H.W.F. *The Greatness That Was Babylon* Mentor 1968
Schaeffer, C. *The Cuneiform Texts of Ras Shamra—Ugarit* Oxford 1939
Scholem, G. *On the Kabbalah and its Symbolism* Routledge & Kegan Paul 1965
Smith, Robertson. *The Religion of the Semites* Black 1894
Strong, D. & Garstang, J. *The Syrian Goddess* Constable 1913
Vieyra, M. "Istar de Nineve" *Revue d'Assyriologie* Vol. 51 1957

AFRICA

Arnott, K. *African Myths and Legends Retold* Oxford University Press 1962
Bleek, W.H. & Lloyd, L.C. *Specimens of Bushman Folklore* Allen and Unwin 1911
Crowther, S. & Taylor, J.C. *The Gospel on the Banks of the Niger* London 1859
Forde, D. *African Worlds* Oxford University Press 1954

Herskovits, M.J. *Dahomean Narrative* Northwestern University Press 1938
Hollis, Claude. *The Nandi* Oxford University Press 1909
Itayemi, P. & Gurrey, P. *Folk Tales and Fables* Penguin 1953
Knappert, Jan. *Myths and Legends of the Congo* Heinemann 1971
Krige, E.J. *The Realm of a Rain Queen* Oxford 1943
Ladner, Joyce. *Tomorrow's Tomorrow, The Black Woman* Doubleday 1971
Little, K.L. *The Mende of Sierra Leone* Routledge & Kegan Paul 1951
MacDonald, Duff. *The Heart of Africa* Aberdeen 1882
Marvel, Elinore & Radin, Paul.. *African Folktales and Sculpture* Bollingen Series Pantheon 1952
Parrinder, E.G. *West African Religions* Epworth London 1949
Rattray, R.S. *Ashanti Religion* Oxford 1923
_____ *Religion and Art in Ashanti* Oxford 1927
_____ *Akan—Ashanti Folk Tales* Oxford 1930
Torrend, J. *Bantu Folklore* Routledge & Kegan Paul 1921
Wagner, G. *The Bantu of North Kavirondo* Oxford 1949
Werner, Alice. *Myths and Legends of the Bantu* Harrap 1933

AUSTRALIA AND POLYNESIA

Andersen, J.C. *Myths and Legends of the Polynesians* London 1928
Basedow, H. *The Australian Aboriginal* Adelaide 1925
Beckwith, M. *Hawaiian Mythology* New Haven 1940
Berndt, R.M. *Kunapipi* Melbourne 1951
Cowan, J. *Legends of the Maori* Fine Arts Ltd. Australia 1913
Danks, B. *Melanesians and Polynesians* London 1910
Dawson, J. *Australian Aborigines* Melbourne 1881
Dixon, Roland. "Oceanic Mythology" in *Mythology of All Races* ed. by MacCulloch, J.A. Boston 1928
Elkin, A.P. & Berndt, R. and C. *Art in Arnhem Land* Chicago 1950
Emerson, N.B. *Pele and Hiiaka* Honolulu 1915
Gill, Wm. W. *Myths and Songs from the South Pacific* London 1876
Gray, George. *Polynesian Mythology* n.d.
Handy, E.S.C. *Polynesian Religion* Bishop Museum 1927
Hiroa, Te Rangi. *The Coming of the Maori* Wellington, N.Z. 1950
Howitt, A.W. *The Native Tribes of South East Australia* London 1904
Izett, J. *Traditions of the Maori People* Wellington, N.Z. n.d.
Layard, J. *Stone Men of Malekula* London 1942
Lewis, A.B. *The Melanesians* University of Chicago Press 1951
Mullins, J. *The Goddess Pele* Tongg Publishing Hawaii 1977
Smith, P.S. *Hawaiiki, The Original Home of the Maori* London 1921
Smith, Ramsay. *Myths and Legends of the Australian Aboriginals* Harrap n.d.

Spencer, B. & Gillen, F.J. *The Arunta* London 1927
Williamson, R.W. *Religion and Social Organization in Central Polynesia* Cambridge 1937

ANATOLIA

Akurgal, Ekrem. *Art of the Hittites* Thames & Hudson 1962
Bennett, F. *Religious Cults Associated with the Amazons* Columbia University Press 1912
Bittel, Kurt. *Hattusha, the Capital of the Hittites* Oxford 1970
Blegen, Carl. *Troy* Princeton 1950
Cadoux, C.J. *Ancient Smyrna* Blackwell 1938
Esin, U. & Benedict, P. "Recent Developments in the Prehistory of Anatolia" *Current Anthropology* 1963
Frankfort, H. *Asia Minor and the Hittites* Pelican 1954
Garstang, J. *The Land of the Hittites* Constable 1910
_____ *The Hittite Empire* Constable 1929
_____ *Prehistoric Mersin* Oxford 1953
Garstang, J. & Gurney, O.R. *The Geography of the Hittite Empire* London 1959
Goetze, A. "Cilicians" *Journal of Cuneiform Studies* Vol. 16 1962
_____ *The Hittite Ritual of Tunnawi* American Oriental Series New Haven 1938
Gurney, O.R. *The Hittites* Penguin 1952
_____ "Hittite Prayers of Mursili II" *Annals of Archaeology and Anthropology* No. 27 Liverpool 1940
Guterbock, H.G. *Hittite Religion* New York 1949
_____ "Hittite Prayers to the Sun" *Journal of American Oriental Society* 1958
Hardy, R.S. "The Old Hittite Kingdom" *American Journal of Semitic Languages* 1941
Haspels, C.H. *The Highlands of Phrygia* Princeton University Press 1971
Laroche, E. "Tarhunda" *Revue Hittite and Asianique* 1958
Lloyd, Seton. *Early Anatolia* Thames & Hudson 1961
_____ *Early Highland Peoples of Anatolia* Thames & Hudson 1967
Mellaart, J. "Anatolian Chronology in Early Middle and Bronze Age" *Anatolian Studies Journal* 1957
_____ *Anatolia* Cambridge 1962
_____ *Earliest Civilizations of the Near East* Thames & Hudson 1965
_____ *Catal Huyuk* Thames & Hudson 1967
_____ "Excavations at Hacilar" *Anatolian Studies Journal* 1961
_____ "Excavations at Catal Huyuk" *Anatolian Studies Journal* 1964
Ramsay, W.M. *Cities and Bishropics of Phrygia* Clarendon 1895

Ransome, H. *The Sacred Bee in Ancient Times and Folklore* Allen & Unwin 1937

Sakir, Cevat. *Asia Minor* Ismir 1971

Sayce, A.H. *The Hittites, Story of a Forgotten Empire* London 1892

Schleimann, H. *Troy* London 1884

Van Loon, M.N. *Urartian Art* Istanbul 1966

Vieyra, M. *Hittite Art* London 1953

INDIA

Avalon, Arthur. *Shakti and Shakta* Madras 1929

_____ *Hymns to the Goddess* Madras 1953

_____ *Principles of Tantra* Madras 1955

Banerjea, J.N. *The Development of Hindu Iconography* Calcutta 1946

Basham, A.L. *The Wonder That Was India* Grove 1954

Bharati, Agehananda. *The Tantric Tradition* Rider 1965

Bose, D.N. & Haldar, H.L. *Tantras—Their Philosophy and Occult Secrets* Calcutta 1956

Brown, Norman O. *Saundaryalhari* Harvard Oriental Studies Vol. 43 Cambridge, MA. 1958

Clayton, A.C. *The Rg Veda and Vedic Religion* Madras 1913

Crooke, W. *Popular Religion and Folklore of Northern India* Westminster Press 1896

Dikshitar, V.R.R. *Studies in Tamil Literature and History* London 1930

Farquhar, J.N. *Outline of the Religious Literature of India* Oxford 1920

Hoffmann, H. *The Religions of Tibet* Allen & Unwin 1961

Hopkins, E.W. *Epic Mythology* Strassburg 1915

Konow, S. & Tuxen, P. *The Religion of India* Copenhagen 1949

Langdon, Stephen. *The Script of Harappa and Mohenjo Daro and its Connection With Other Scripts* London 1934

MacDonell, A.A. *Vedic Mythology* Strassburg 1897

_____ *Hymns from the Rg Veda* London 1922

MacKay, Ernest. *The Indus Civilization* London 1935

MacKenzie, Donald. *Indian Myth and Legend* Gresham n.d.

Marshall, Sir John. *Mohenjo Daro and the Indus Civilization* 3 Vols. Probsthain 1931

Muir, J. *Original Sanskrit Texts on the Origin and History of the People of India* London 1874

Muller, F.M. & Oldenberg, H. *Rg Veda Hymns* Oxford 1897

O'Flaherty, W.D. *Hindu Myths* Penguin 1975

Piggott, Stuart. *Prehistoric India* Penguin 1950

Pillai, M.S.P. *Tamil Literature* Tinnevelly 1929

Rafy, Mrs. M. *Folktales of the Khasis*
Renou, L. *Religions of Ancient India* London 1953
Roy, P.C. *The Mahabharata* Calcutta 1935
Sastri, H. *Origin and Cult of Tara* Archaeological Survey of India n.d.
Thompson, E.J. & Spencer, A.M. *Bengali Religious Lyrics* Oxford 1923
Whitehead, H. *The Village Gods of India* Calcutta 1916
Wheeler, Sir Mortimer. *The Indus Civilization* Cambridge 1953
Wilson, H.H. *The Great Mother* Oriental Translation Fund 1840
Zimmer, H. *Myth and Symbols in Indian Art* Bollingen Series 1946

SUMER

Braidwood, R.J. *Prehistoric Investigations of Iraqi Kurdistan* University of Chicago Press 1960
Chiera, Edward. *Sumerian Religious Texts* Upland, Penn. 1924
Cornwall, P.B. "Two Letters from Dilmun" *Journal of Cuneiform Studies* No. 6 1952
Crawford, O.G.S. *The Eye Goddess* Phoenix 1957
Delougaz, P. *The Temple Oval at Khafajah* University of Chicago 1940
_____ *Pre-Sargonic Temple in the Diyala Region* Chicago 1942
Evans, G. "Ancient Mesopotamian Assemblies" *Journal of American Oriental Society* No. 78 1958
Frankfort, H. *Cylinder Seals* Macmillan 1939
_____ *Archaeology and the Sumerian Problem* Chicago 1932

Handcock, P. *Mesopotamian Archaeology* Macmillan 1912
Harris, Rivkah. "Naditu Women of Sippar I & II *Journal of Cuneiform Studies* Vol. 15 & 16 1962
Hinz, Walther. *The Lost World of Elam* New York University Press 1973
Jacobsen, Th. "Formative Tendencies in Sumerian Religion" in *The Bible and the Ancient Near East* ed. by Wright, G.E. Doubleday 1961
Kramer, S.N. *Sumerian Mythology* University of Pennsylvania 1944
_____ *Sumerian Myths, Epics and Tales* Princeton 1957
_____ *History Begins at Sumer* Doubleday 1958
_____ *The Sumerians, Their History, Culture, and Character* University of Chicago 1963
_____ *The Sacred Marriage Rite* Indiana University Press 1969
Langdon, Stephen. *The Sumerian Epic of Paradise* University of Pennsylvania 1915
_____ *Tammuz and Ishtar* Oxford 1918
Lloyd, Seton. *Mesopotamia, Excavations at Sumerian Sites* London 1936
_____ *Ruined Cities of Iraq* Department of Antiquities Iraq 1942
Mallowan, M.E.L. *Twenty-Five Years of Mesopotamian Discovery* British School of Archaeology Iraq 1956
Mason, Herbert. *Gilgamesh* Mentor 1972

Moortgat, A. *The Art of Ancient Mesopotamia* Phaidon 1967
Oppenheim, A.L. *Ancient Mesopotamia* Chicago 1964
Parrot, Andre. *Sumer* Thames & Hudson 1960
Perkins, A.L. *The Comparative Archaeology of Early Mesopotamia* University of Chicago Press 1949
Roux, G. *Ancient Iraq* London 1966
Sandars, N.K. *Poems of Heaven and Hell from Ancient Mesopotamia* Penguin 1971
Van Buren, E.D. "The Sacred Marriage in Early Times in Mesopotamia" *Orientalia* Vol. 13 1944
Von Oppenheim, M. *Tell Halaf* Putnam 1931
Woolley, Leonard. *History Unearthed* Benn 1958
_____ *Excavations at Ur* Crowell 1965
_____ *A Forgotten Kingdom* Norton 1968

EGYPT

Albright, W.F. "The Early Alphabetic Inscriptions from Sinai" *Bulletin of the School of Oriental Research* Vol. 110 April 1948
Allen, T.G. *The Egyptian Book of the Dead* University of Chicago Press 1960
Anthes, R. "Egyptian Mythology in the Third Millenium" *Journal of Near Eastern Studies* Vol. 18 1959
Apuleius, Lucius. *The Golden Ass* trans. Wm. Adlington ed. by Harry Schnur Crowell Collier 1962
Boscawen, W. *Egypt and Chaldea* London 1894
Breasted, J.H. *Ancient Records of Egypt* 4 Vols. New York 1906-07
_____ *The Development of Religion and Thought in Ancient Egypt* London 1912
Budge, E.A. Wallis. *Egyptian Book of the Dead* British Museum 1895
_____ *Egyptian Magic* Kegan Paul 1901
_____ *The Gods of the Egyptians* Methuen 1904
_____ *The Dwellers of the Nile* Religious Tract Society 1926
Cerny, J. *Ancient Egyptian Religion* London 1952
De Buck, A. & Gardiner, H. *Egyptian Coffin Texts* Chicago 1935
Edwards, I.E.S. *The Pyramids of Egypt* Penguin 1947
Emery, W. *Archaic Egypt* Penguin 1961
Erman, Adolf. *The Literature of the Ancient Egyptians* London 1927
_____ *Life in Ancient Egypt* Dover 1971
Evans, Sir Arthur. *The Early Nilotic, Libyan and Egyptian Relations with Minoan Crete* Macmillan 1925
Faulkner, R.D. *The Ancient Egyptian Pyramid Texts* Oxford 1969

Flinders-Petrie, Wm. *Egypt and Israel* London 1925
_____ *Life in Ancient Egypt* Constable 1923
_____ *Religious Life in Ancient Egypt* Constable 1924
Frankfort, H. *Ancient Egyptian Religion* New York 1948
Gardiner, A.H. *Egyptian Grammar* Oxford 1927
_____ *The Astarte Papyrus* Griffiths Institute Oxford 1936
Harris, J.R. *The Legacy of Egypt* Oxford 1971
Lichtheim, M. *Ancient Egyptian Literature* University of California 2 Vols. 1973, 1976
MacKenzie, Donald. *Egyptian Myths and Legends* Gresham London n.d.
Mercer, S. *The Religion of Ancient Egypt* Luzac 1949
_____ *The Pyramid Texts in Translation and Commentary* New York 4 Vols. 1952
Morenz, S. *Egyptian Religion* Methuen 1973
Murray, Margaret. *The Splendour That Was Egypt* Sidgewick-Jackson 1972
Piankoff, A. "The Theology in Ancient Egypt" *Antiquity and Survival* 1956
Rundle Clark, R.T. *Myth and Symbol in Ancient Egypt* London 1959
Sayce, A.H. *The Religion of Ancient Egypt and Babylon* Clark 1902
Van Seters, J. *The Hyksos* New Haven 1966
Witt, R.E. *Isis in the Graeco-Roman World* Thames and Hudson 1971

NATIVE AMERICAN—NORTH AMERICA

Alexander, H.B. "Indian Mythology" in *Mythology of All Races* ed. by MacCulloch, J.A. Boston 1928
Bancroft, H.H. *The Native Races of the Pacific States* New York 1876
Bada, J.F. "New Evidence for the Antiquity of Man in North America" *Science* Vol. 184 1974
Bandi, H.G.. *Eskimo Prehistory* University of Washington Press 1958
Beauchamp, W.M. *History of the New York Iroquois* N.Y. State Museum Bulletin 1905
Benedict, Ruth. *Patterns of Culture* Houghton Mifflin 1934
_____ *Zuni Mythology* AMS Press 1935
Boas, F. *Folktales of the Salishan and Sahaptin Tribes* American Folklore Society 1917
_____ *Keresan Texts* American Ethnological Society 1928
_____ *The Central Eskimo* University of Nebraska Press 1964
Brown, J.K. "Economic Organization and the Position of Women among the Iroquois" *Ethnohistory* Vol. 17 1970
Bunzel, R. *Zuni Origin Myths* Bureau of American Ethnology No. 47 1929
Caldwell, J.R. & Hall, R.L. *Hopewellian Studies* Springfield, Illinois State Museum 1970

Canfield, Wm. *Legends of the Iroquois* New York 1902
Curtis, E.S. *The North American Indian* Cambridge, MA n.d.
Downs, J.F. *The Navajo* Holt, Rinehart & Winston 1972
Drucker, P. *Indians of the Northwest Coast* McGraw Hill 1955
Emerson, E.R. *Indian Myths* Boston 1884
Farb, Peter. *Man's Rise to Civilization* Dutton 1968
Hagan, W.T. *American Indians* University of Chicago Press 1961
Haury, E.W. *The Hohokam* University of Arizona Press 1976
Hewitt, J.N.B. *Iroquoian Cosmogony* Bureau of American Ethnology
    Vol. 21 1903
Hippler, A.E. "The Athabascans of Interior Alaska" *American Anthro-
    pology* Vol. 75 1973
Jahoda, G. *The Trail of Tears* Holt, Rinehart & Winston 1975
Jennings, J.D. *Prehistory of North America* McGraw Hill 1974
Marriott, A. & Rachlin, C. *Plains Indian Mythology* Crowell 1975
McFeat, T. *Indians of the North Pacific Coast* University of Washington
    Press 1966
Morgan, L.H. *Ancient Society* Meridian 1963
_____ *League of the He De No Sau Nee* Corinth 1962
Opler, M.E. *Myths and Tales of the Jicarilla Apache* American Folklore
    Society 1938
Parsons, E.C. *Pueblo Indian Religion* University of Chicago Press 1939
Rasmussen, Knud. *The Eagle's Gift* Doubleday 1932
Stubbs, Stanley. *A Bird's Eye View of the Pueblos* University of
    Oklahoma 1950
Swanton, J.R. "The Indian Tribes of North America" *Bureau of
    American Ethnology* 1946
Thompson, Stith. *Tales of the North American Indians* University of
    Indiana Press 1929
Tyler, Hamilton A. *Pueblo Gods and Myths* University of Oklahoma
    1964
Waters, Frank. *Book of the Hopi* Ballantine 1963
_____ *Masked Gods* Ballantine 1970

JAPAN

Anesaki, Masaharu. "History of the Japanese Religion" in *Mythology
    of All Races* ed. by MacCulloch, J.A. Boston 1928
Aston, W.G. *History of Japanese Literature* London 1909
_____ *Shinto, the Way of the Gods* London 1905
_____ *Nihongi, Chronicles of Japan from the Earliest Times to
    A.D. 697* Allen and Unwin 1956
Batchelor, John. *The Ainu and their Folklore* London 1901
_____ *Notes on the Ainu* Asiatic Society of Japan Stanford 1958

Chamberlain, B.H. *Kojiki, Record of Ancient Matters* Asiatic Society of
    Japan 1883
Davis, F.H. *Myths and Legends of Japan* Harrap 1913
Dorson, R.M. *Folk Legends of Japan* Tuttle 1962
Eliseev, S. *Asiatic Mythology* Harrap 1932
Etter, Carl. *Ainu Folklore* Wilcox and Follett 1949
MacKenzie, Donald. *Myths of China and Japan* Gresham London 1923
McAlpine, Helen & Wm. *Japanese Tales and Legends* Oxford 1958
Phillipi, D.L. *Norito, A New Translation of the Ancient Japanese Ritual*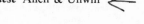
    Prayers Kokugakuin University 1959
Sansom, George. *A History of Japan to 1334* Stanford 1958
Satow, Ernest. *Ancient Japanese Rituals* Asiatic Society of Japan Vol.
    II. 1927
Seki, Keigo. *Folktales of Japan* University of Chicago Press
Smith, R.G. *Ancient Tales and Folklore of Japan* Black London 1908
Wheeler, Post. *The Sacred Scriptures of the Japanese* Allen & Unwin
    1952

SCANDINAVIAN

Auden, W.H. & Taylor, P.B. *The Elder Edda* Faber & Faber 1969
Bellows, Henry. *The Poetic Edda* American Scandinavian Foundation
    1923
Brodeur, A.G. *The Prose Edda of Snorri Sturluson* Scandinavian Classics
    1916
Christiansen, R.Th. *Studies in Irish and Scandinavian Folktales* Copen-
    hagen 1959
Craigie, Wm. *The Art of Poetry in Iceland* Oxford 1937
_____ *Scandinavian Folklore* London 1896
Davidson, H.R.E. *Gods and Myths of Northern Europe* Pelican 1964
_____ *Scandinavian Mythology* Hamlyn 1969
Glob, P.V. *The Bog People* Faber & Faber 1969
Halliday, W.R. *Indo-European Folk Tales* Cambridge University Press
    1933
Hollander, Lee M. ed. *The Skalds* University of Michigan Press 1968
Holmberg, Uno. "Finno Ugric, Siberian Mythology" in *Mythology of
    All Races* ed. by MacCulloch, J.A. Boston 1928
Kirby, W.F. *Kalevala* Dent 1907
Magnusson, M. & Palsson, H. *The Vinland Sagas, the Norse Discovery
    of America* Penguin 1965
Powell, G.E.J. & Magnusson, E. *Icelandic Legends* London 1864
Rydberg, Viktor. *Teutonic Mythology* Swan Sonnenschein 1891
Simpson, Jacqueline. *Icelandic Folktales and Legends* University of Cal-
    ifornia Press 1972

Sleeman, J.H. *Agricola and Germania* Cambridge 1958
Sturluson, Snorri. *The Prose Edda* translation by Young, Jean I. Bowes
and Bowes Cambridge 1954
Tacitus. *Germania* translation by Mattingly, H. Penguin 1948
Turville-Petre, E.O.G. *Myth and Religion of the North* Weidenfeld &
Nicolson 1964

GREEK AND AEGEAN

Alexiou, Stylianos. *Ancient Crete* Thames & Hudson 1967
_____ *Minoan Civilization* Heraklion 1969
Ames, D. *Greek Mythology* Hamlyn 1963
Avery, C. *The New Century Classical Handbook* Appleton Century
Crofts 1962
Bennett, F. *Religious Cults Associated With the Amazons* Columbia
1912
Butterworth, E.A. *Some Traces of the Pre-Olympian World* De Gruyter
1966
Casson, S. *Essays in Aegean Archaeology* Oxford 1927
Catling, H.W. *Patterns of Settlement in Bronze Age Cyprus* Lund 1963
Dempsey, T. *Delphic Oracle* Blackwell 1918
Di Cesnola, L.P. *Cyprus, its Ancient Cities, Tombs and Temples* Murray
1877
Dikaios, P. *Khirokitia* Oxford University Press 1953
Drees, Ludwig. *Olympia* Paul Mall Press 1971
Evans, Sir Arthur. *The Mycenaean Tree and Pillar Cult* Macmillan 1901
_____ *The Earlier Religions of Greece in Light of Cretan Discov-*
eries Macmillan 1925
_____ *The Palace of Minos at Knossos* Macmillan 1936
Farnell, L.R. *The Cults of the Greek States* 5 Vols. Clarendon 1896
Flaceliere, R. *Greek Oracles* Elek 1965
Gjerstad, E. *Studies of Prehistoric Cyprus* Uppsala 1926
Glotz, G. *The Aegean Civilization* Routledge & Kegan Paul 1925
Graves, R. *The Greek Myths* 2 Vols. Penguin 1955
Guthrie, G. *The Greeks and their Gods* Methuen 1950
Harrison, J.E. *Prologomena to the Study of Greek Religion* Cambridge
1903
_____ *Themis* Cambridge 1912
Higgins, R. *Minoan and Mycenaean Art* Praeger 1967
Hood, Sinclair. *The Minoans, Crete in the Bronze Age* Thames & Hud-
son 1971
Hopper, R.J. *The Acropolis* Macmillan 1971
Hoyle, P. *Delphi* Cassell 1967
Hutchinson, R.W. *Prehistoric Crete* Penguin 1962
Huxley, G.L. *Early Sparta* Faber & Faber 1962
Karageorghis, V. *Mycenaean Art from Cyprus* Barrie & Jenkins 1970

Karakatsanis, A. *Museums and Collections in Greece* Athens 1970
Kitto, H.D.F. *The Greeks* Penguin 1951
Marinatos, S. *Crete and Mycenae* Thames & Hudson 1960
Matz, F. *Crete and Early Greece* Methuen 1962
Miliades, Y. *A Concise Guide to the Acropolis Museum* Athens 1971
Mylonas, G. *Eleusis and the Eleusinian Mysteries* Princeton 1961
Nilsson, M. *The Minoan-Mycenaean Religion and its Survival in Greek Religion* Lund 1927
Parke, H.W. *Greek Oracles* Hutchinson 1967
Pendlebury, J. *The Archaeology of Crete* Methuen 1939
Persson, A.W. *The Religion of Greece in Prehistoric Times* University of California Press 1942
Petracos, B. *Delphi* Delphi Museum 1971
Poulsen, F. *Delphi* Glyndendal 1921
Rose, H.J. *A Handbook of Greek Mythology* Methuen 1928
_____ *Gods and Heroes of the Greeks* Meridian 1958
Sakellariou, A. *Prehistoric Collections* Athens 1970
Sandars, N.K. *The Sea Peoples* Thames & Hudson 1978
Schleimann, H. *Mycenae* London 1878
Seltman, C. *The Twelve Olympians* Pan 1952
_____ *Women in Antiquity* Pan 1956
Spretnak, C. *Lost Goddesses of Early Greece* Moon 1978 *
Von Matt, L. *Ancient Crete* Thames & Hudson 1967
Willetts, R.F. *Cretan Cults and Festivals* Barnes and Noble 1962

GENERAL

Bacon, E. *Vanished Civilizations* Thames & Hudson 1963
Braidwood, R.J. *Prehistoric Men* University of Chicago 1948
Brandon, S.G.F. *Creation Legends of the Near East* Hodder Stoughton 1963
Bulfinch, Thomas. *Bulfinch's Mythology* Tilton 1881
Chiera, E. *They Wrote on Clay* Chicago 1938
Childe, Gordon. *New Light on the Most Ancient East* Norton 1969
Cole, S. *The Neolithic Revolution* British Museums 1970
Colum, Padraic. *Myths of the World* Grosset & Dunlap 1930
Crossland, R.A. "Immigrants from the North" *Cambridge Ancient History* Vol. I Cambridge 1970
Daniels, Glyn. *Malta* Thames & Hudson 1957
Dawson, Christopher. *Age of the Gods* Murray 1928
Dawson, D. *The Story of Prehistoric Civilizations* Franklin Watts 1951
Ehrich, R.W. *Relative Chronologies on Old World Archaeology* Chicago 1954
Finegan, J. *Light from the Ancient East* Princeton 1946

* Beacon 1981

Frankfort, Henri. *Kingship and the Gods* Chicago 1948
_____ *The Birth of Civilization in the Near East* Doubleday 1951
_____ *The Problems of Similarities in Ancient Near Eastern Religions* Clarendon 1951
_____ *The Art and Architecture of the Ancient Orient* Penguin 1954
Frazer, J. *The Golden Bough* Macmillan 12 Vols. 1911-15
Frobenius, L. *The Childhood of Man* Seeley 1909
Gadd, C.J. *Ideas of Divine Rule in the Ancient Near East* Oxford 1933
Garcia, L. & Galloway, J. & Lommel, A. *Prehistoric and Primitive Art* Thames and Hudson 1969
Gaster, T. *Thespis* Doubleday 1950
Gimbutas, M. *The Gods and Goddesses of Old Europe* Thames & Hudson 1974
Gordon, Cyrus. *The Ancient Near East* Norton 1962
_____ *The Common Backgrounds of the Greek and Hebrew Civilizations* Norton 1962
_____ *Forgotten Scripts* Penguin 1968
Gray, John. *Archaeology of the Old Testament World* Nelson 1962
_____ *Near Eastern Mythology* Hamlyn 1969
Graziozi, P. *Paleolithic Art* Faber & Faber 1960
Guido, M. *Sardinia* Thames & Hudson 1963
Guilliame, A. *Islam* Penguin 1952
Hall, H.R. *The Ancient History of the Near East* Methuen 1913
Hamilton, Edith. *Mythology* Mentor 1955
Harrison, R.K. *Ancient World* English Universities Press 1971
Hartland, E.S. *Primitive Society* Methuen 1921
Hawkes, J. *Dawn of the Gods* Chatto & Windus 1958
_____ *Prehistory: History of Mankind, Cultural and Scientific Development* Mentor 1965
_____ *The First Great Civilizations* Hutchinson 1973
Hooke, S.H. *Myth and Ritual* Oxford University Press 1933
_____ *Myth, Ritual and Kingship* Oxford 1958
_____ *Middle Eastern Mythology* Penguin 1963
James, E.O. *The Origins of Religion* Heritage 1937
_____ *Prehistoric Religion* Thames & Hudson 1957
_____ *Myth and Ritual in the Ancient Near East* Thames & Hudson 1958
_____ *The Cult of the Mother Goddess* Thames & Hudson 1959
_____ *The Ancient Gods* Weidenfeld & Nicolson 1960
_____ *Seasons, Feasts and Festivals* Thames & Hudson 1961
Kramer, S.N. ed. *Mythologies of the Ancient World* Doubleday 1961
Larousse. *New Larousse Encyclopedia of Mythology* ed. by Guirand, F. Hamlyn 1960
Leach, M. *Standard Dictionary of Folklore* Funk & Wagnalls 1949

_____ *The Beginning* Funk & Wagnalls 1956

Lissner, I. *The Living Past* Putnam 1957

Lloyd, Seton. *Foundations in the Dust* Oxford 1947

_____ *Mounds of the Near East* Thames & Hudson 1961

Lommel, A. *Prehistoric and Primitive Man* McGraw Hill 1966

Maringer, Johannes. *The Gods of Prehistoric Man* Knopf 1960

McEvedy, Colin. *The Penguin Atlas of Ancient History* Penguin 1967

Menan, Aubrey. *Cities in the Sand* Thames & Hudson 1972

Murray, M. *The Witch Cult of Western Europe* Clarendon 1921

_____ *The Genesis of Religion* Routledge & Kegan Paul 1963

Norbeck, E. *Religion in Primitive Society* Harper 1961

Osborn, H.F. *Men of the Old Stone Age* Scribner's 1916

Piggott, S. *The Dawn of Civilization* Thames & Hudson 1961

Powell, T.G.E. *Prehistoric Art* Praeger 1966

Pritchard, J.B. *Palestinian Figures in Relation to Certain Goddesses Known Through Literature* Kraus-Thompson 1943

_____ *Ancient Near Eastern Texts Relating to the Old Testament* Princeton 1950

_____ *The Ancient Near East* Princeton 1958

_____ *Archaeology and the Old Testament* Princeton 1958

_____ *The Ancient Near East in Pictures* Princeton 1969

Stone, Merlin. *When God Was A Woman* Dial 1976

Spiegelberg, F. *Living Religions of the World* Thames & Hudson 1957

Van Over, Raymond. *Sun Songs* Mentor 1980

Vitaliano, D. *Legends of the Earth* Indiana University Press 1973

Von Cles-Reden, Sybelle. *The Realm of the Great Goddess* Thames & Hudson 1961

Warner, Rex. ed. *Encyclopedia of World Mythology* Phoebus 1971

Wright, G.E. ed. *The Bible and the Ancient Near East* Doubleday 1961

RITUALS AND COMMEMORATIONS YOU MAY WANT TO REMEMBER (from Vol. II)

New Year's Day—(mid-June) Heliacal rising of the star Sothis (Sirius), possibly related to the Festival of Lights at Sais. See Neit, Isis, Hathor/Egyptian Section.

New Year's Day—(autumn) The yearly judgment of people by the Laws of Nidaba. See Nina (Nanshe)/Sumerian section.

New Year's Day—(Dec. 21-22, Winter Solstice) Original New Year for Scandinavians.

New Moon—The fixing of the destinies. See Inanna/Sumerian section and Artemis/Greek Section. (Possibly related to Shapatu rites in Babylon. See Ishtar, Shekhina/Semitic Section—Vol. I).

Dawn—The arrival of Ushas as enlightenment. See Ushas/Indian Section.

The Birth of a Baby—Decreeing its future. See Nerthus—Urth (the Norns)/Scandinavian Section, and Hathor/Egyptian Section.

Menarche ritual—See Changing Woman/Native American Section.

Death rituals—See Neit, Seshat/Egyptian Section, and Ereshkigal/Sumerian Section.

Spring Equinox—(first day of Nisan) See Aphrodite/Greek Section. (Probably related to Spring Festival for Kybele. See Anatolian Section—Vol. I).

May 1st—Rowan Witch Day, possibly related to the return of Iduna and the Celtic Beltane fires. See Iduna and introduction/Scandinavian Section.

June—Vestalia in Rome, in honour of Vesta. See Hestia/Greek Section.

August 21—September 20—The reign of Virginal Justice. See Themis and Dike/Greek Section.

September 21—October 20—the reign of Mother Justice. See Themis and Dike/Greek Section.

September 20—30 (Greek month of Boedromion) The rituals of Eleusis and the Thesmophorias for Demeter and Kore. See Greek Section.

October 31st—November 1st—The Alfablot rite for Holla (Hella) to raise the souls of the dead. See Hella, Nerthus and Urth/Scandinavian Section.

Winter Solstice—The probable emergence of the Sun Goddess from the cave. The decoration of the Sakaki tree. See Amaterasu/Japanese Section.